DEPT.H™

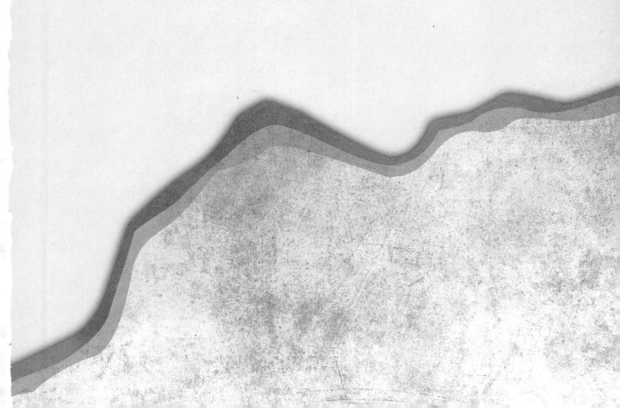

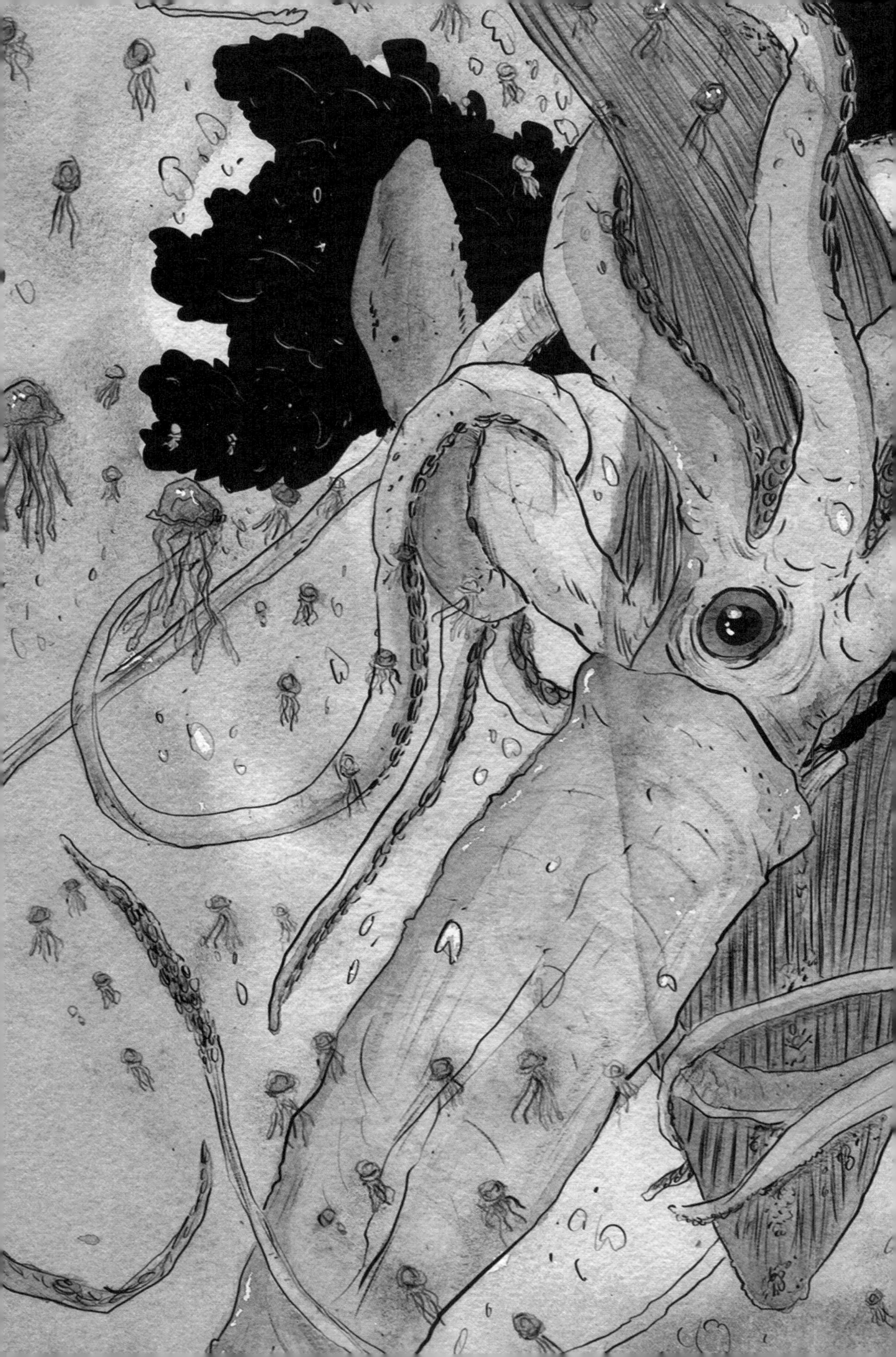

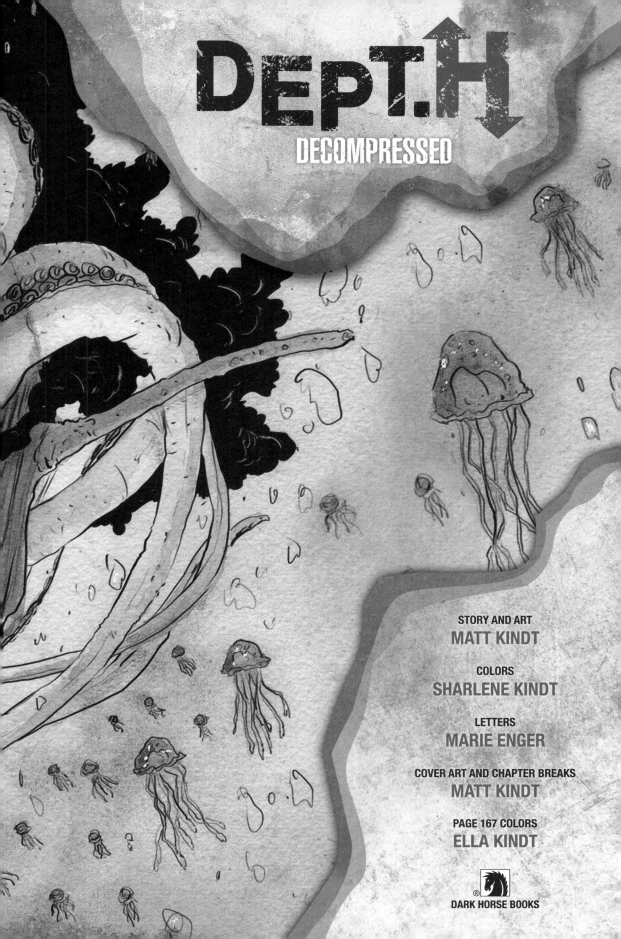

DEPT.H
DECOMPRESSED

STORY AND ART
MATT KINDT

COLORS
SHARLENE KINDT

LETTERS
MARIE ENGER

COVER ART AND CHAPTER BREAKS
MATT KINDT

PAGE 167 COLORS
ELLA KINDT

DARK HORSE BOOKS

PRESIDENT AND PUBLISHER
MIKE RICHARDSON

EDITOR
DANIEL CHABON

ASSOCIATE EDITOR
CARDNER CLARK

DESIGNER
ETHAN KIMBERLING

DIGITAL ART TECHNICIAN
ALLYSON HALLER

Neil Hankerson, Executive Vice President • Tom Weddle, Chief Financial Officer
Randy Stradley, Vice President of Publishing • Nick McWhorter, Chief Business
Development Officer • Matt Parkinson, Vice President of Marketing • David
Scroggy, Vice President of Product Development • Dale LaFountain, Vice Pres-
ident of Information Technology • Cara Niece, Vice President of Production and
Scheduling • Mark Bernardi, Vice President of Book Trade and Digital Sales
Ken Lizzi, General Counsel • Dave Marshall, Editor in Chief • Davey Estrada,
Editorial Director • Scott Allie, Executive Senior Editor • Chris Warner, Senior
Books Editor • Cary Grazzini, Director of Specialty Projects • Lia Ribacchi, Art
Director • Vanessa Todd, Director of Print Purchasing • Matt Dryer, Director of
Digital Art and Prepress • Michael Gombos, Director of International Publishing
and Licensing

Published by Dark Horse Books
A division of Dark Horse Comics, Inc.
10956 SE Main Street
Milwaukie, OR 97222

First edition: January 2018
ISBN 978-1-61655-991-5

10 9 8 7 6 5 4 3 2 1
Printed in China

International Licensing: (503) 905-2377
Comic Shop Locator Service: comicshoplocator.com

This volume collects the Dark Horse Comics series *Dept. H* issues #13–#18.

Names: Kindt, Matt, author, artist. | Kindt, Sharlene, colorist. | Enger,
  Marie, letterer.
Title: Dept. H / story and art, Matt Kindt ; colors, Sharlene Kindt ;
  letters, Marie Enger ; cover art and chapter breaks Matt Kindt.
Description: First edition. | Milwaukie, OR : Dark Horse Books, 2018-
  Contents: v. 3. Decompressed.
Identifiers: LCCN 2016034697 | ISBN 9781616559915 (v. 3 : hardback)
Subjects: LCSH: Comic books, strips, etc. | BISAC: COMICS & GRAPHIC NOVELS /
  Crime & Mystery.
Classification: LCC PN6727.K54 D47 2017 | DDC 741.5/973--dc23
LC record available at https://lccn.loc.gov/2016034697

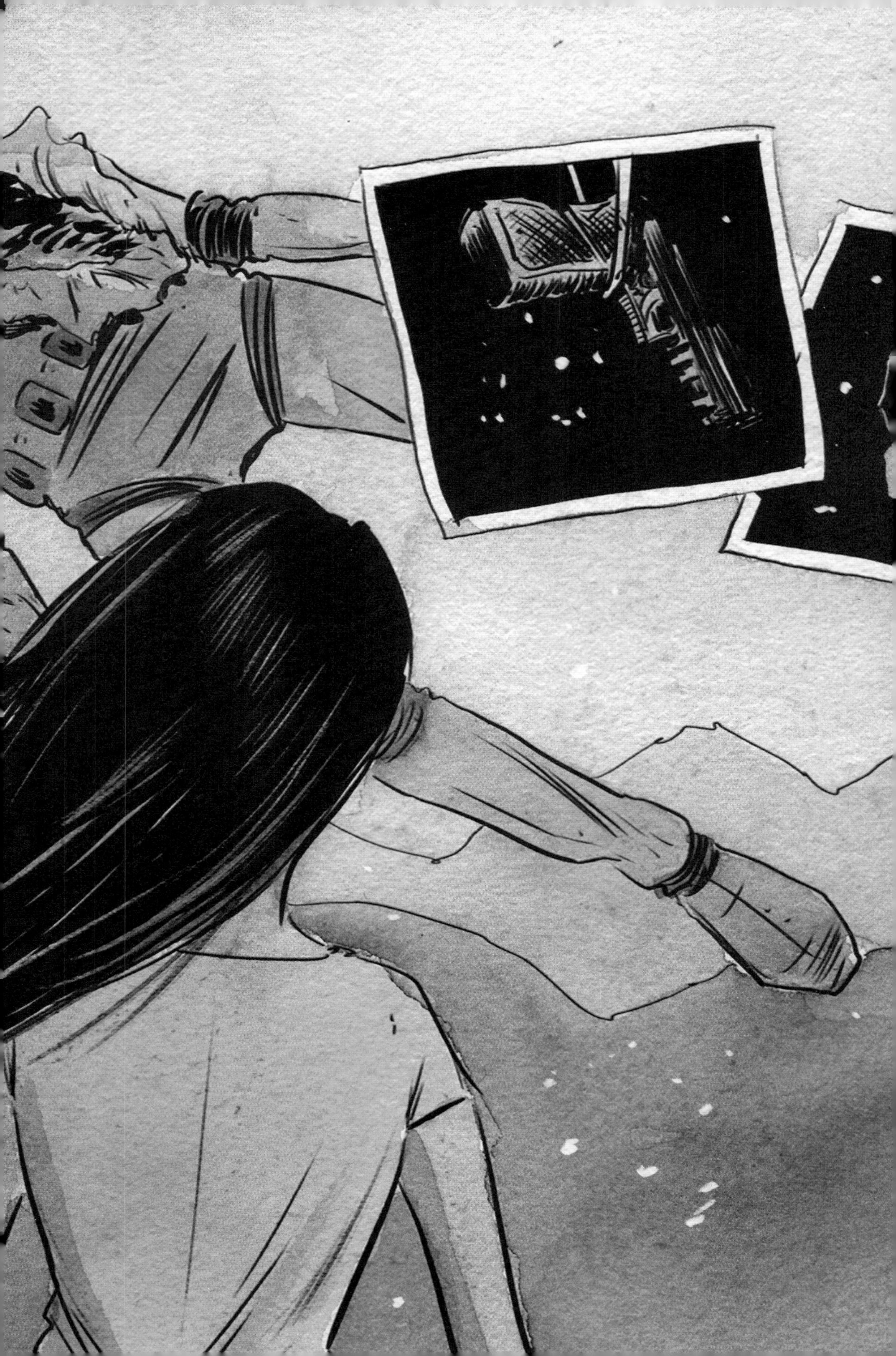

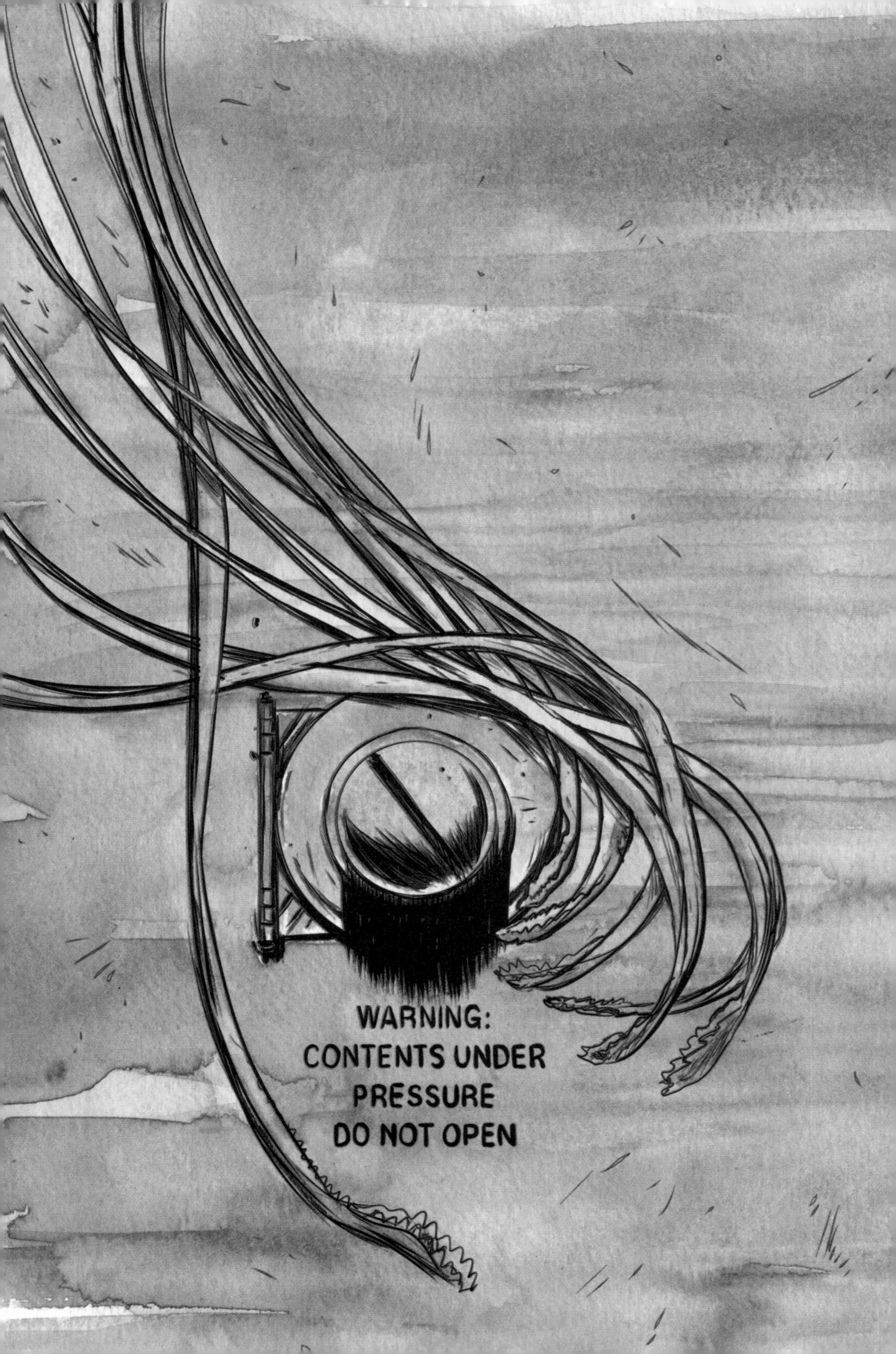
WARNING:
CONTENTS UNDER
PRESSURE
DO NOT OPEN

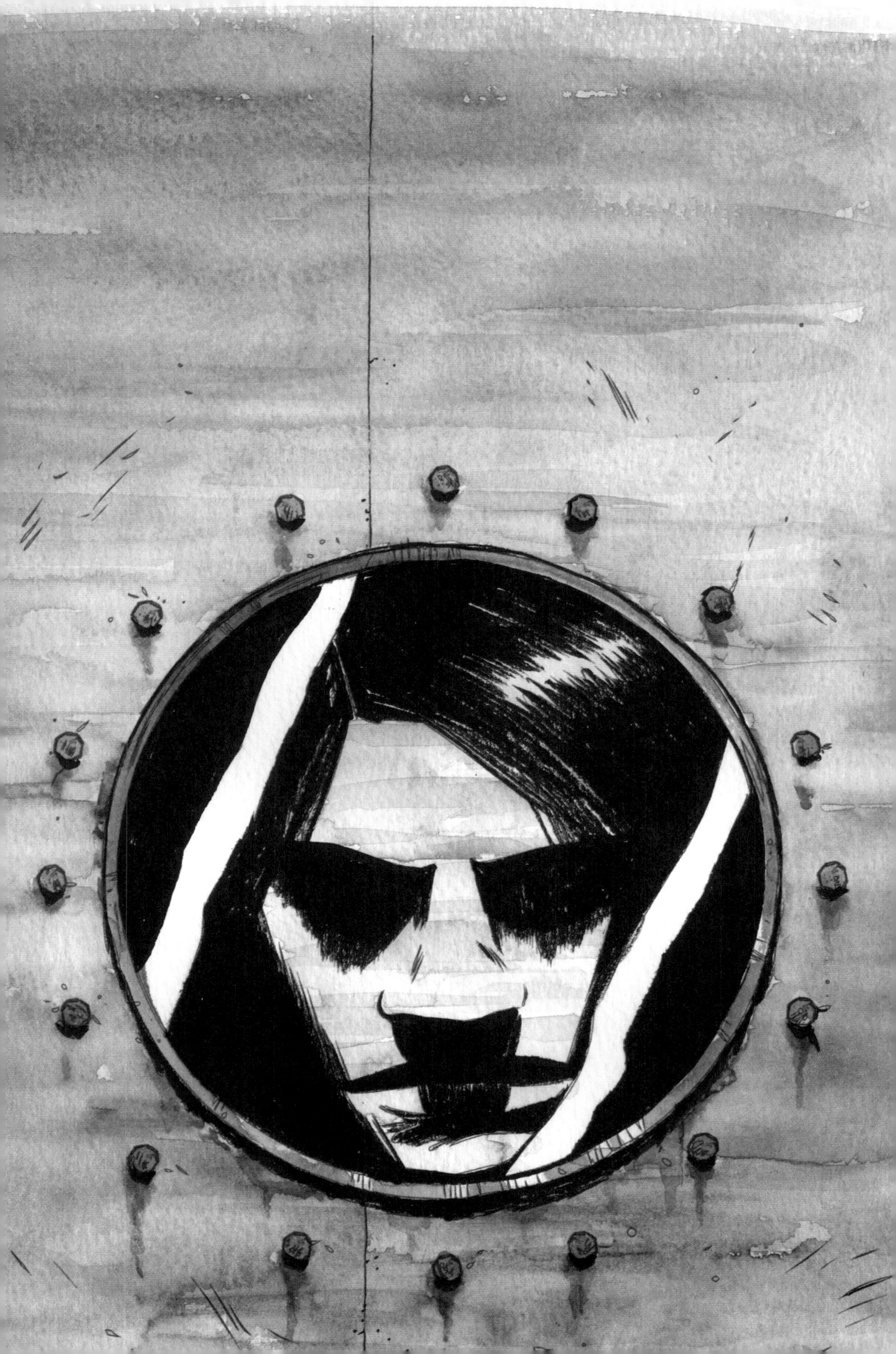

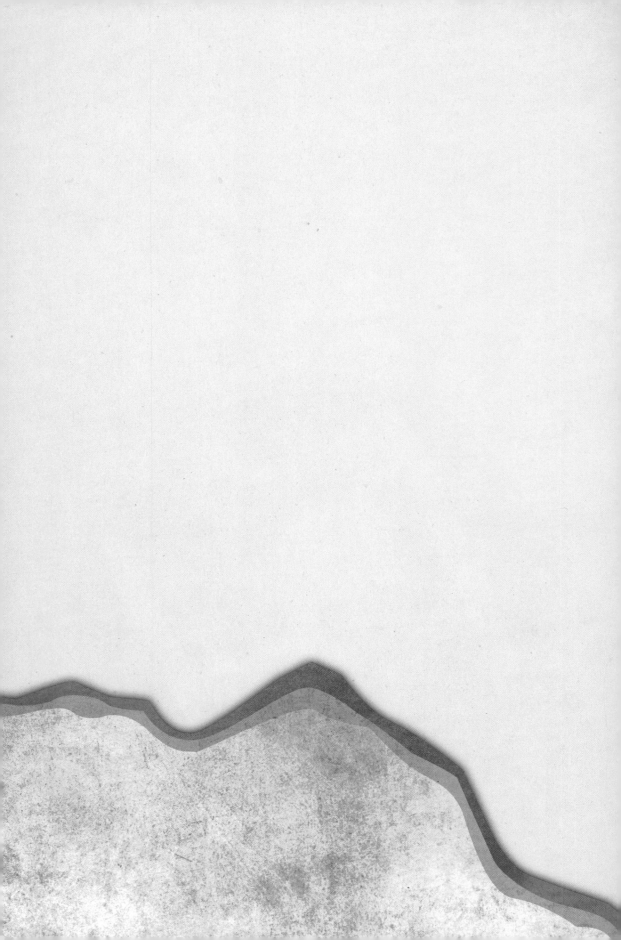

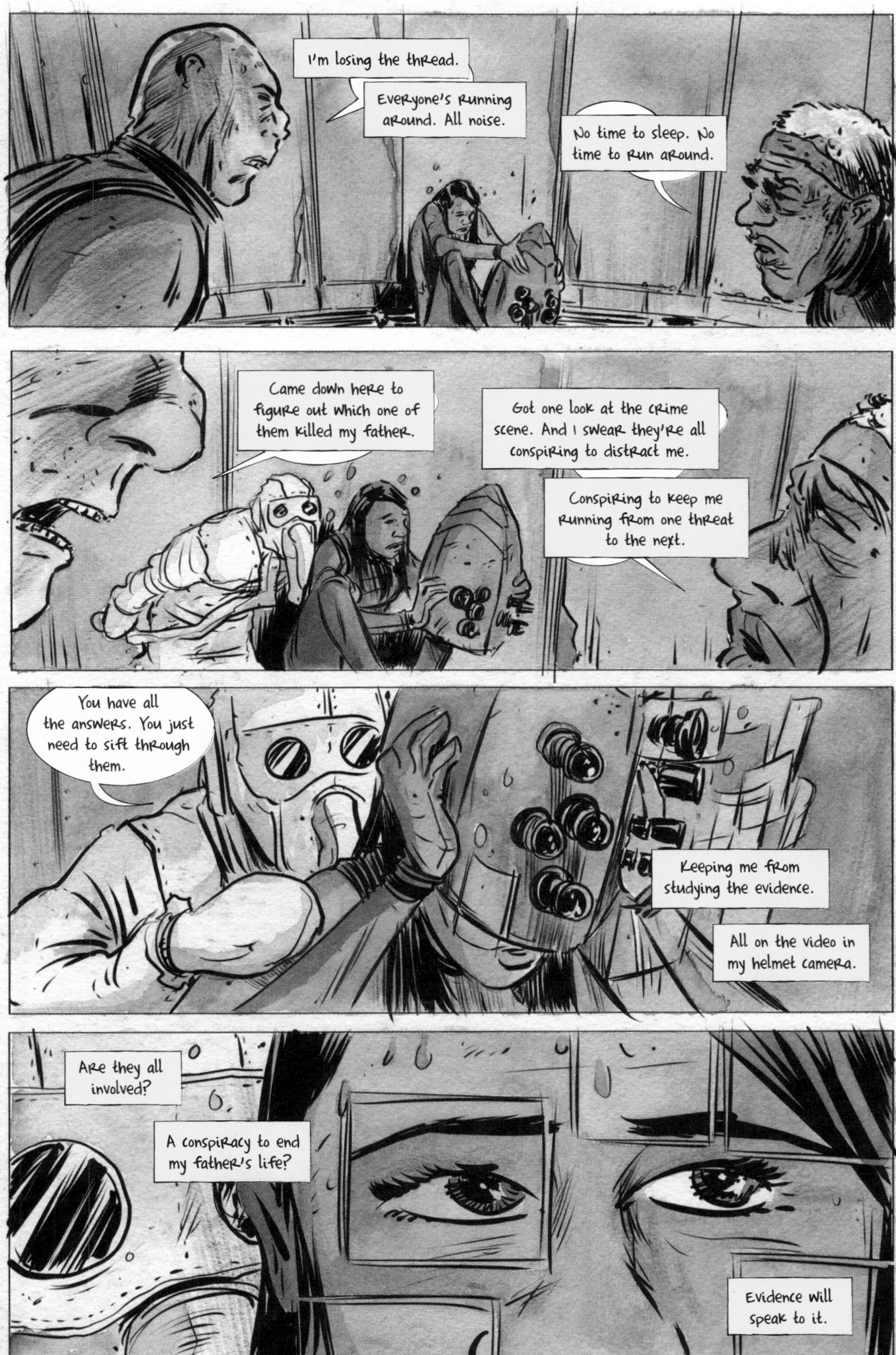
I'm losing the thread.
Everyone's running around. All noise.
No time to sleep. No time to run around.
Came down here to figure out which one of them killed my father.
Got one look at the crime scene. And I swear they're all conspiring to distract me.
Conspiring to keep me running from one threat to the next.
You have all the answers. You just need to sift through them.
Keeping me from studying the evidence.
All on the video in my helmet camera.
Are they all involved?
A conspiracy to end my father's life?
Evidence will speak to it.

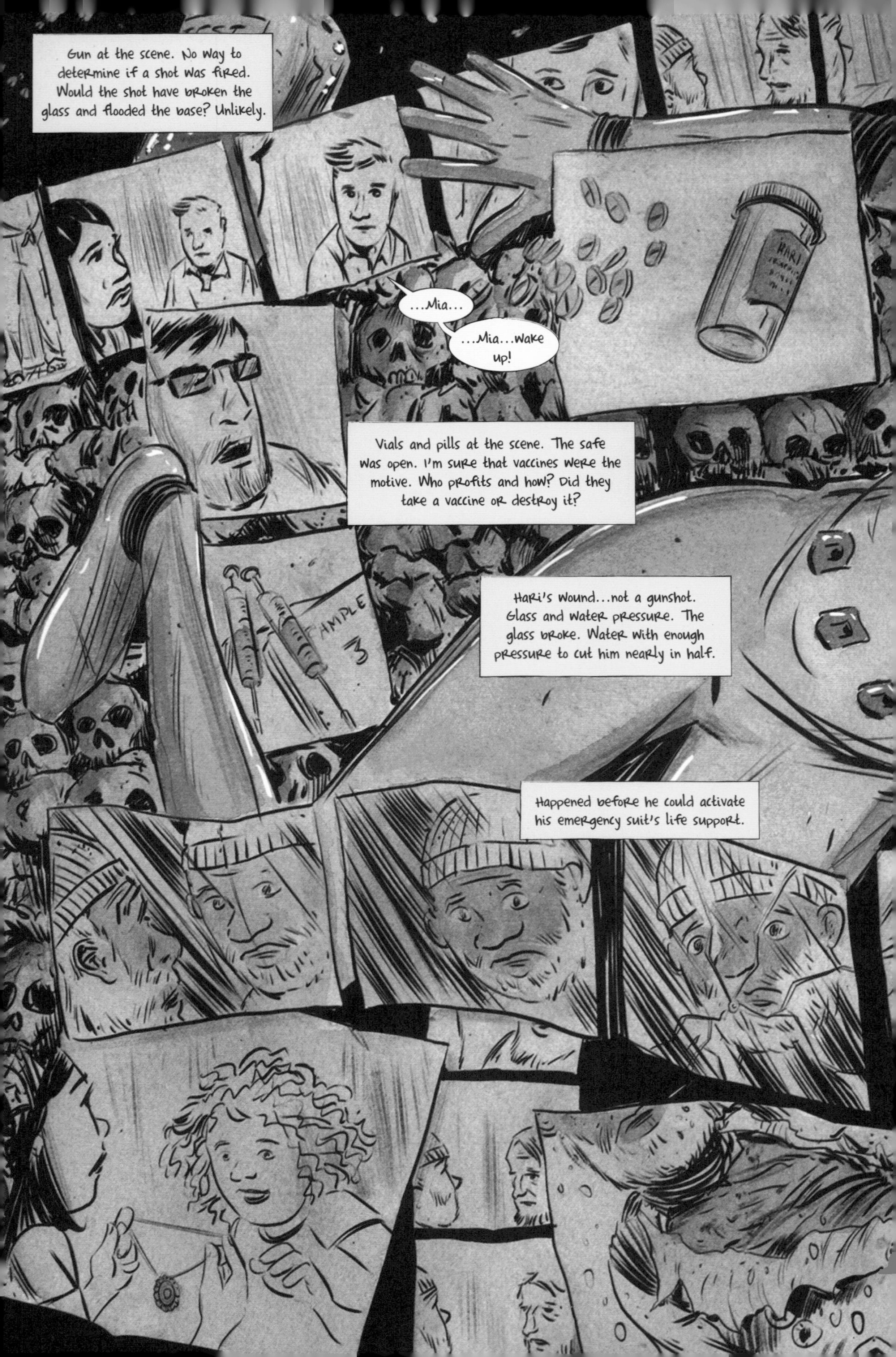
Gun at the scene. No way to determine if a shot was fired. Would the shot have broken the glass and flooded the base? Unlikely.
...Mia...
...Mia...wake up!
Vials and pills at the scene. The safe was open. I'm sure that vaccines were the motive. Who profits and how? Did they take a vaccine or destroy it?
SAMPLE 3
Hari's wound...not a gunshot. Glass and water pressure. The glass broke. Water with enough pressure to cut him nearly in half.
Happened before he could activate his emergency suit's life support.

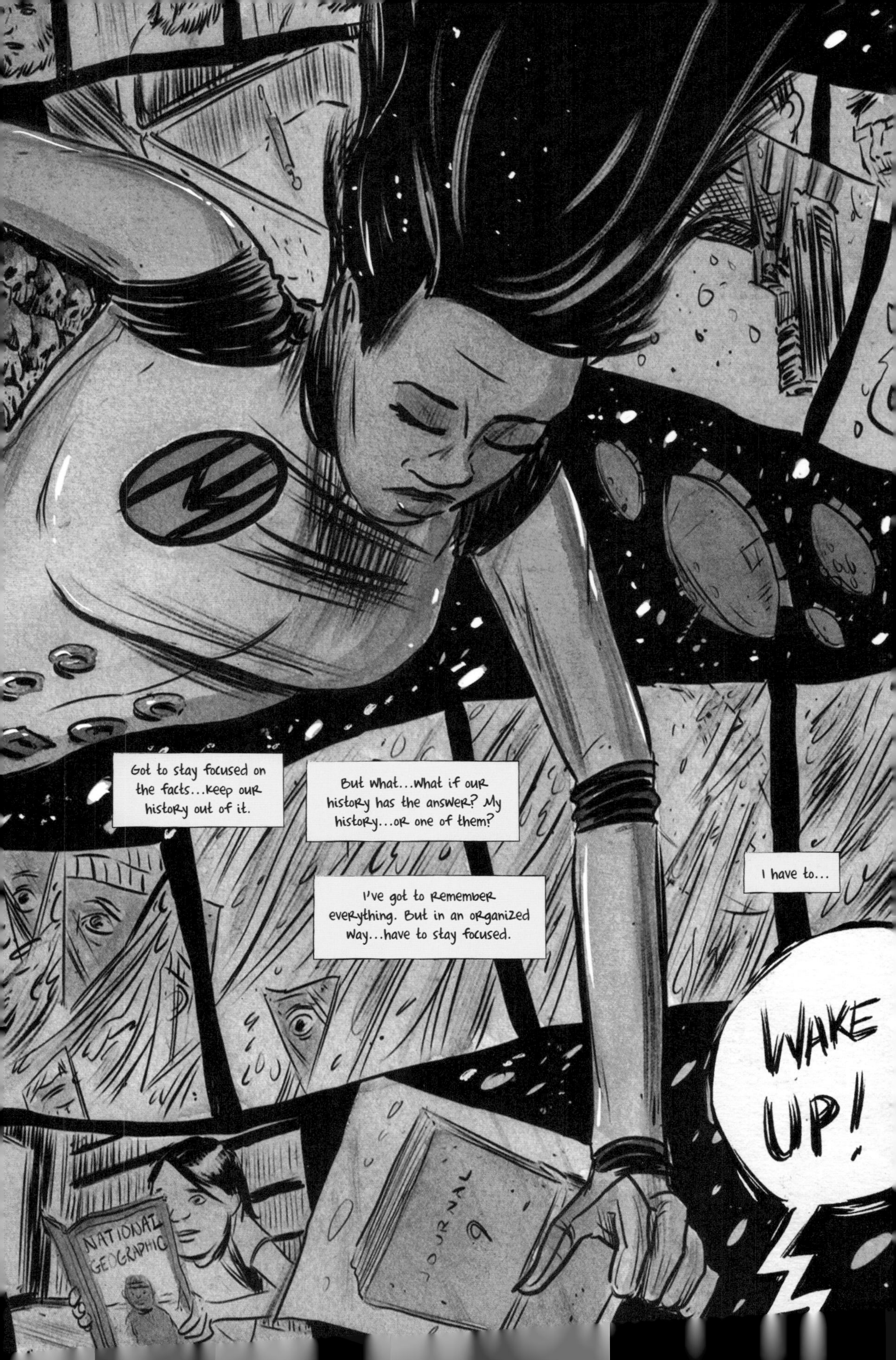
Got to stay focused on the facts...keep our history out of it.
But what...what if our history has the answer? My history...or one of them?
I've got to remember everything. But in an organized way...have to stay focused.
I have to...
WAKE UP!
NATIONAL GEOGRAPHIC
JOURNAL

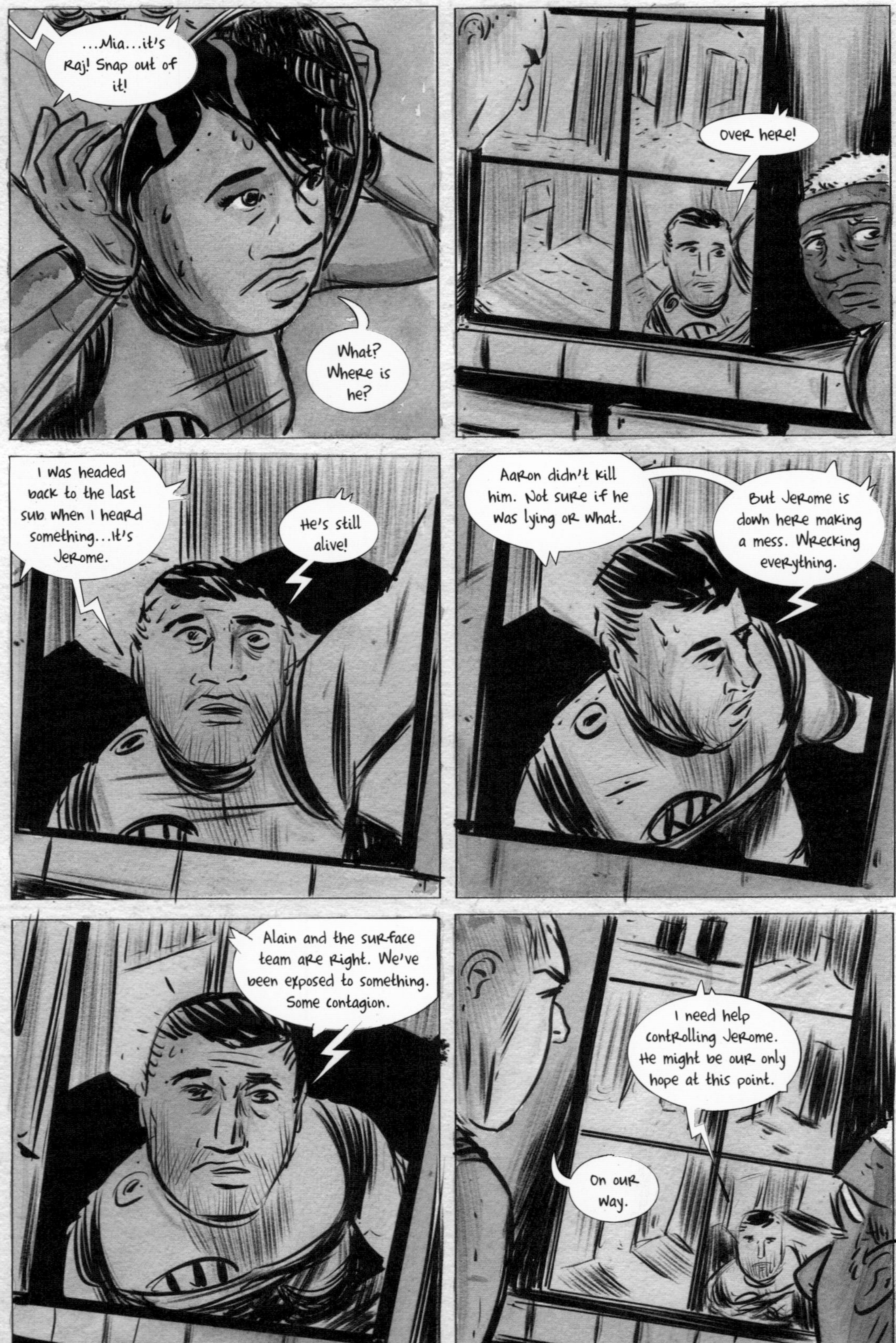
...Mia...it's Raj! Snap out of it!
What? Where is he?
Over here!
I was headed back to the last sub when I heard something...It's Jerome.
He's still alive!
Aaron didn't kill him. Not sure if he was lying or what.
But Jerome is down here making a mess. Wrecking everything.
Alain and the surface team are right. We've been exposed to something. Some contagion.
I need help controlling Jerome. He might be our only hope at this point.
On our way.

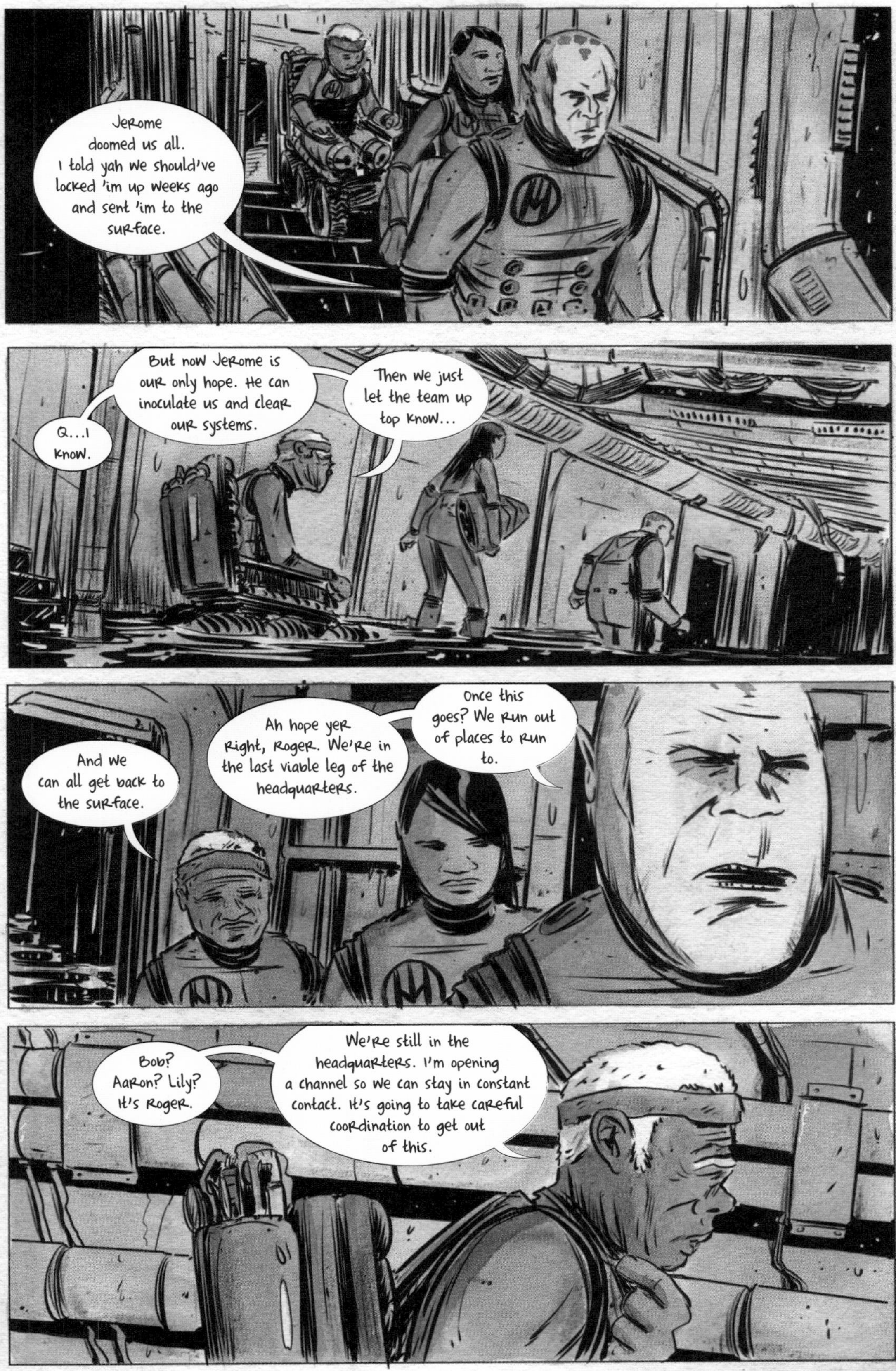
Jerome doomed us all. I told yah we should've locked 'im up weeks ago and sent 'im to the surface.
Q...I know.
But now Jerome is our only hope. He can inoculate us and clear our systems.
Then we just let the team up top know...
And we can all get back to the surface.
Ah hope yer right, Roger. We're in the last viable leg of the headquarters.
Once this goes? We run out of places to run to.
Bob? Aaron? Lily? It's Roger.
We're still in the headquarters. I'm opening a channel so we can stay in constant contact. It's going to take careful coordination to get out of this.

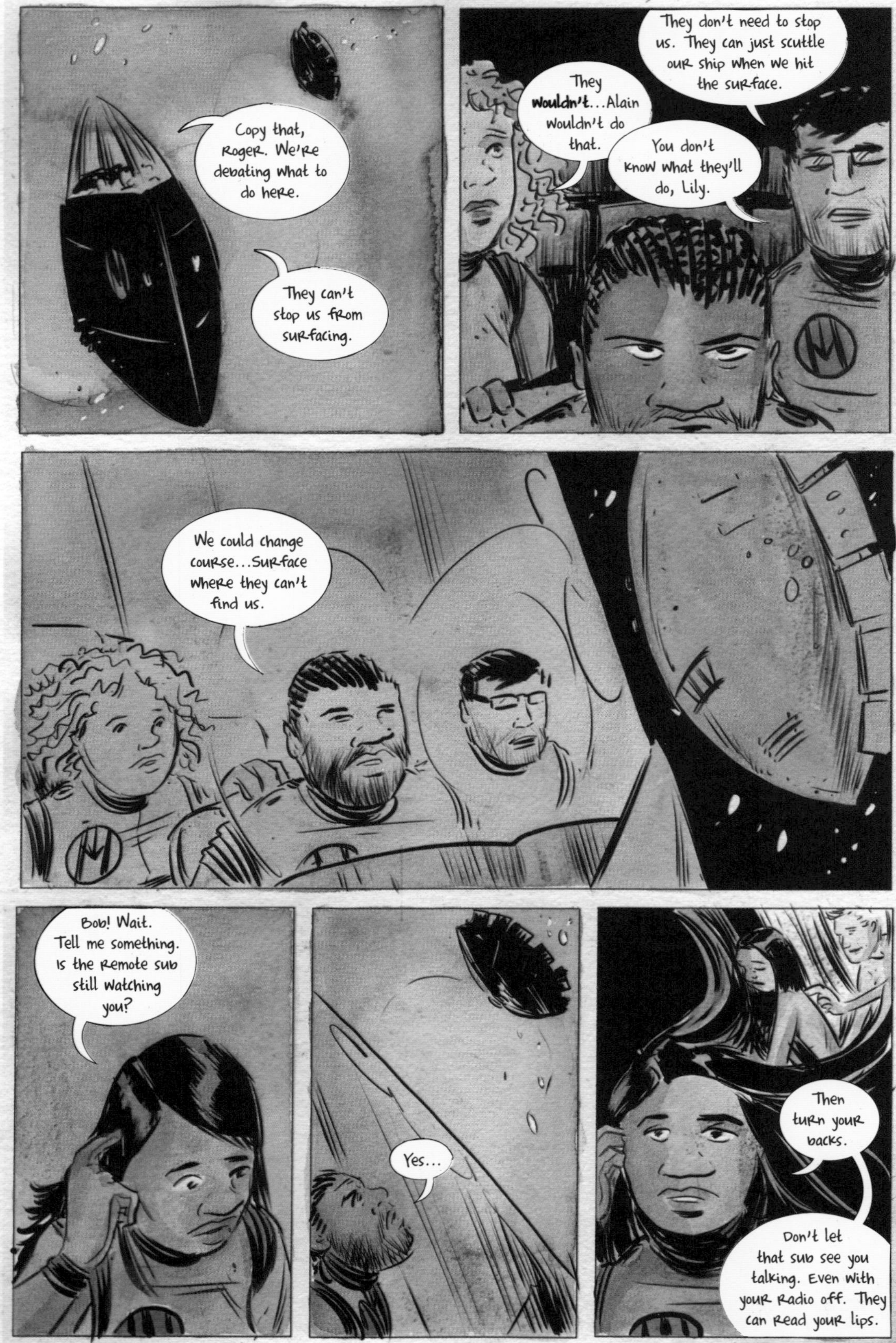
Copy that, Roger. We're debating what to do here.
They can't stop us from surfacing.
They don't need to stop us. They can just scuttle our ship when we hit the surface.
They **wouldn't**...Alain wouldn't do that.
You don't know what they'll do, Lily.
We could change course...Surface where they can't find us.
Bob! Wait. Tell me something. Is the remote sub still watching you?
Yes...
Then turn your backs.
Don't let that sub see you talking. Even with your radio off. They can read your lips.

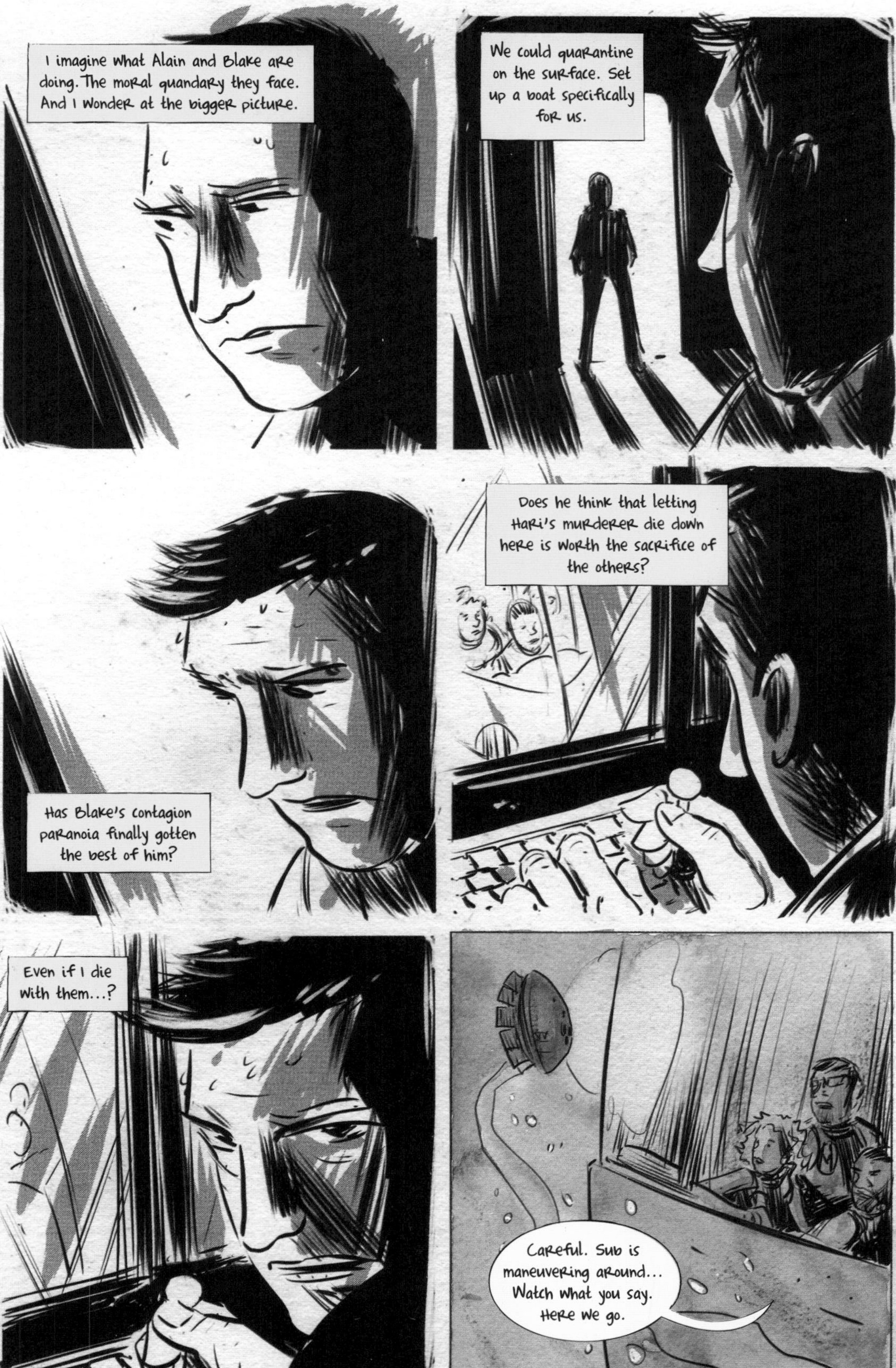
I imagine what Alain and Blake are doing. The moral quandary they face. And I wonder at the bigger picture.
We could quarantine on the surface. Set up a boat specifically for us.
Has Blake's contagion paranoia finally gotten the best of him?
Does he think that letting Hari's murderer die down here is worth the sacrifice of the others?
Even if I die with them...?
Careful. Sub is maneuvering around... Watch what you say. Here we go.

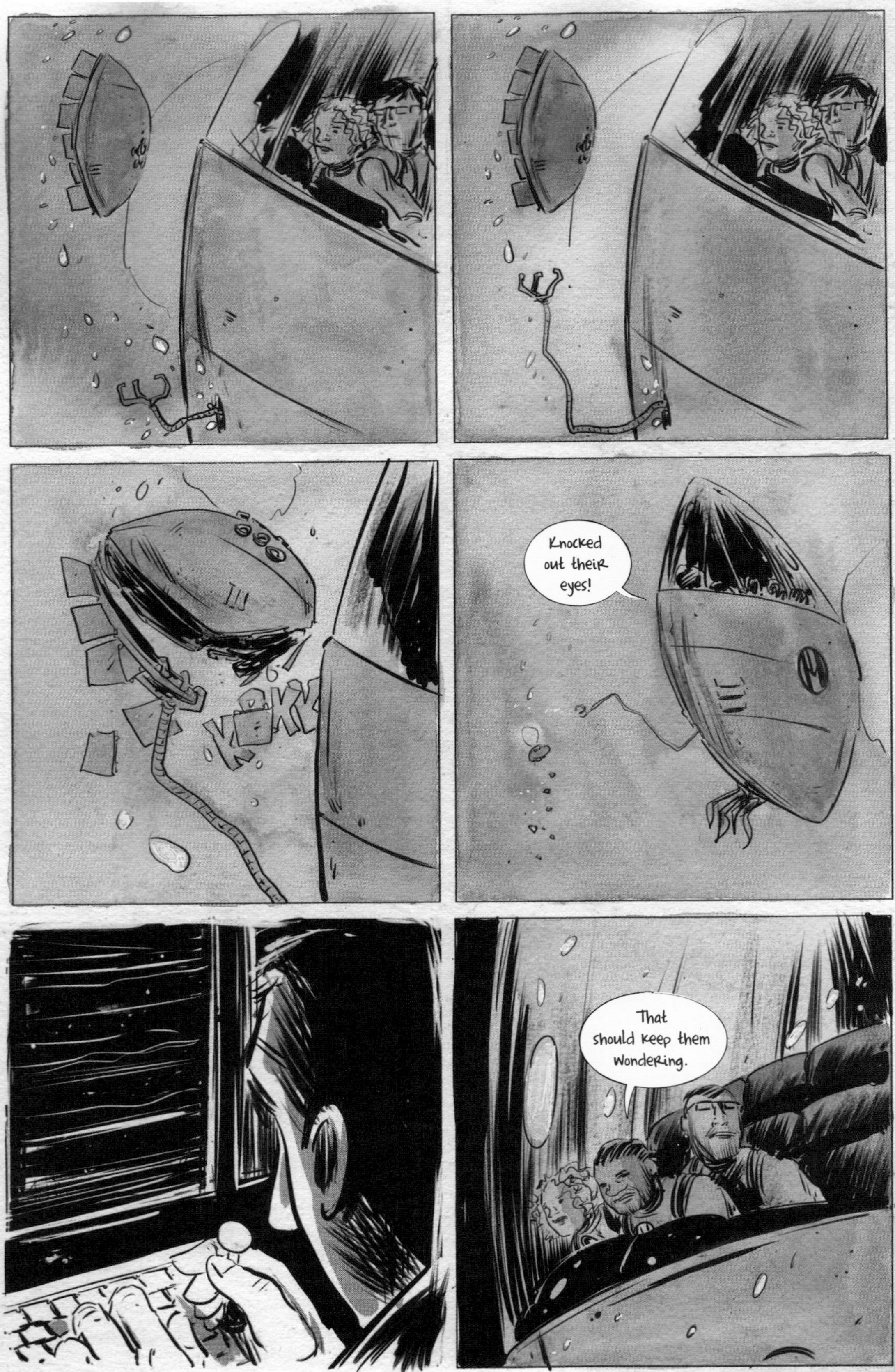
Knocked out their eyes!
That should keep them wondering.

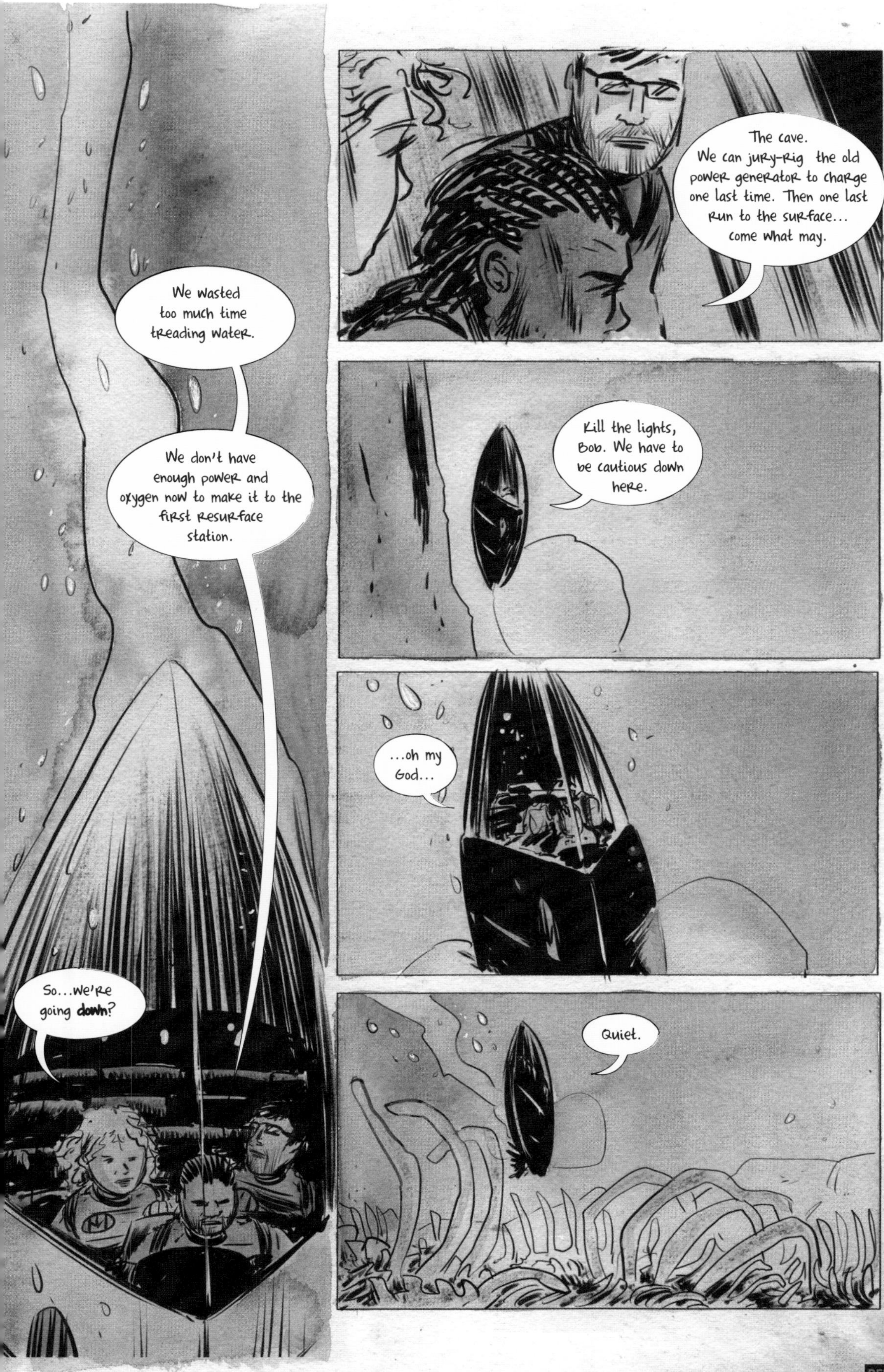
We wasted too much time treading water.
We don't have enough power and oxygen now to make it to the first resurface station.
So...we're going **down**?
The cave. We can jury-rig the old power generator to charge one last time. Then one last run to the surface... come what may.
Kill the lights, Bob. We have to be cautious down here.
...oh my God...
Quiet.

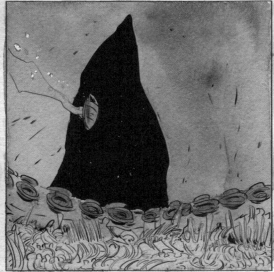

What the hell was that? Did you guys know that was down here?

Aaron?

Yeah. We saw some...strange things down here.

There's a reason why Hari quarantined this area.

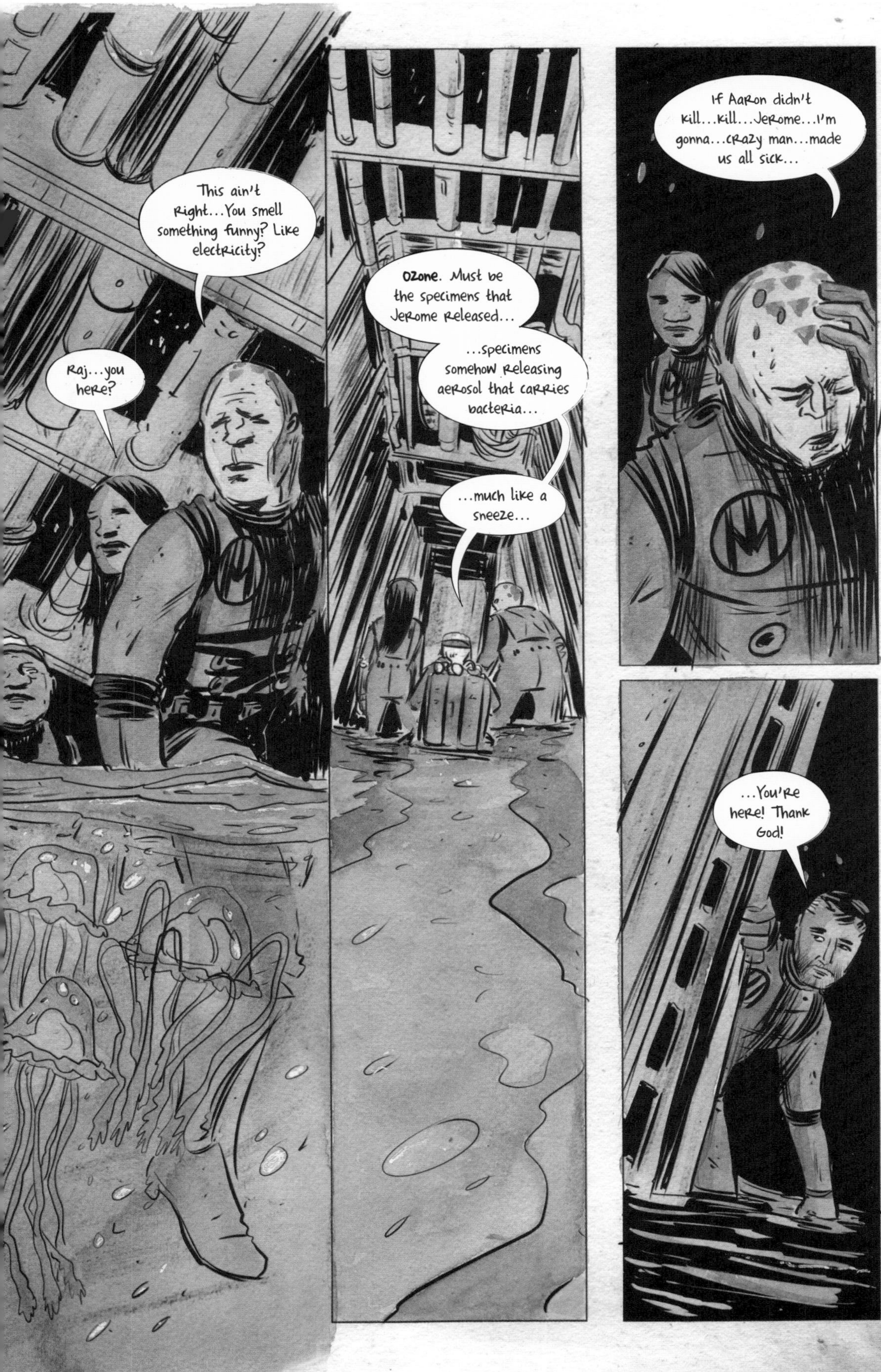
This ain't right...You smell something funny? Like electricity?
Raj...you here?
OZone. Must be the specimens that Jerome released...
...specimens somehow releasing aerosol that carries bacteria...
...much like a sneeze...
If Aaron didn't kill...kill...Jerome...I'm gonna...crazy man...made us all sick...
...You're here! Thank God!

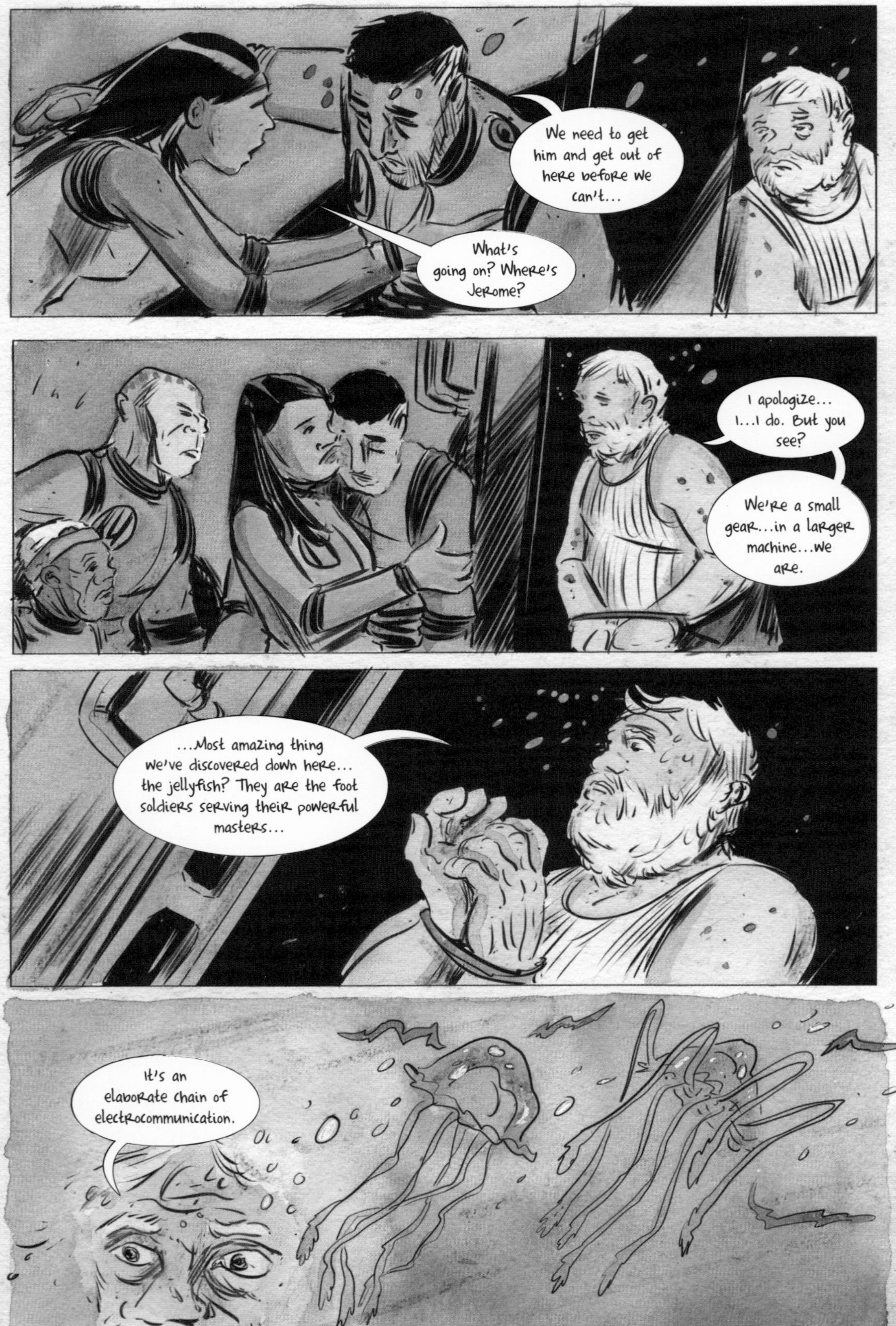
We need to get him and get out of here before we can't...
What's going on? Where's Jerome?
I apologize... I...I do. But you see?
We're a small gear...in a larger machine...we are.
...Most amazing thing we've discovered down here... the jellyfish? They are the foot soldiers serving their powerful masters...
It's an elaborate chain of electrocommunication.

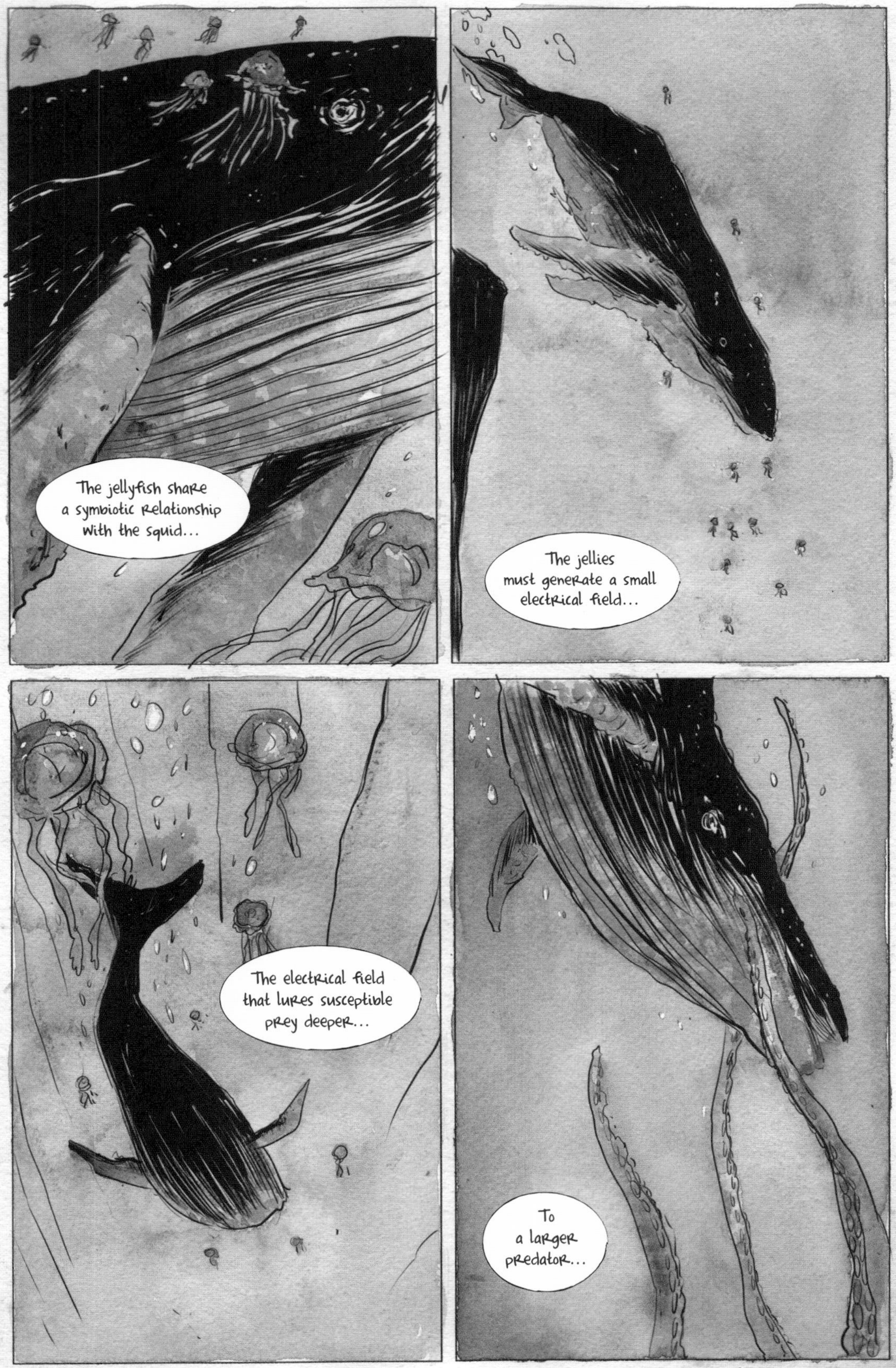
The jellyfish share a symbiotic relationship with the squid...
The jellies must generate a small electrical field...
The electrical field that lures susceptible prey deeper...
To a larger predator...

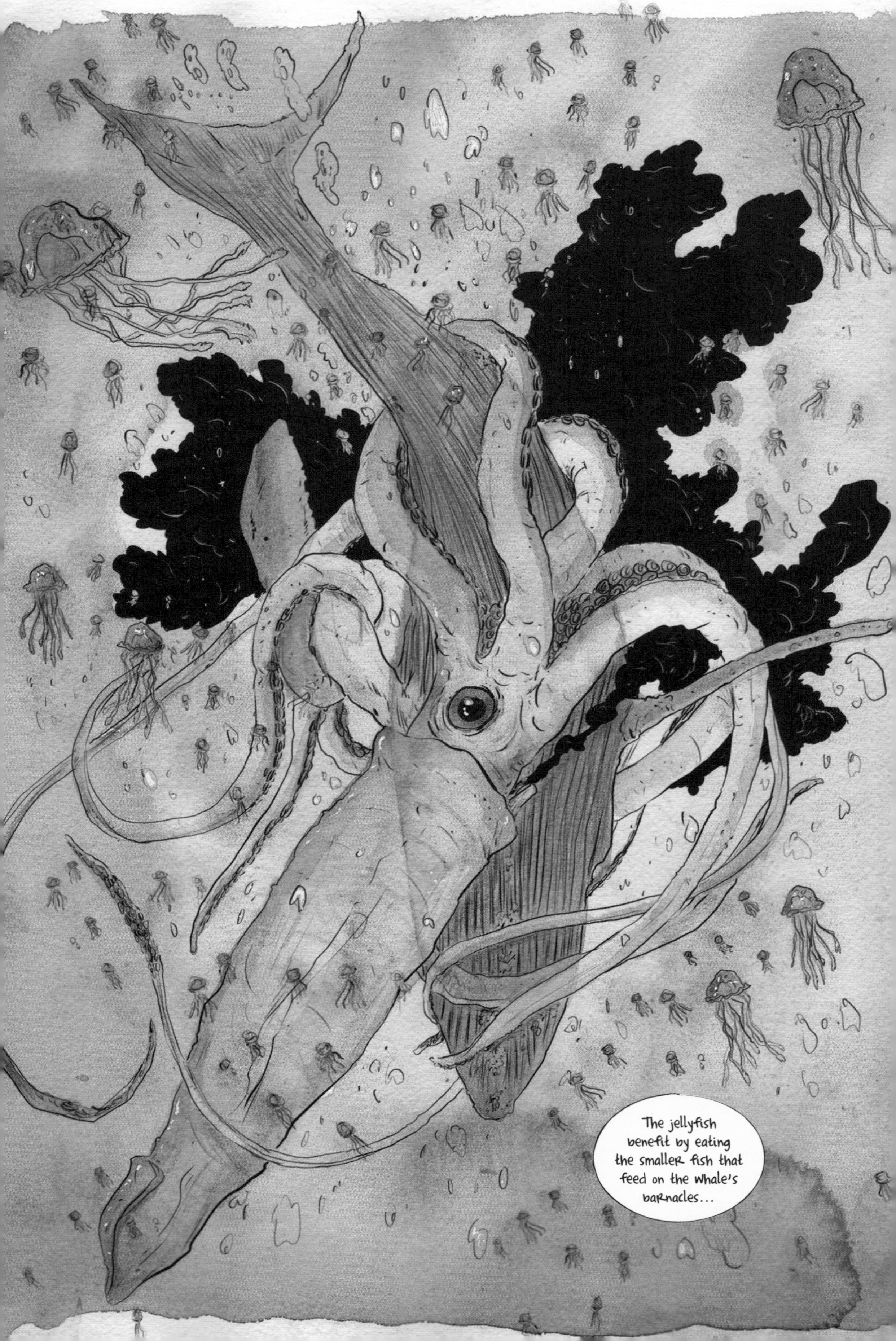
The jellyfish benefit by eating the smaller fish that feed on the whale's barnacles...

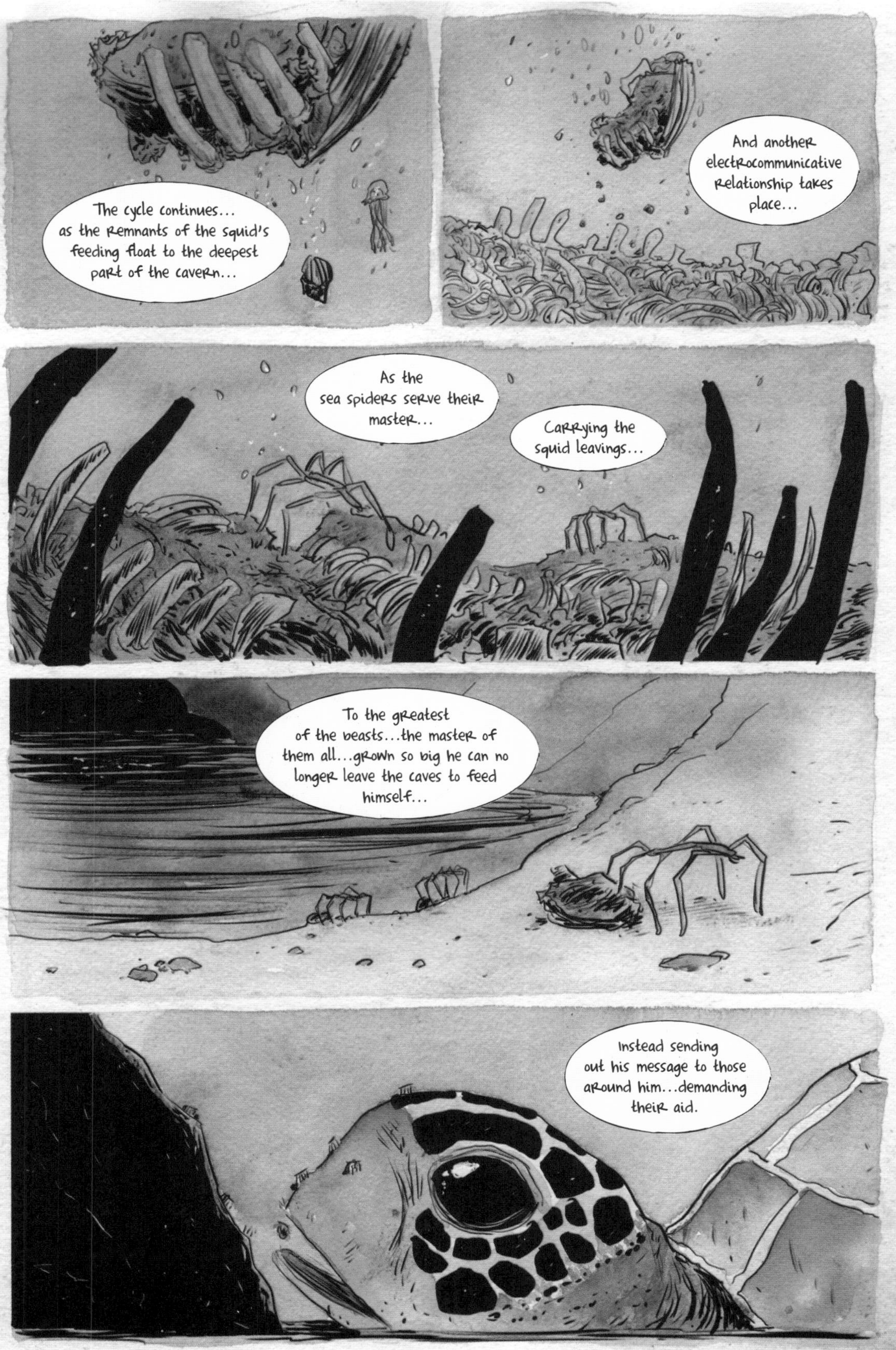

The cycle continues... as the remnants of the squid's feeding float to the deepest part of the cavern...
And another electrocommunicative relationship takes place...
As the sea spiders serve their master...
Carrying the squid leavings...
To the greatest of the beasts...the master of them all...grown so big he can no longer leave the caves to feed himself...
Instead sending out his message to those around him...demanding their aid.

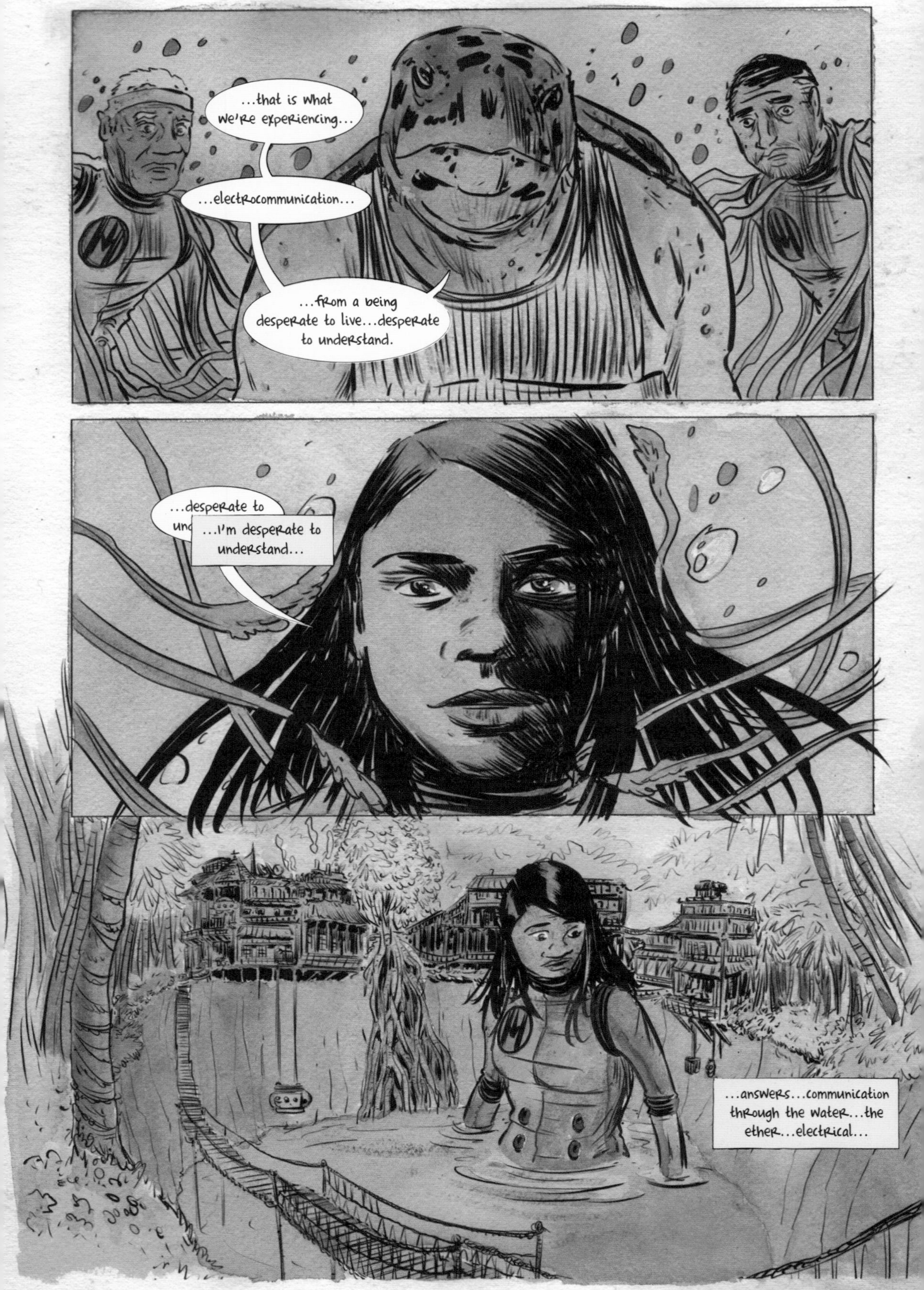
...that is what we're experiencing...
...electrocommunication...
...from a being desperate to live...desperate to understand.
...desperate to und
...I'm desperate to understand...
...answers...communication through the water...the ether...electrical...

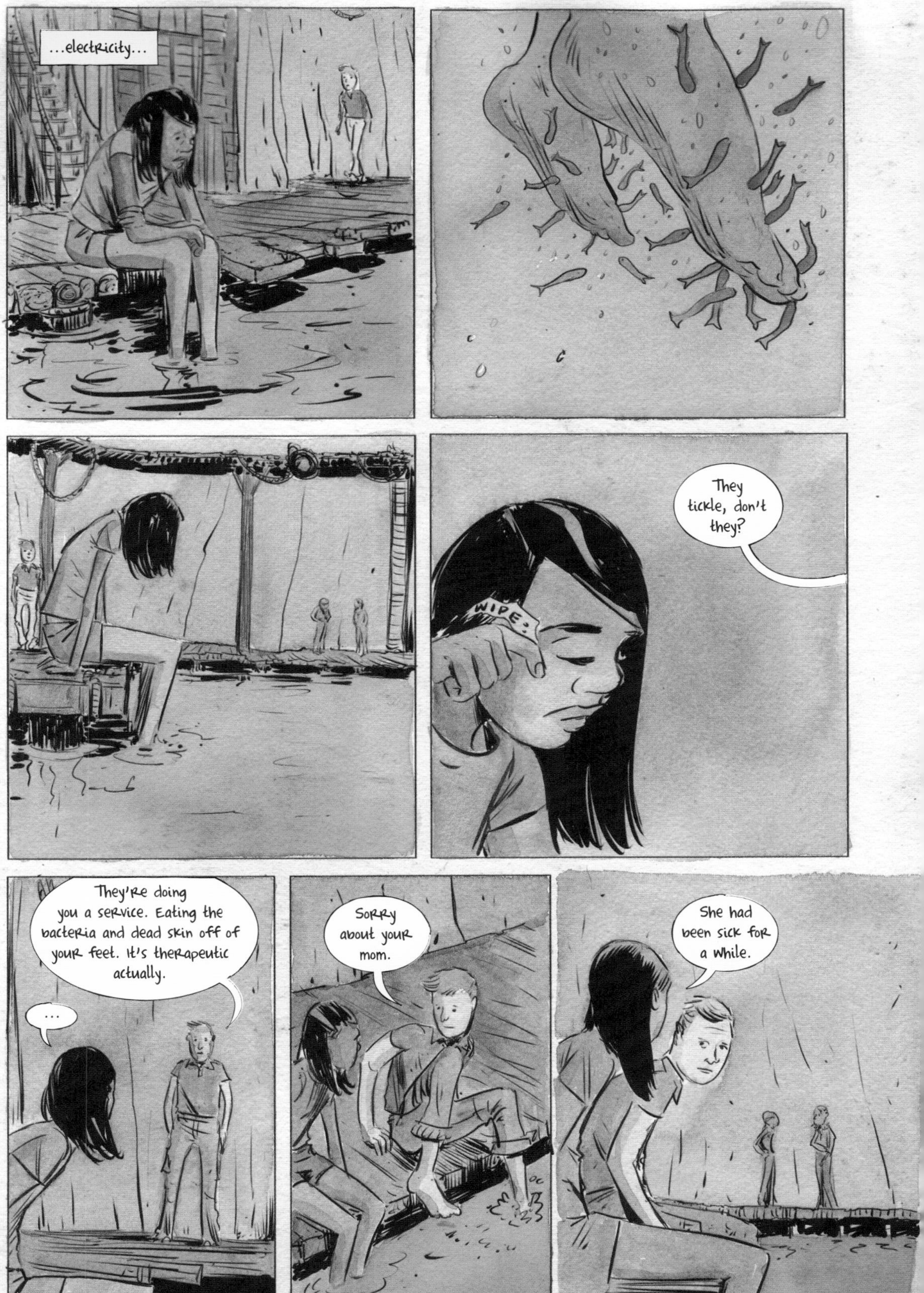

...electricity...
They tickle, don't they?
WIPE:
They're doing you a service. Eating the bacteria and dead skin off of your feet. It's therapeutic actually.
...
Sorry about your mom.
She had been sick for a while.

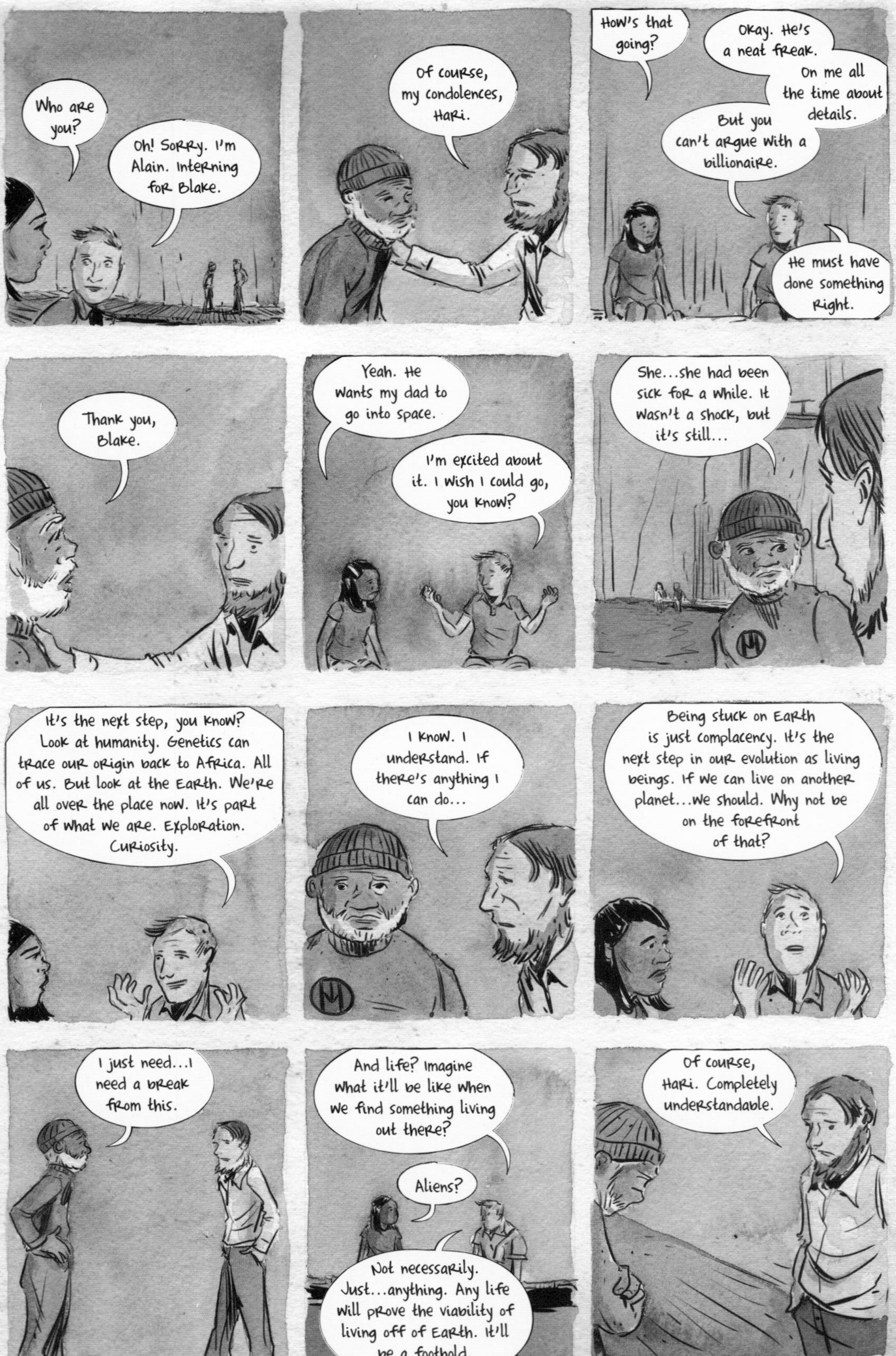
Who are you?
Oh! Sorry. I'm Alain. Interning for Blake.
Of course, my condolences, Hari.
How's that going?
Okay. He's a neat freak.
On me all the time about details.
But you can't argue with a billionaire.
He must have done something right.
Thank you, Blake.
Yeah. He wants my dad to go into space.
I'm excited about it. I wish I could go, you know?
She...she had been sick for a while. It wasn't a shock, but it's still...
It's the next step, you know? Look at humanity. Genetics can trace our origin back to Africa. All of us. But look at the Earth. We're all over the place now. It's part of what we are. Exploration. Curiosity.
I know. I understand. If there's anything I can do...
Being stuck on Earth is just complacency. It's the next step in our evolution as living beings. If we can live on another planet...we should. Why not be on the forefront of that?
I just need...I need a break from this.
And life? Imagine what it'll be like when we find something living out there?
Aliens?
Not necessarily. Just...anything. Any life will prove the viability of living off of Earth. It'll be a foothold.
Of course, Hari. Completely understandable.

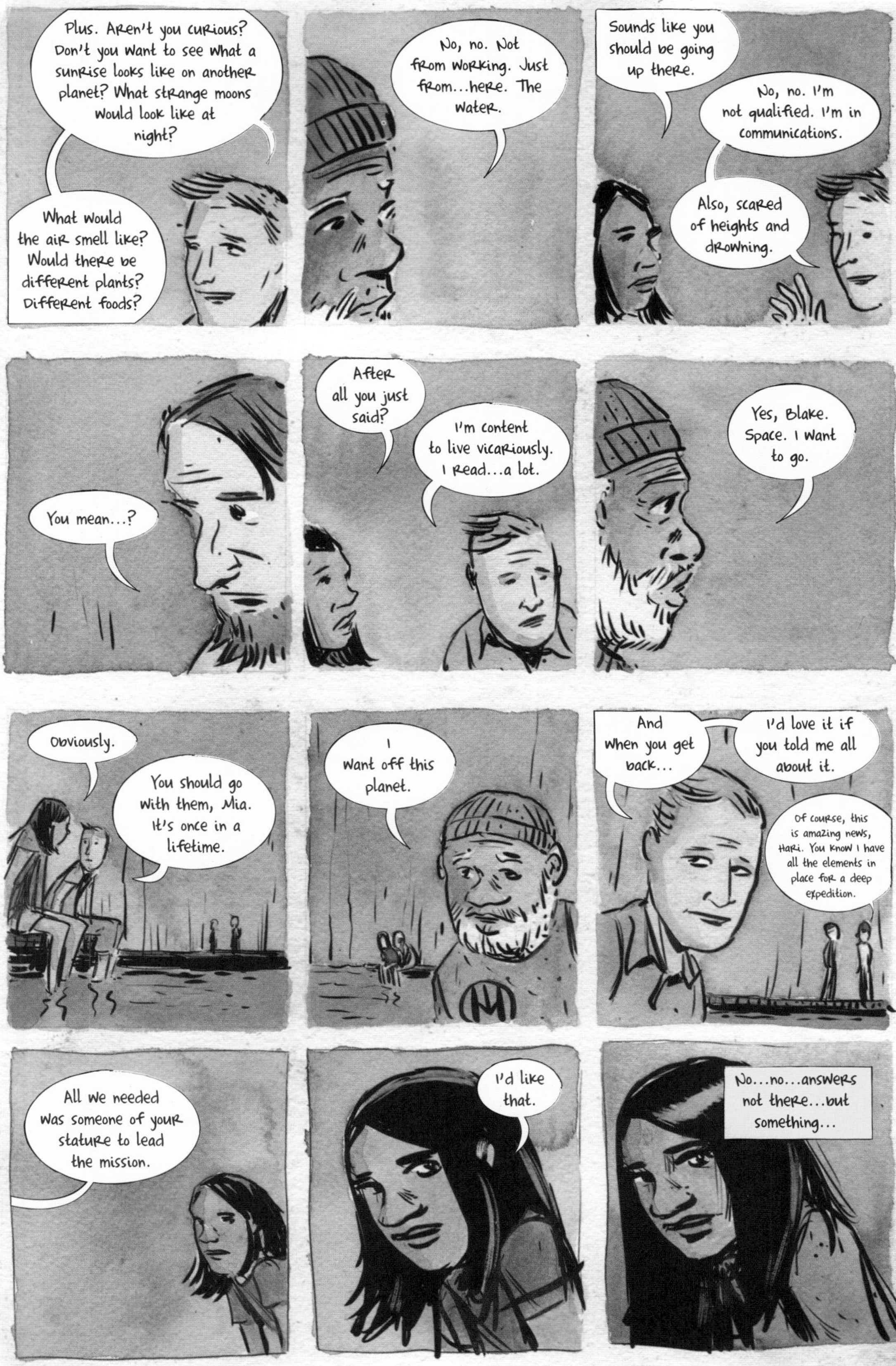
Plus. Aren't you curious? Don't you want to see what a sunrise looks like on another planet? What strange moons would look like at night?
What would the air smell like? Would there be different plants? Different foods?
No, no. Not from working. Just from...here. The water.
Sounds like you should be going up there.
No, no. I'm not qualified. I'm in communications.
Also, scared of heights and drowning.
You mean...?
After all you just said?
I'm content to live vicariously. I read...a lot.
Yes, Blake. Space. I want to go.
Obviously.
You should go with them, Mia. It's once in a lifetime.
I want off this planet.
And when you get back...
I'd love it if you told me all about it.
Of course, this is amazing news, Hari. You know I have all the elements in place for a deep expedition.
All we needed was someone of your stature to lead the mission.
I'd like that.
No...no...answers not there...but something...

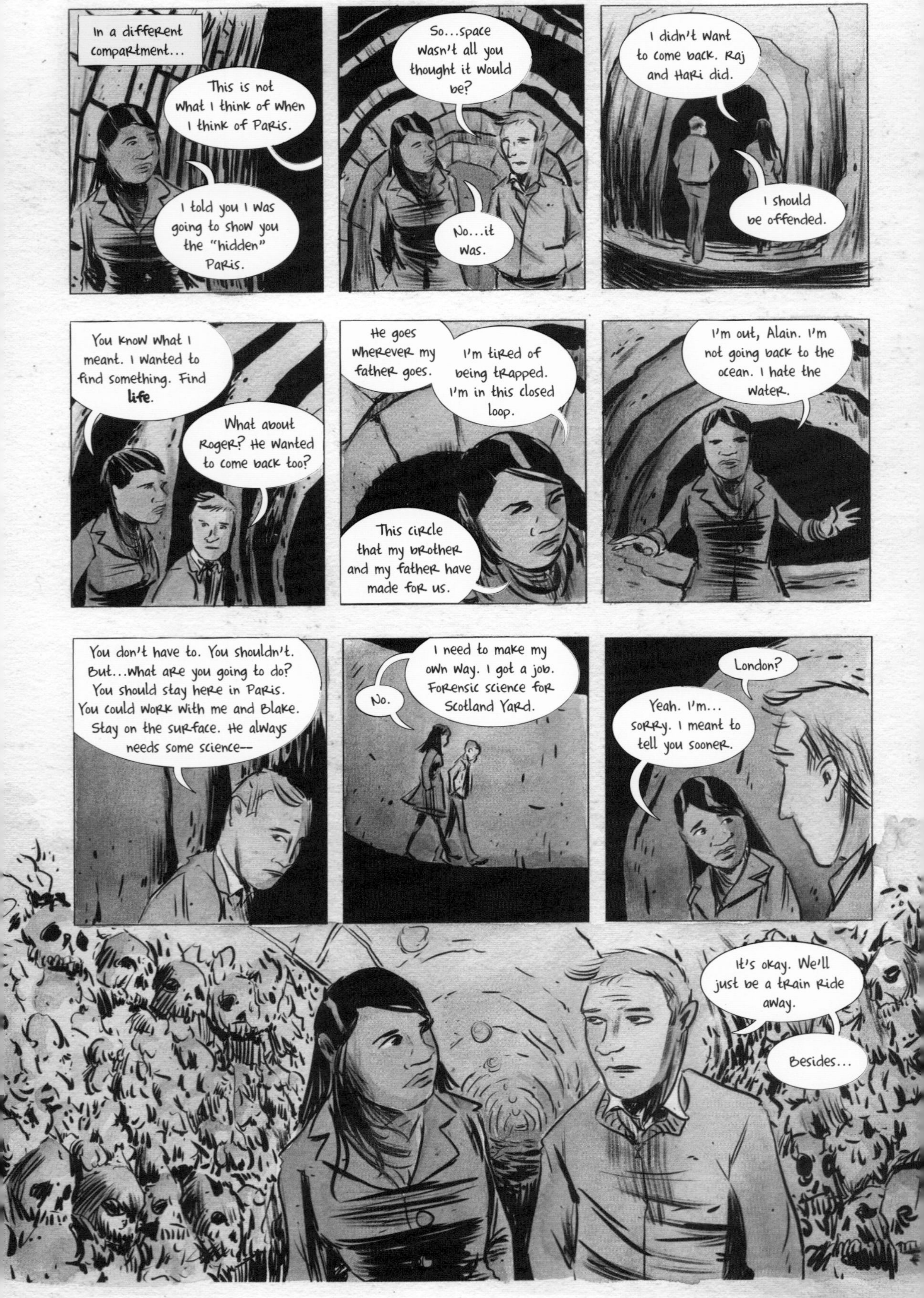
In a different compartment...
This is not what I think of when I think of Paris.
I told you I was going to show you the "hidden" Paris.
So...space wasn't all you thought it would be?
No...it was.
I didn't want to come back. Raj and Hari did.
I should be offended.
You know what I meant. I wanted to find something. Find **life**.
What about Roger? He wanted to come back too?
He goes wherever my father goes.
I'm tired of being trapped. I'm in this closed loop.
This circle that my brother and my father have made for us.
I'm out, Alain. I'm not going back to the ocean. I hate the water.
You don't have to. You shouldn't. But...what are you going to do? You should stay here in Paris. You could work with me and Blake. Stay on the surface. He always needs some science--
No.
I need to make my own way. I got a job. Forensic science for Scotland Yard.
London?
Yeah. I'm... sorry. I meant to tell you sooner.
It's okay. We'll just be a train ride away.
Besides...

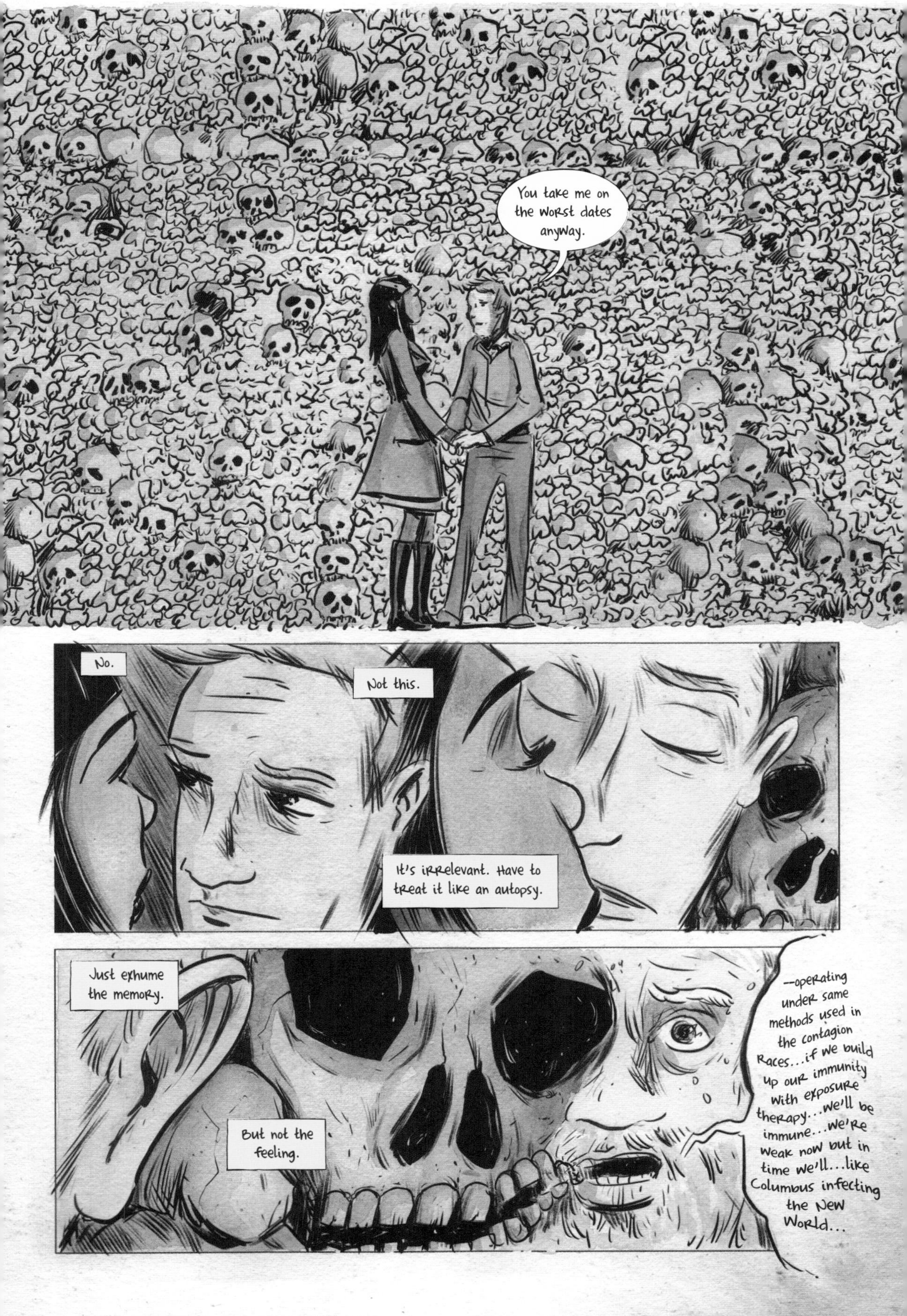
You take me on the worst dates anyway.
No.
Not this.
It's irrelevant. Have to treat it like an autopsy.
Just exhume the memory.
But not the feeling.
--operating under same methods used in the contagion races...if we build up our immunity with exposure therapy...we'll be immune...we're weak now but in time we'll...like Columbus infecting the New World...

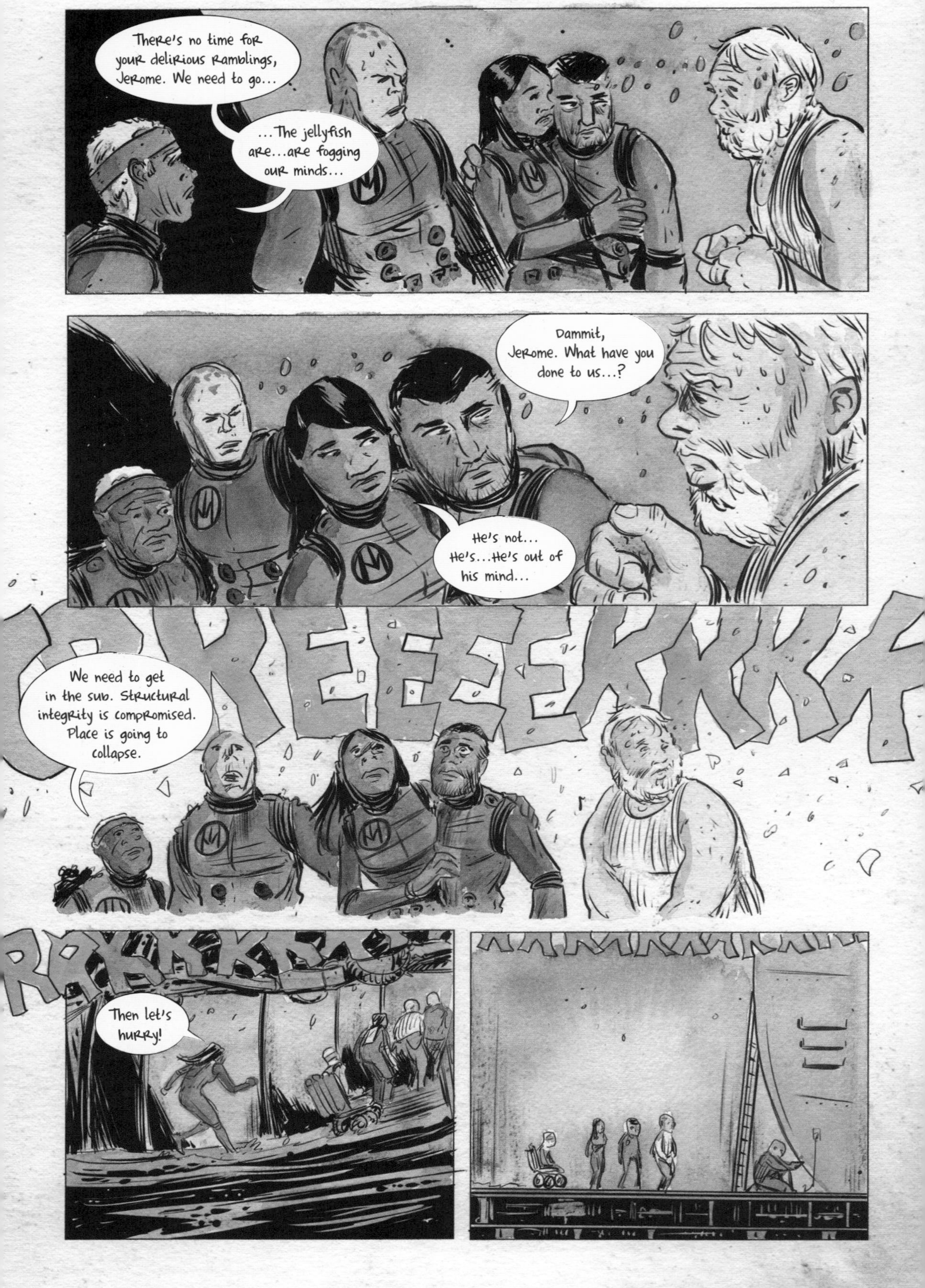
There's no time for your delirious ramblings, Jerome. We need to go...
...The jellyfish are...are fogging our minds...
Dammit, Jerome. What have you done to us...?
He's not... He's...He's out of his mind...
We need to get in the sub. Structural integrity is compromised. Place is going to collapse.
Then let's hurry!

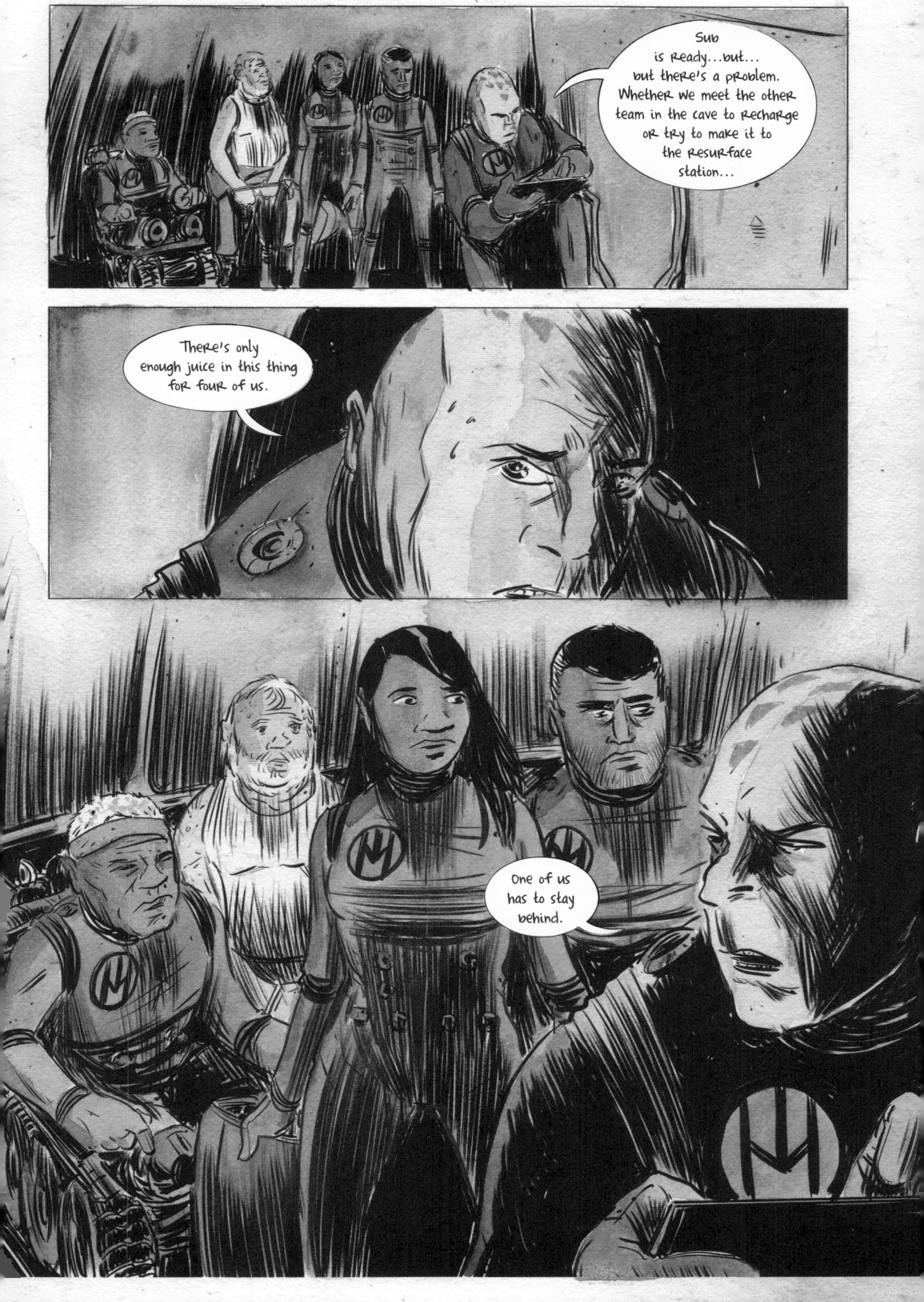
Sub is ready...but... but there's a problem. Whether we meet the other team in the cave to recharge or try to make it to the resurface station...
There's only enough juice in this thing for four of us.
One of us has to stay behind.

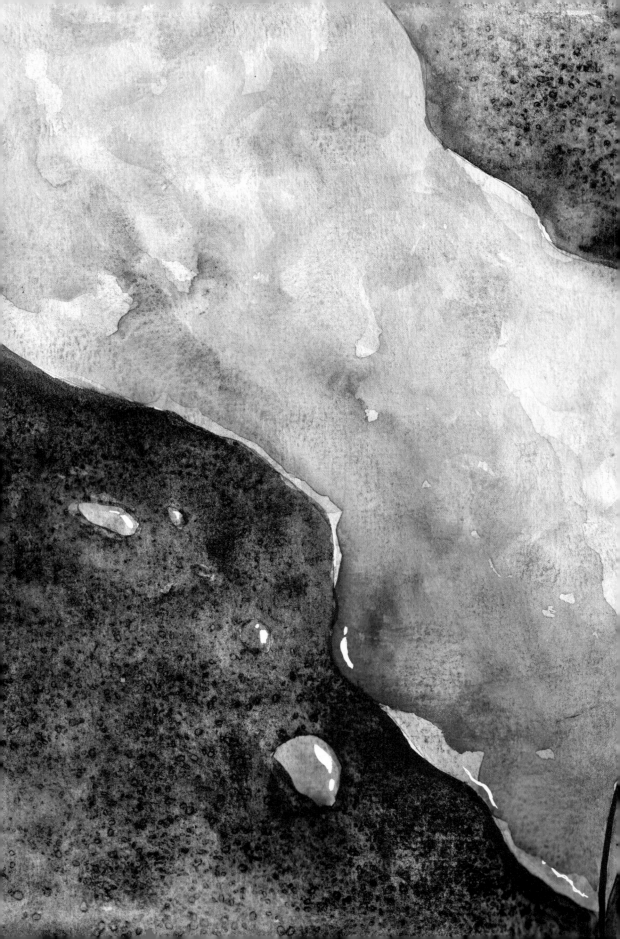

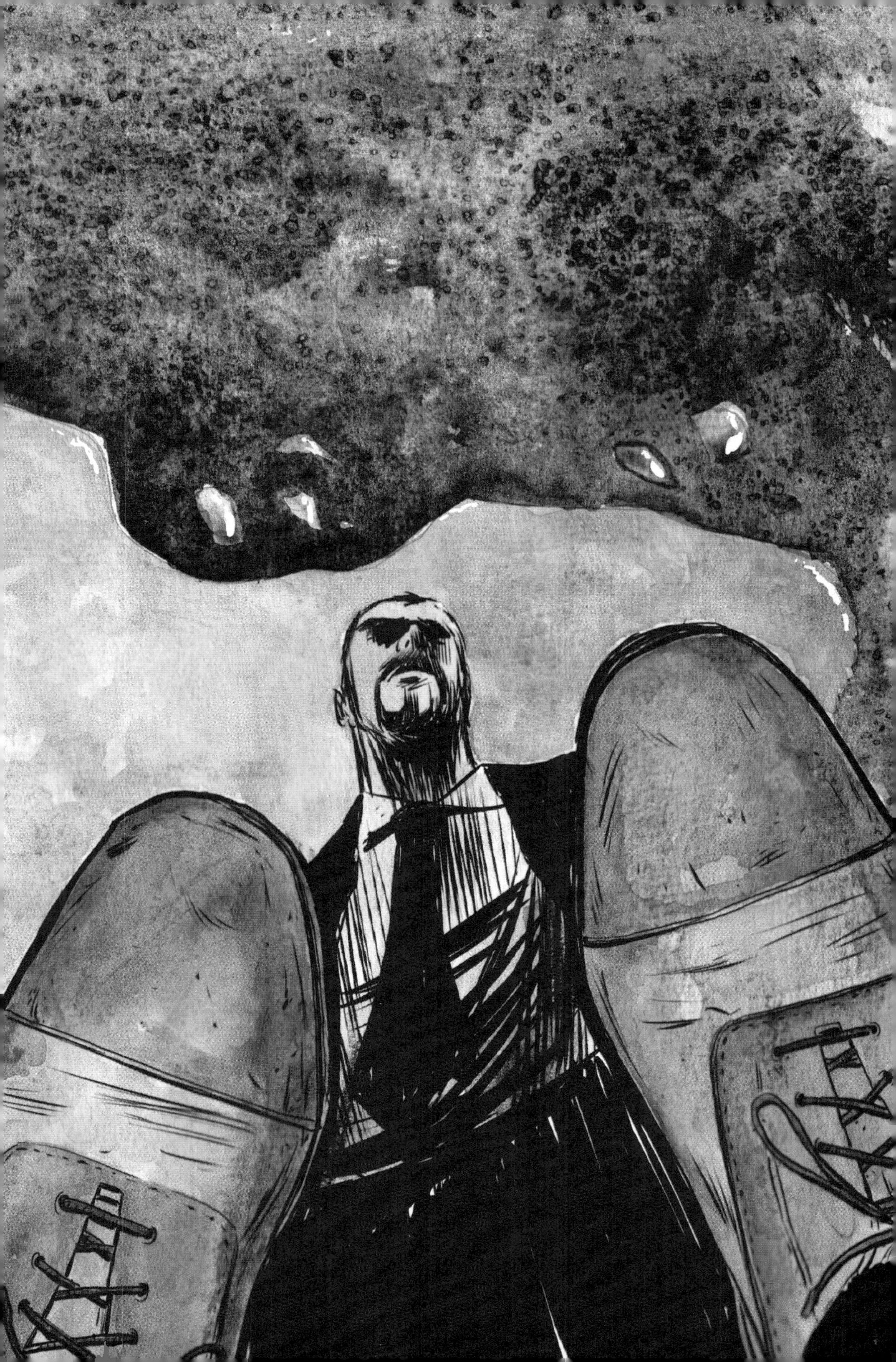

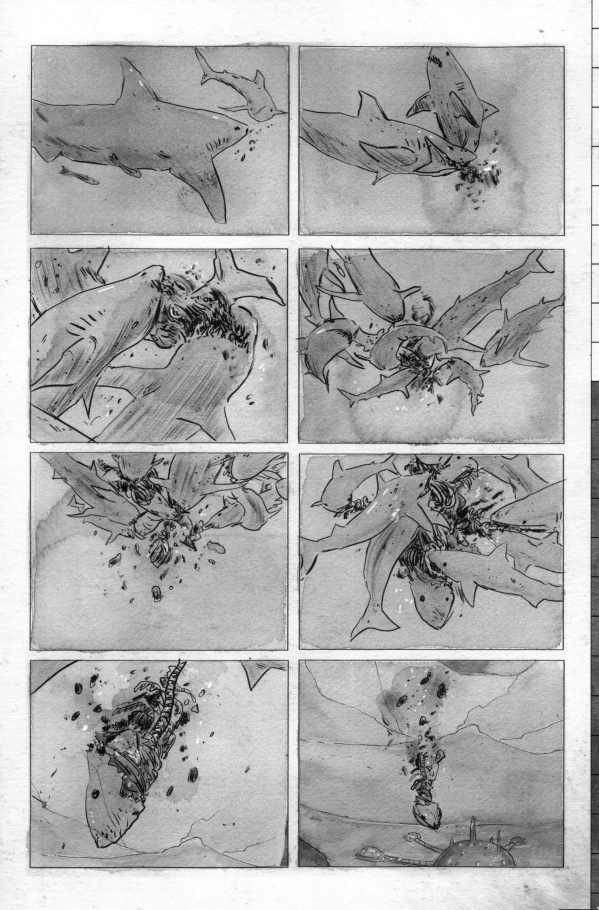

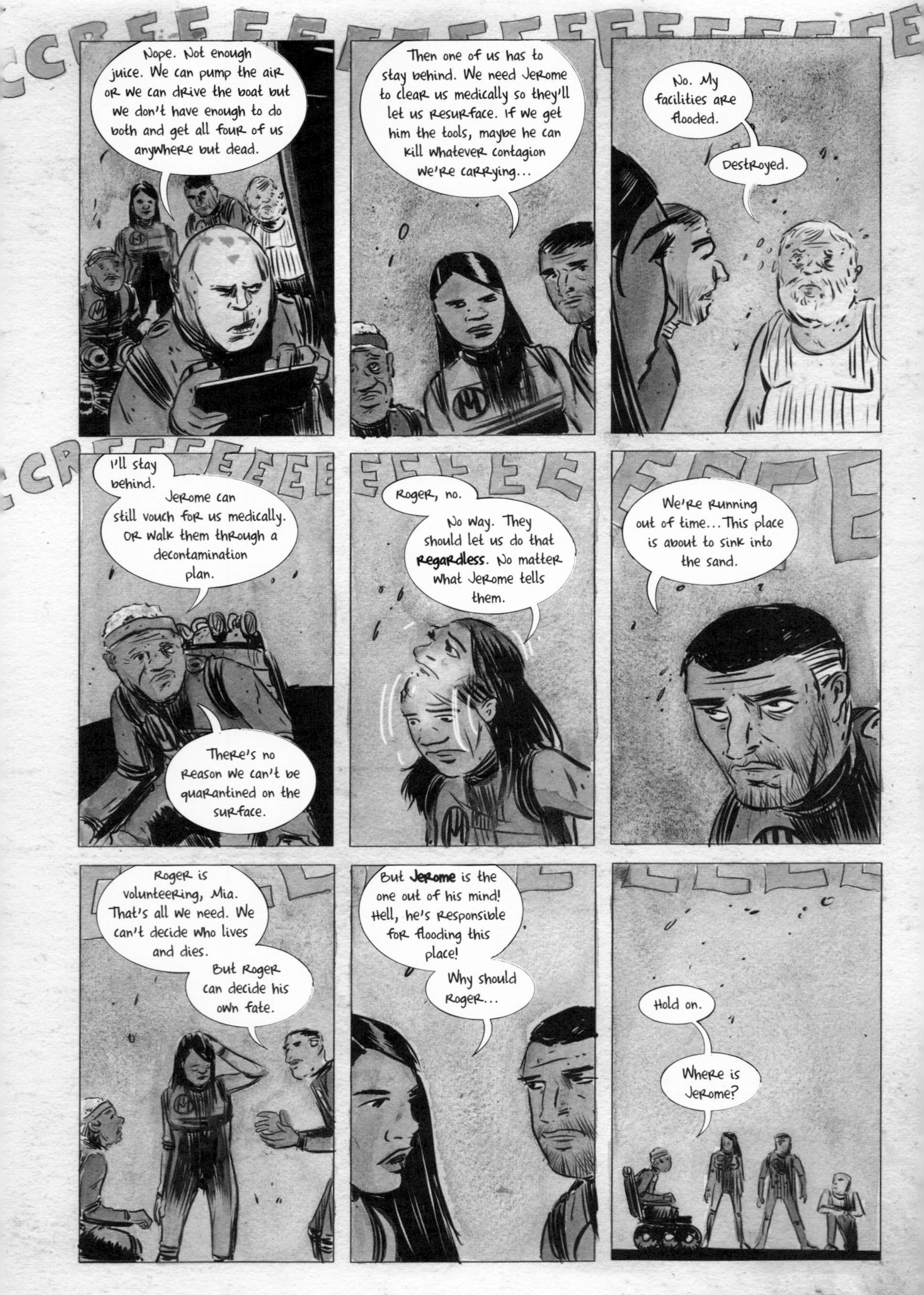
Nope. Not enough juice. We can pump the air or we can drive the boat but we don't have enough to do both and get all four of us anywhere but dead.
Then one of us has to stay behind. We need Jerome to clear us medically so they'll let us resurface. If we get him the tools, maybe he can kill whatever contagion we're carrying...
No. My facilities are flooded.
Destroyed.
I'll stay behind.
Jerome can still vouch for us medically. Or walk them through a decontamination plan.
There's no reason we can't be quarantined on the surface.
Roger, no.
No way. They should let us do that **regardless**. No matter what Jerome tells them.
We're running out of time... This place is about to sink into the sand.
Roger is volunteering, Mia. That's all we need. We can't decide who lives and dies.
But Roger can decide his own fate.
But **Jerome** is the one out of his mind! Hell, he's responsible for flooding this place!
Why should Roger...
Hold on.
Where is Jerome?

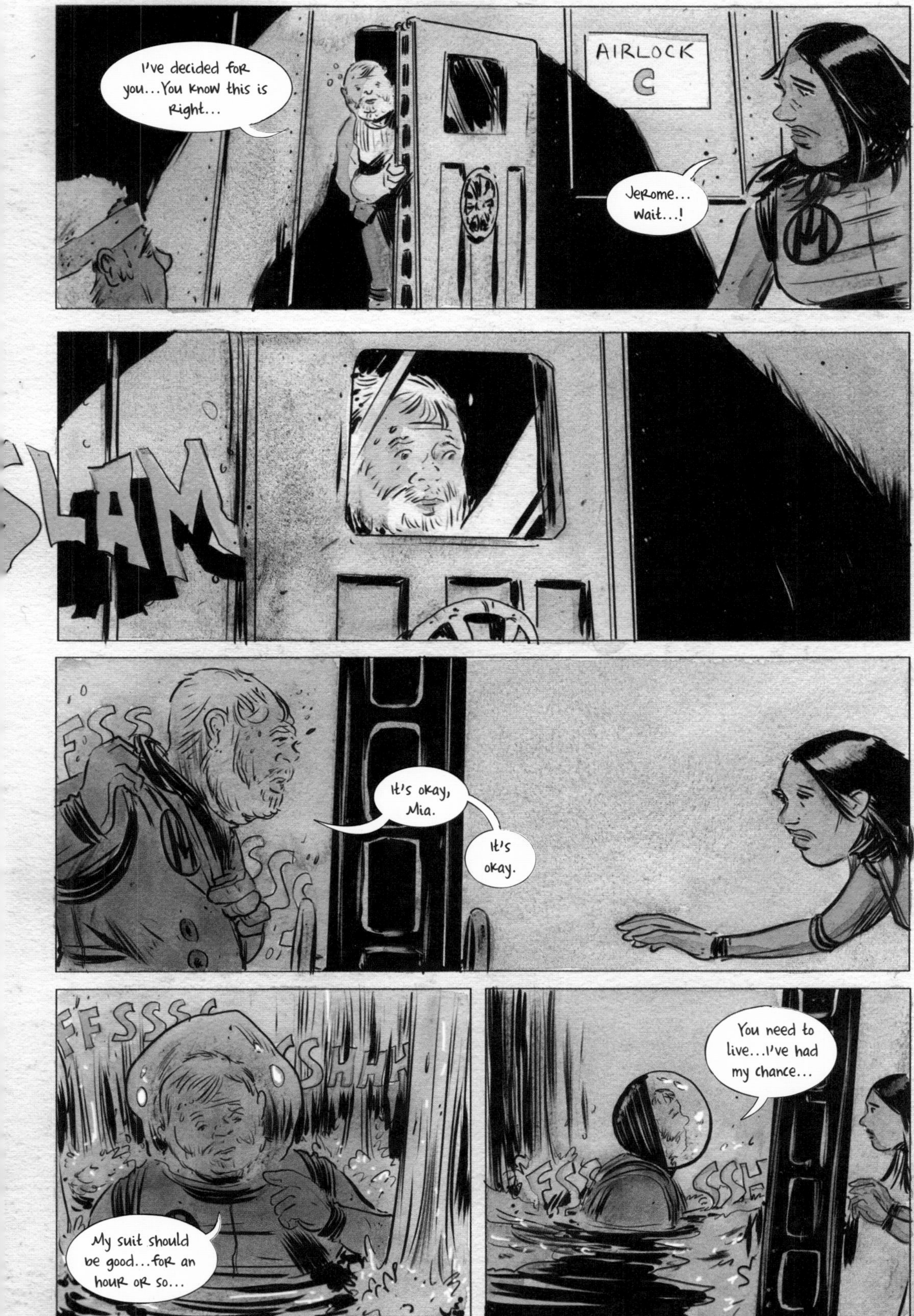
I've decided for you...You know this is Right...
AIRLOCK C
Jerome... Wait...!
SLAM
It's okay, Mia.
It's okay.
My suit should be good...for an hour or so...
You need to live...I've had my chance...

...I had an epiphany down here, Mia...I'll tell you all I know...

I serve a larger purpose now...and hopefully I can serve yours as well...

...Your father didn't understand... how small our role really is...

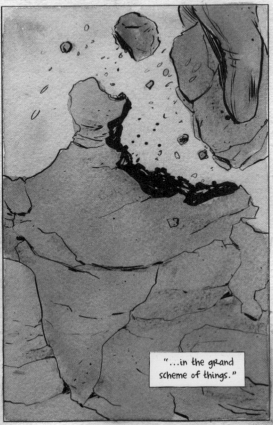

"...in the grand scheme of things."

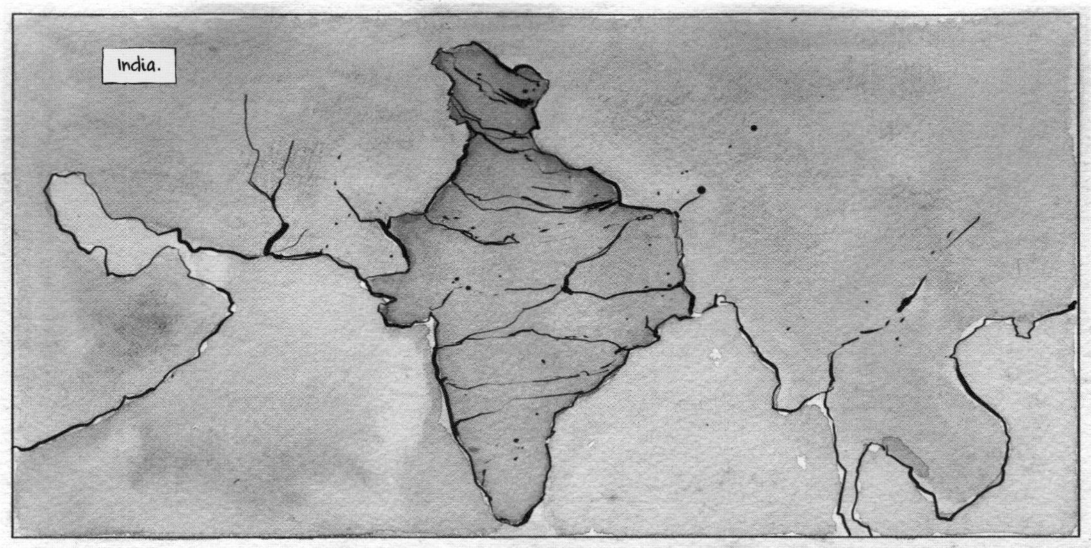
India.

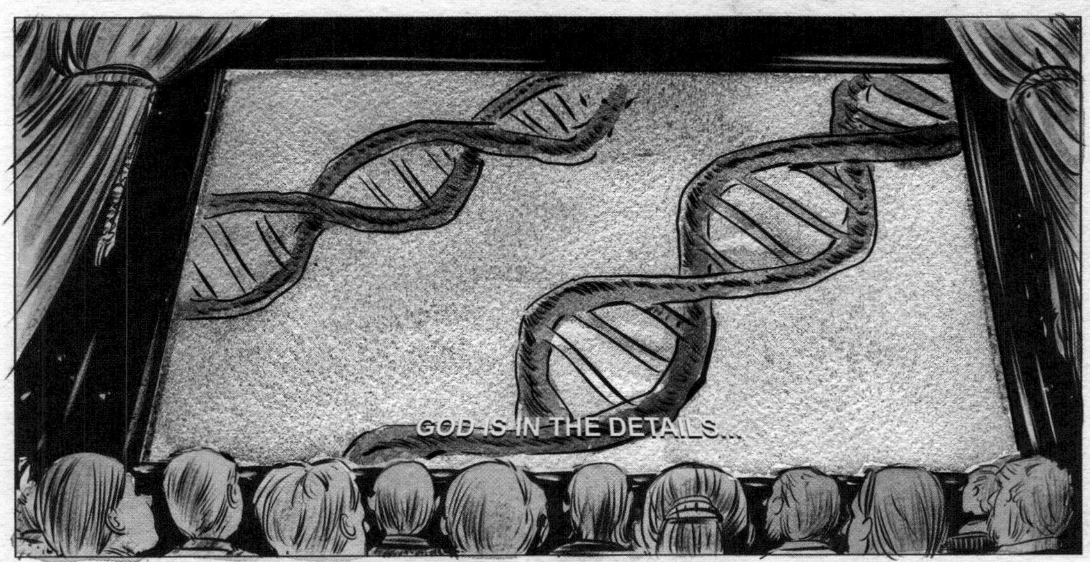
GOD IS IN THE DETAILS...

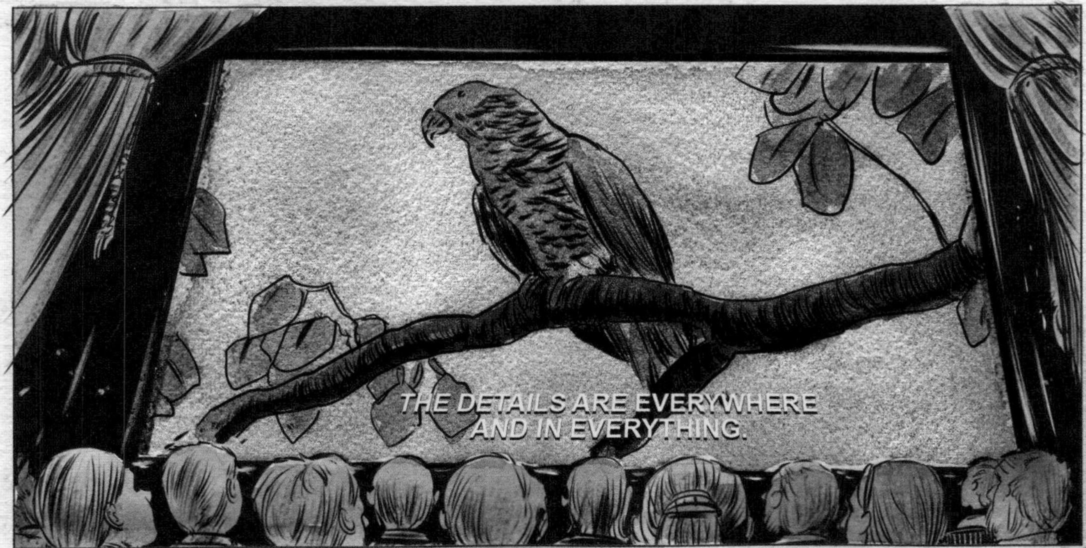
THE DETAILS ARE EVERYWHERE
AND IN EVERYTHING.

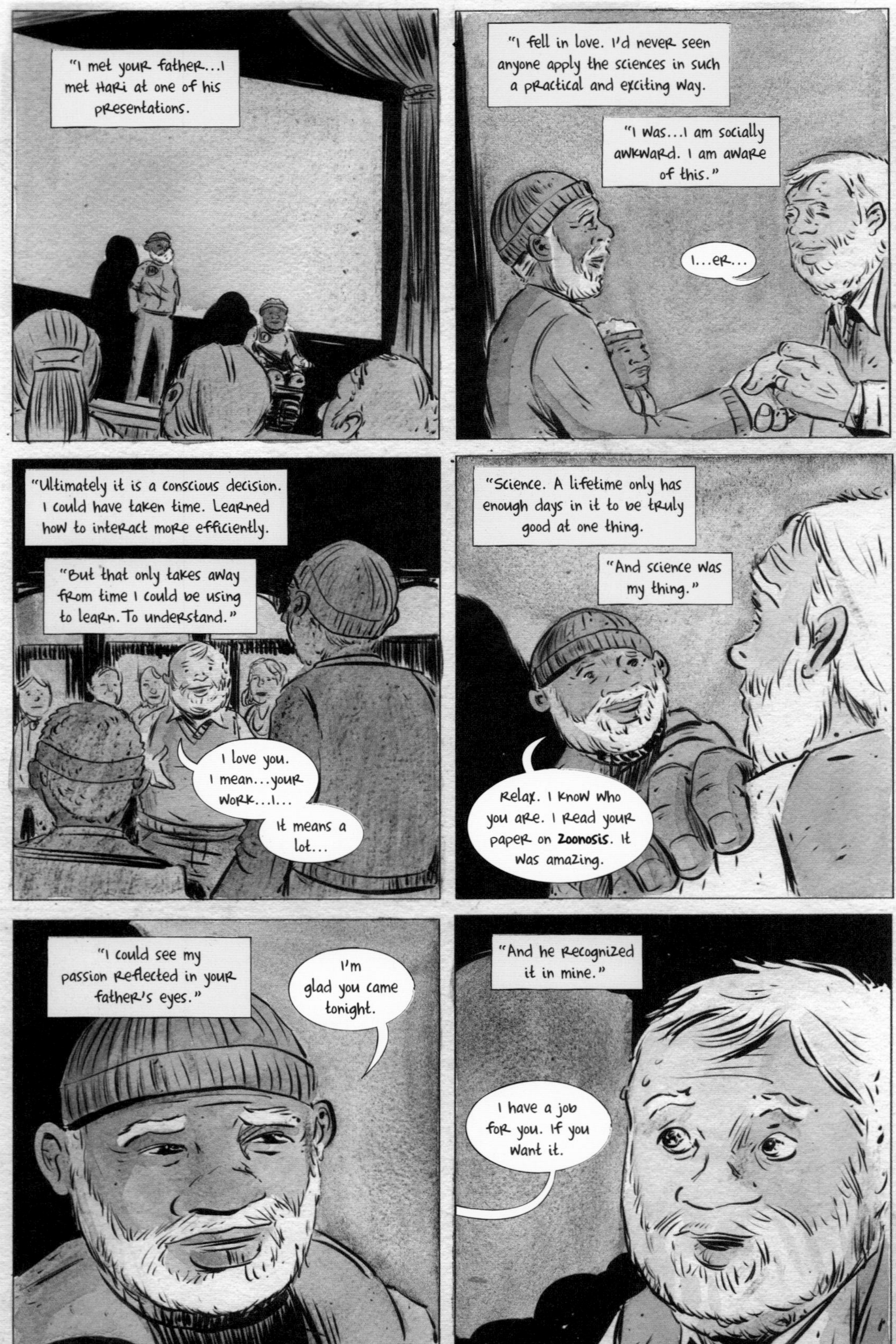
"I met your father...I met Hari at one of his presentations.
"I fell in love. I'd never seen anyone apply the sciences in such a practical and exciting way.
"I was...I am socially awkward. I am aware of this."
I...er...
"Ultimately it is a conscious decision. I could have taken time. Learned how to interact more efficiently.
"But that only takes away from time I could be using to learn. To understand."
I love you. I mean...your work...I...
It means a lot...
"Science. A lifetime only has enough days in it to be truly good at one thing.
"And science was my thing."
Relax. I know who you are. I read your paper on **Zoonosis**. It was amazing.
"I could see my passion reflected in your father's eyes."
I'm glad you came tonight.
"And he recognized it in mine."
I have a job for you. If you want it.

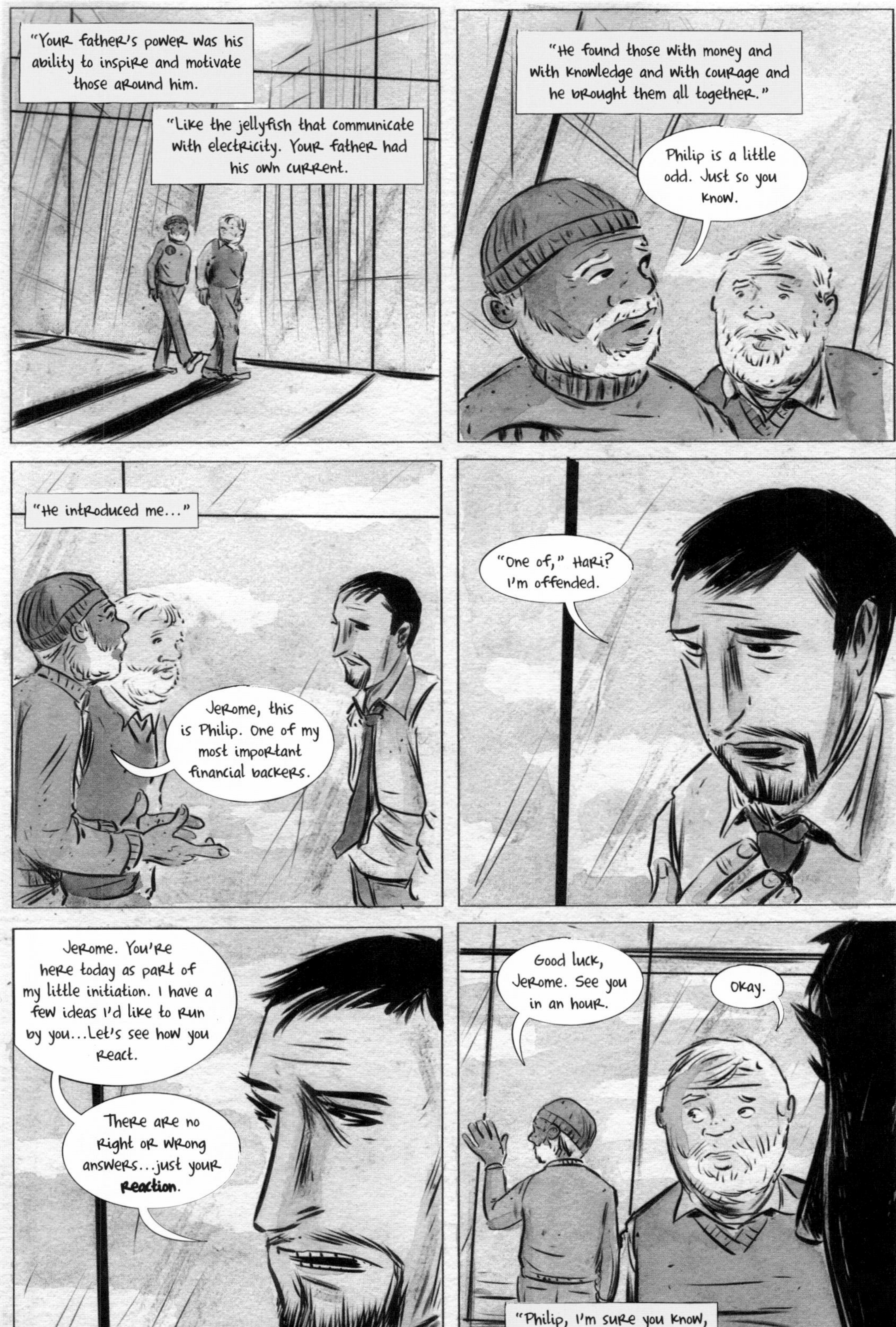
"Your father's power was his ability to inspire and motivate those around him.
"Like the jellyfish that communicate with electricity. Your father had his own current.
"He found those with money and with knowledge and with courage and he brought them all together."
Philip is a little odd. Just so you know.
"He introduced me..."
Jerome, this is Philip. One of my most important financial backers.
"One of," Hari? I'm offended.
Jerome. You're here today as part of my little initiation. I have a few ideas I'd like to run by you...Let's see how you react.
There are no right or wrong answers...just your **reaction**.
Good luck, Jerome. See you in an hour.
Okay.
"Philip, I'm sure you know, had...interesting ideas."

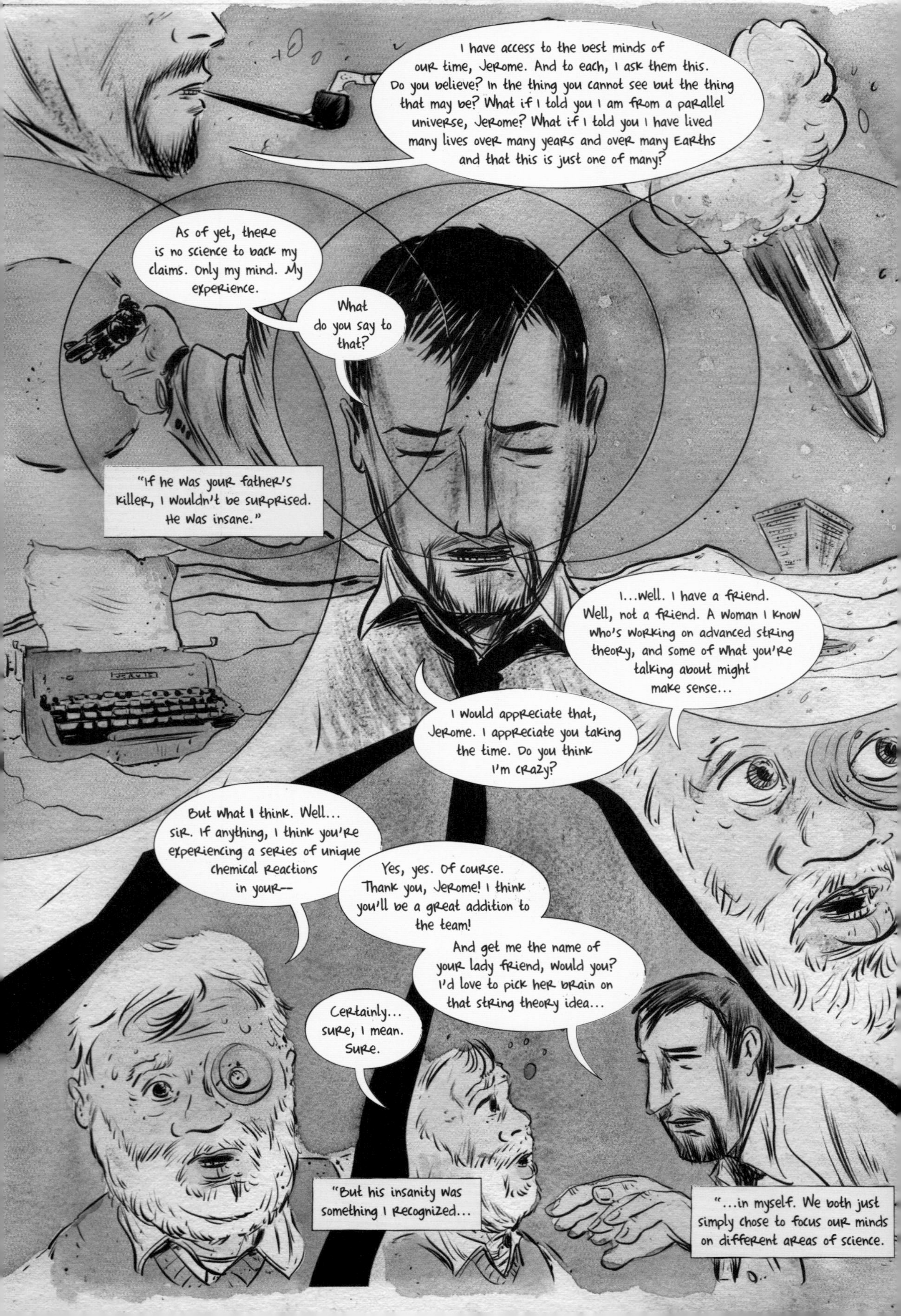
I have access to the best minds of our time, Jerome. And to each, I ask them this. Do you believe? In the thing you cannot see but the thing that may be? What if I told you I am from a parallel universe, Jerome? What if I told you I have lived many lives over many years and over many Earths and that this is just one of many?
As of yet, there is no science to back my claims. Only my mind. My experience.
What do you say to that?
"If he was your father's killer, I wouldn't be surprised. He was insane."
I...well. I have a friend. Well, not a friend. A woman I know who's working on advanced string theory, and some of what you're talking about might make sense...
I would appreciate that, Jerome. I appreciate you taking the time. Do you think I'm crazy?
But what I think. Well... sir. If anything, I think you're experiencing a series of unique chemical reactions in your--
Yes, yes. Of course. Thank you, Jerome! I think you'll be a great addition to the team!
And get me the name of your lady friend, would you? I'd love to pick her brain on that string theory idea...
Certainly... sure, I mean. Sure.
"But his insanity was something I recognized...
"...in myself. We both just simply chose to focus our minds on different areas of science.

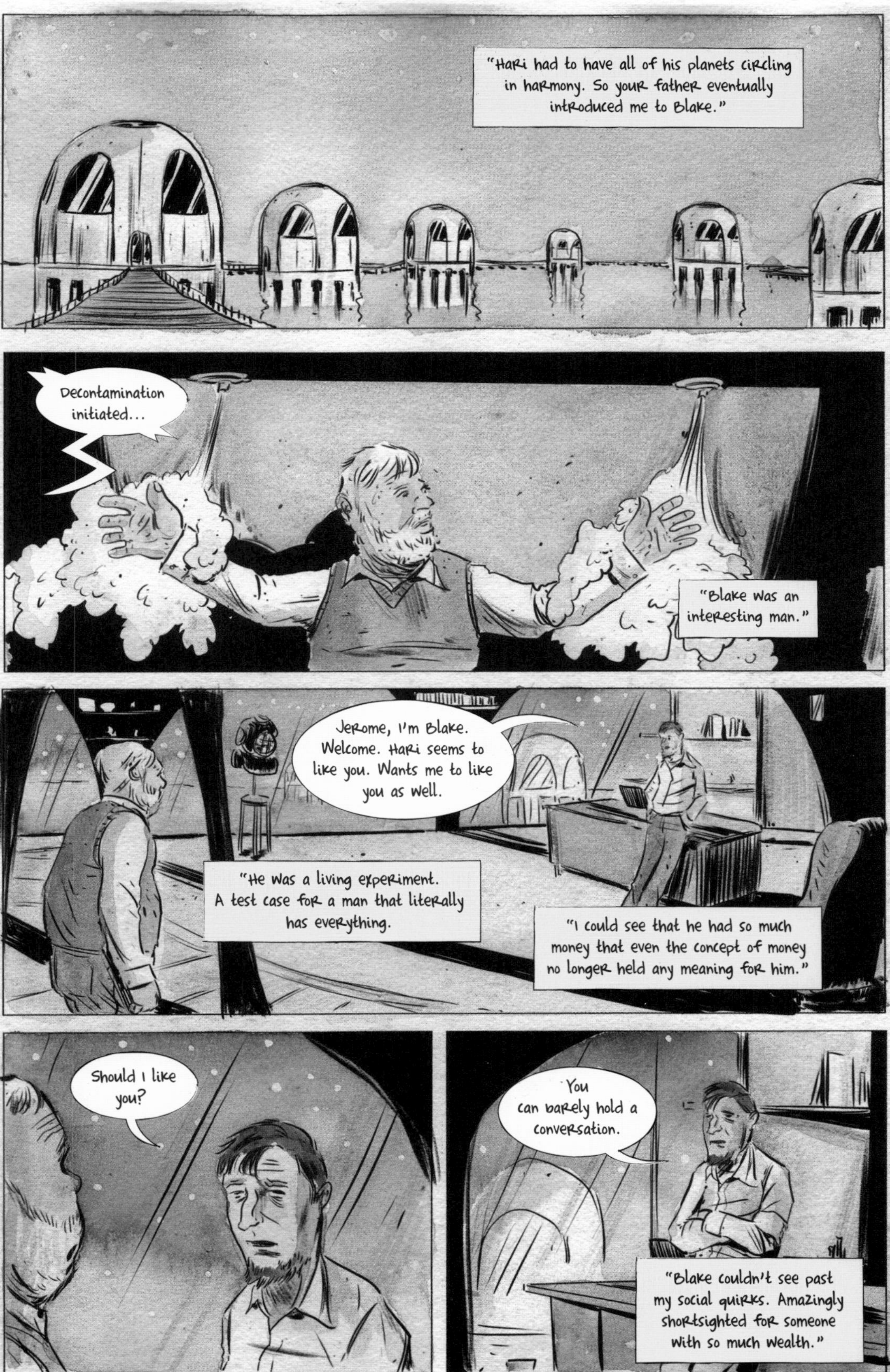
"Hari had to have all of his planets circling in harmony. So your father eventually introduced me to Blake."
Decontamination initiated...
"Blake was an interesting man."
Jerome, I'm Blake. Welcome. Hari seems to like you. Wants me to like you as well.
"He was a living experiment. A test case for a man that literally has everything.
"I could see that he had so much money that even the concept of money no longer held any meaning for him."
Should I like you?
You can barely hold a conversation.
"Blake couldn't see past my social quirks. Amazingly shortsighted for someone with so much wealth."

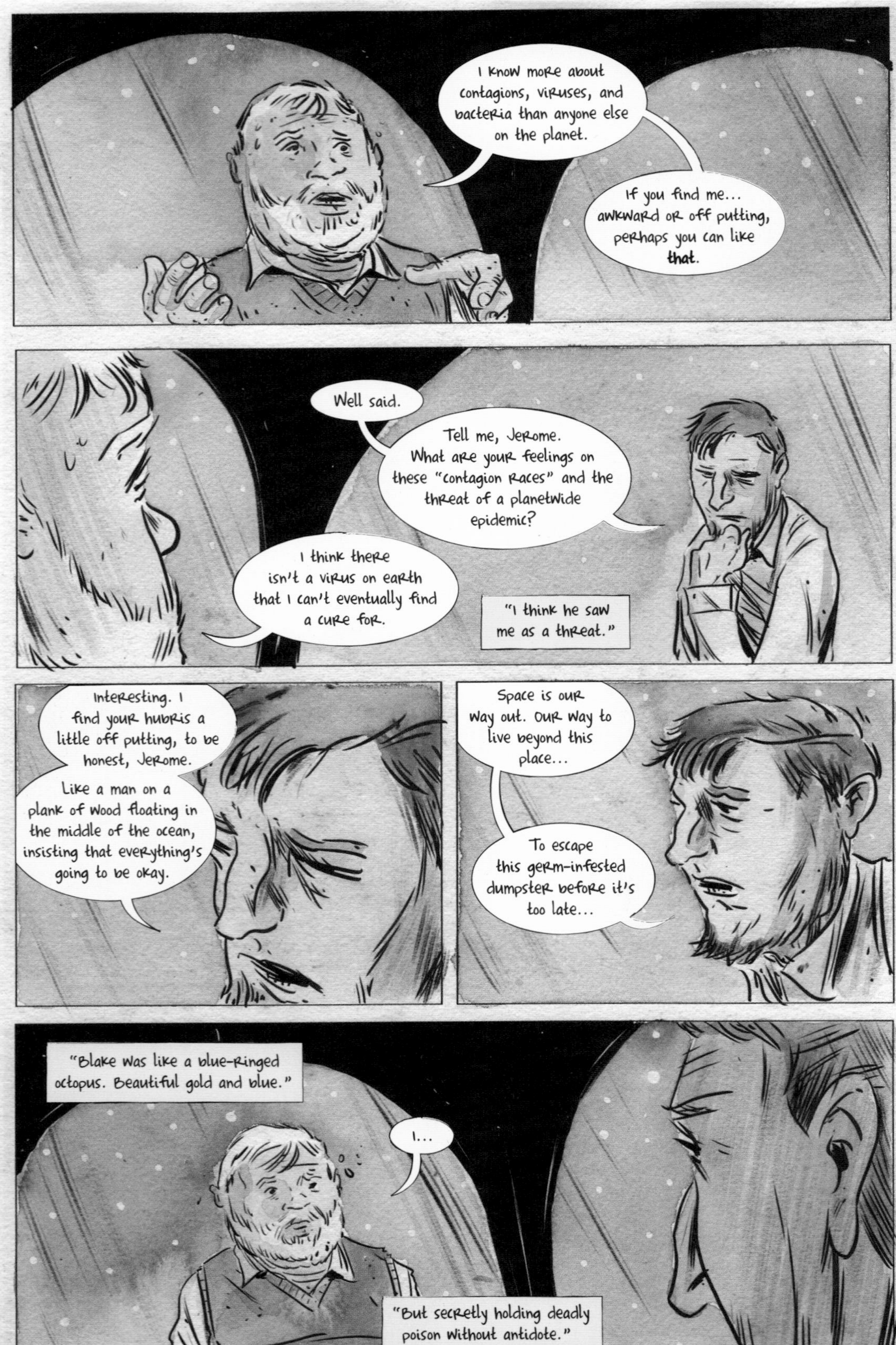
I know more about contagions, viruses, and bacteria than anyone else on the planet.
If you find me... awkward or off putting, perhaps you can like **that**.
Well said.
Tell me, Jerome. What are your feelings on these "contagion races" and the threat of a planetwide epidemic?
I think there isn't a virus on earth that I can't eventually find a cure for.
"I think he saw me as a threat."
Interesting. I find your hubris a little off putting, to be honest, Jerome.
Like a man on a plank of wood floating in the middle of the ocean, insisting that everything's going to be okay.
Space is our way out. Our way to live beyond this place...
To escape this germ-infested dumpster before it's too late...
"Blake was like a blue-ringed octopus. Beautiful gold and blue."
I...
"But secretly holding deadly poison without antidote."

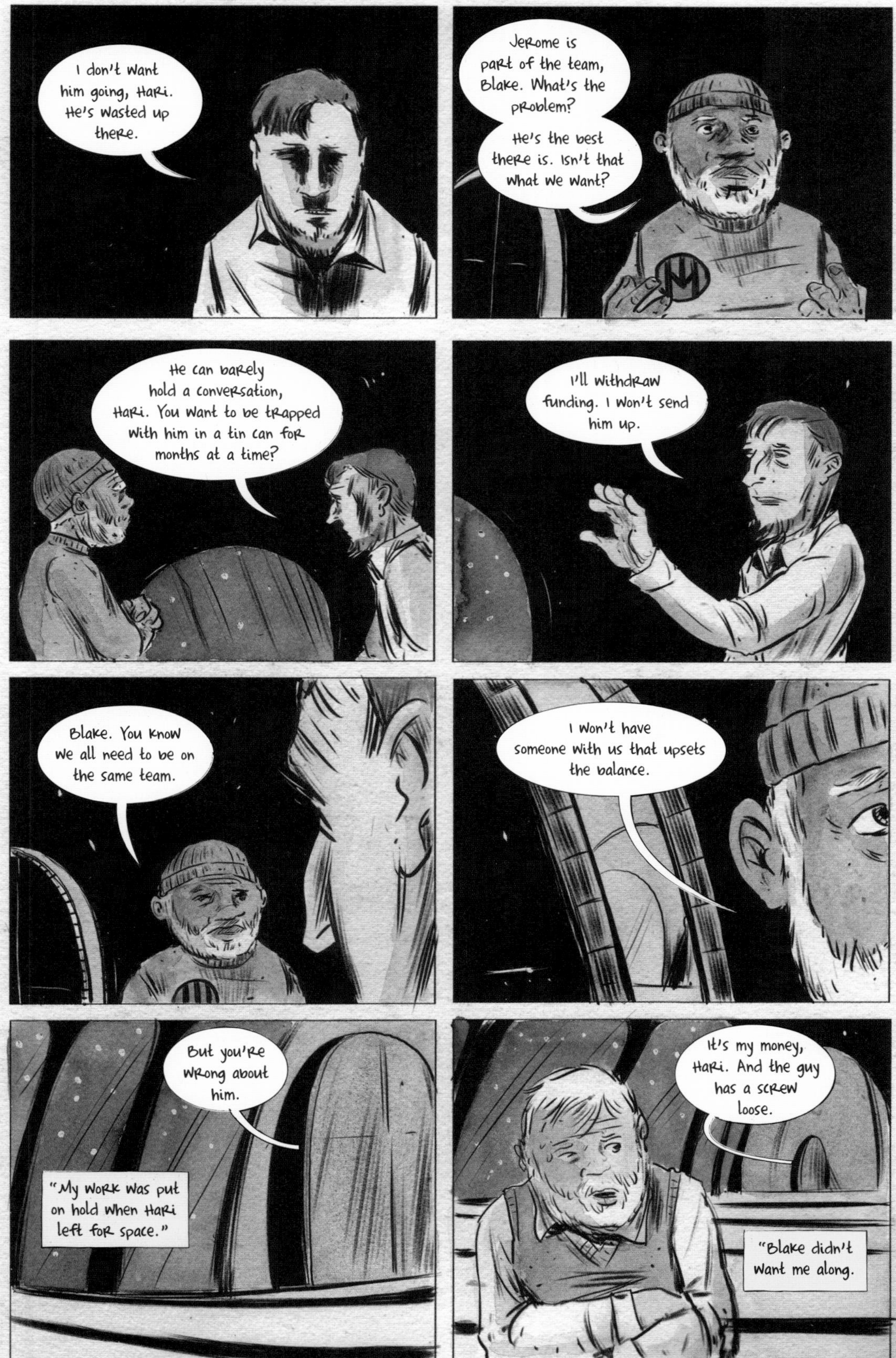
I don't want him going, Hari. He's wasted up there.
Jerome is part of the team, Blake. What's the problem?
He's the best there is. Isn't that what we want?
He can barely hold a conversation, Hari. You want to be trapped with him in a tin can for months at a time?
I'll withdraw funding. I won't send him up.
Blake. You know we all need to be on the same team.
I won't have someone with us that upsets the balance.
But you're wrong about him.
"My work was put on hold when Hari left for space."
It's my money, Hari. And the guy has a screw loose.
"Blake didn't want me along.

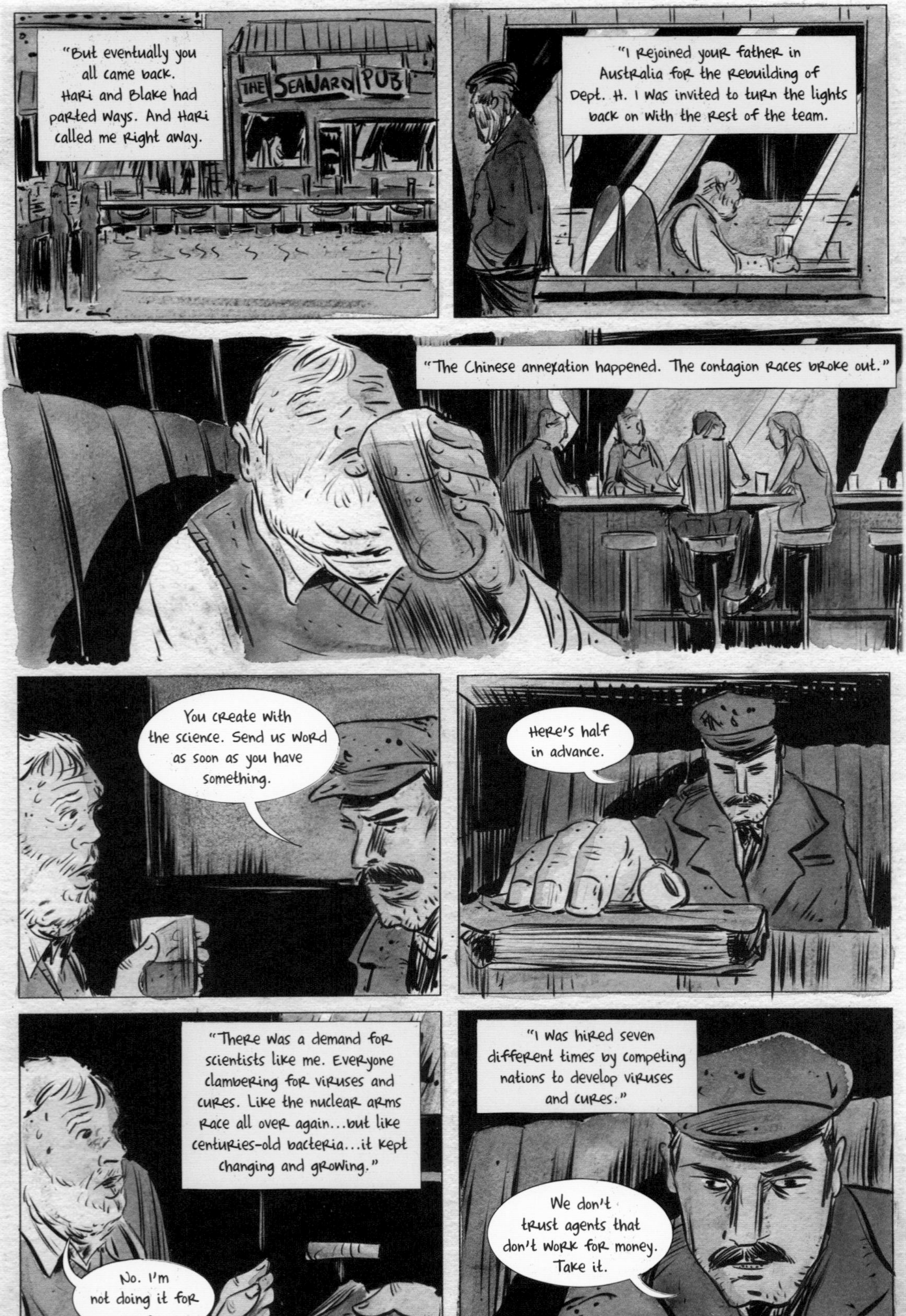
"But eventually you all came back. Hari and Blake had parted ways. And Hari called me right away.
THE SEAWARD PUB
"I rejoined your father in Australia for the rebuilding of Dept. H. I was invited to turn the lights back on with the rest of the team.
"The Chinese annexation happened. The contagion races broke out."
You create with the science. Send us word as soon as you have something.
Here's half in advance.
"There was a demand for scientists like me. Everyone clambering for viruses and cures. Like the nuclear arms race all over again...but like centuries-old bacteria...it kept changing and growing."
No. I'm not doing it for money.
"I was hired seven different times by competing nations to develop viruses and cures."
We don't trust agents that don't work for money. Take it.

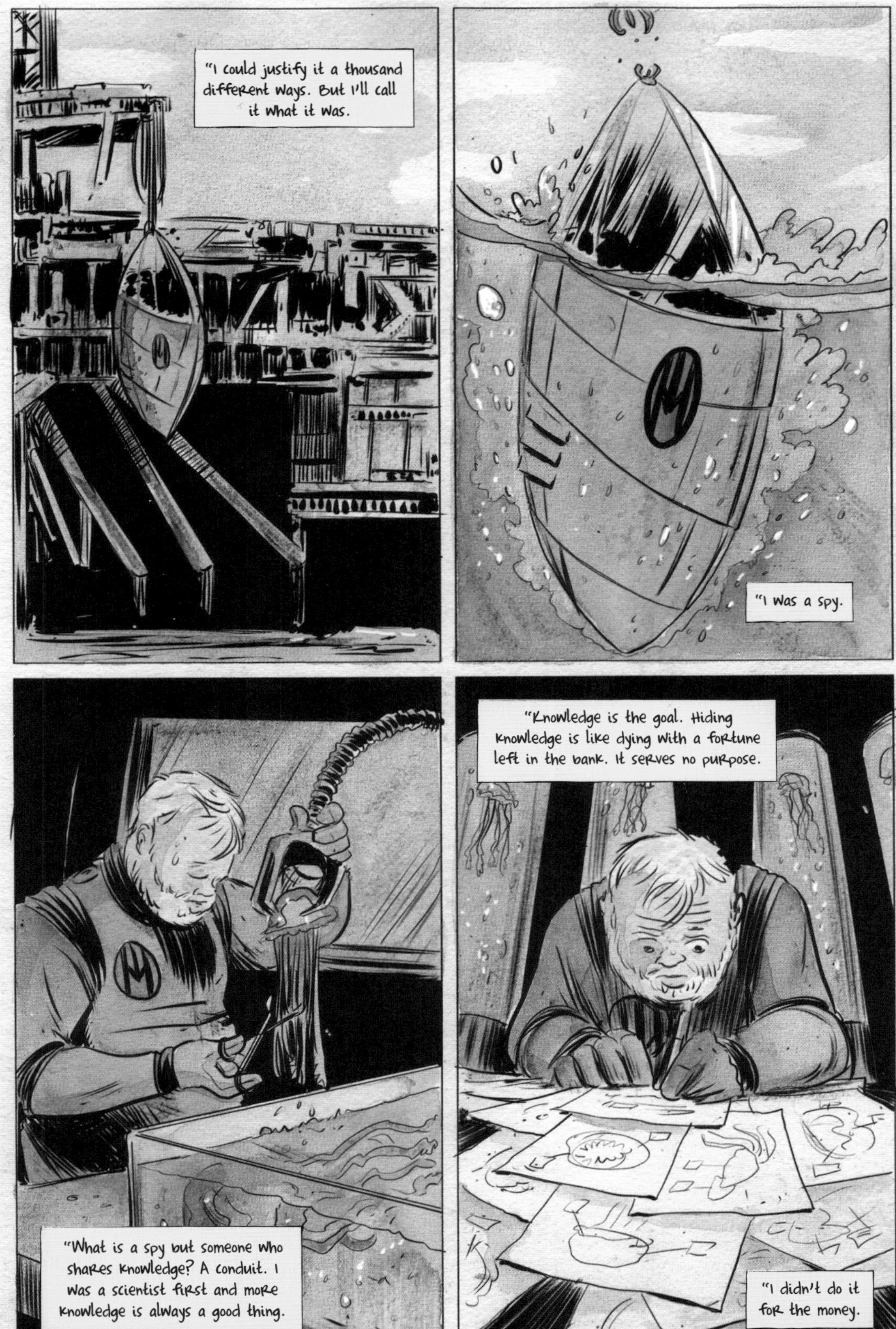
"I could justify it a thousand different ways. But I'll call it what it was.
"I was a spy.
"What is a spy but someone who shares knowledge? A conduit. I was a scientist first and more knowledge is always a good thing.
"Knowledge is the goal. Hiding knowledge is like dying with a fortune left in the bank. It serves no purpose.
"I didn't do it for the money.

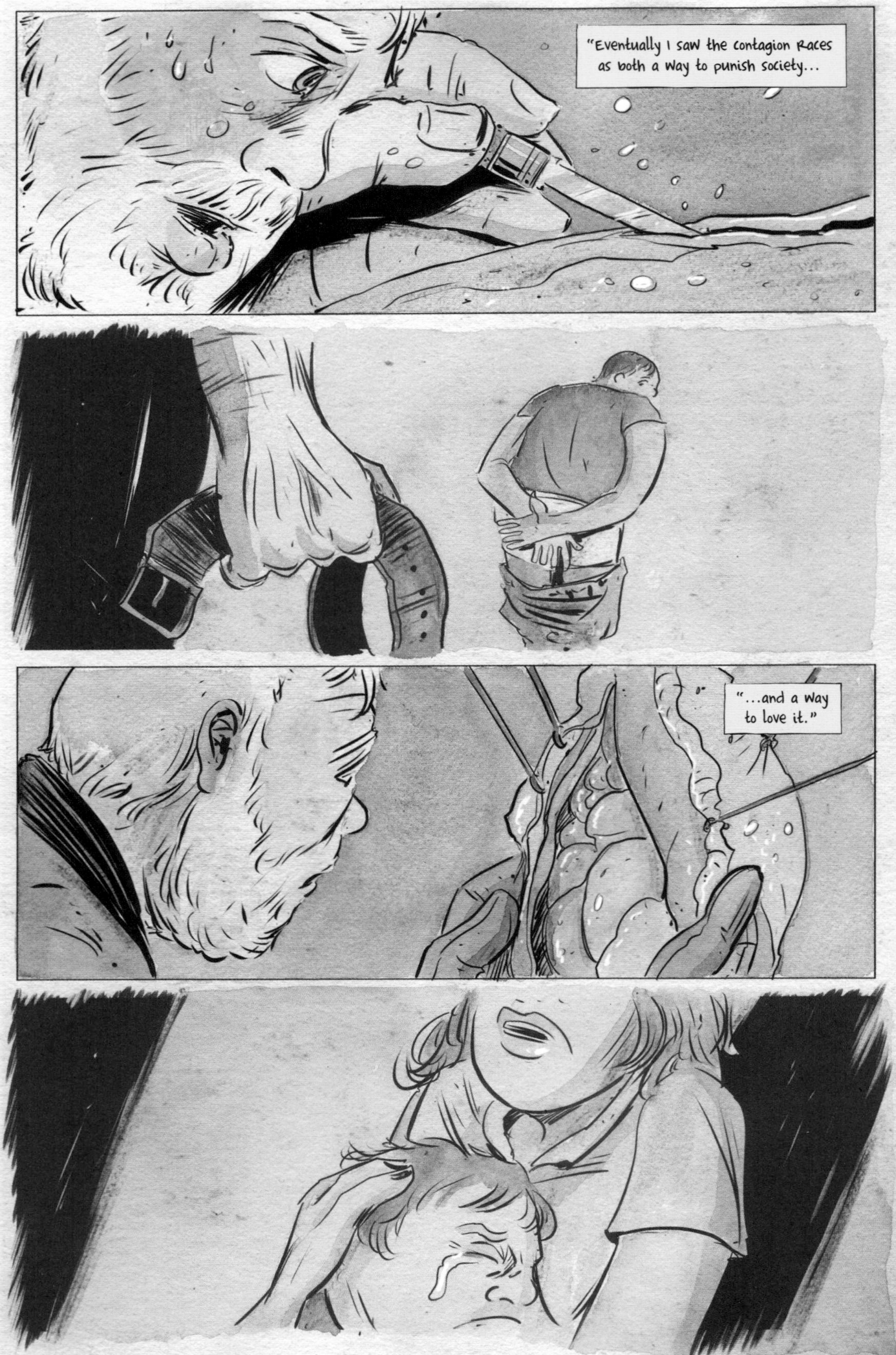
"Eventually I saw the contagion Races as both a way to punish society...
"...and a way to love it."

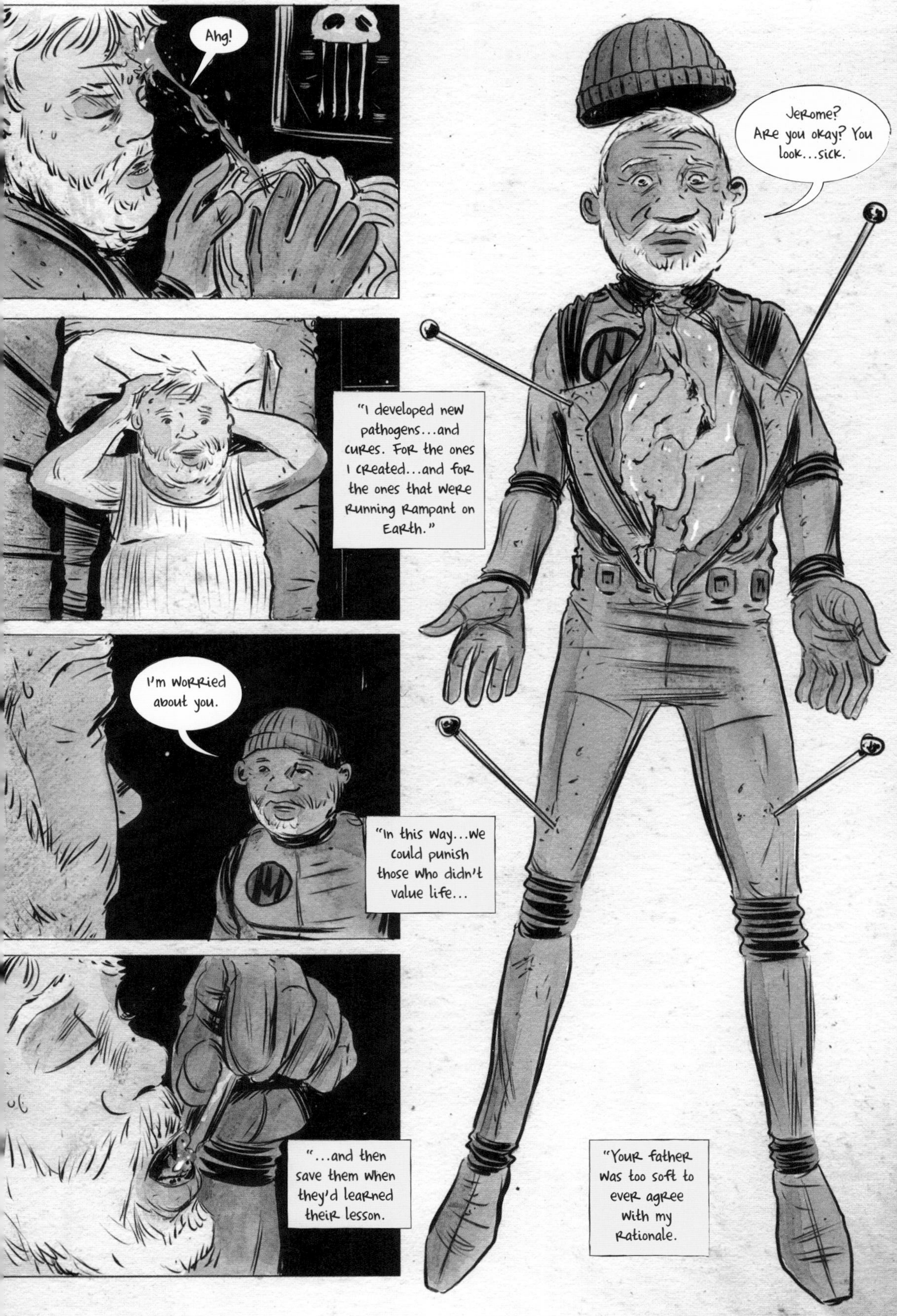
Ahg!
"I developed new pathogens...and cures. For the ones I created...and for the ones that were running rampant on Earth."
I'm worried about you.
"In this way...we could punish those who didn't value life...
"...and then save them when they'd learned their lesson.
Jerome? Are you okay? You look...sick.
"Your father was too soft to ever agree with my rationale.

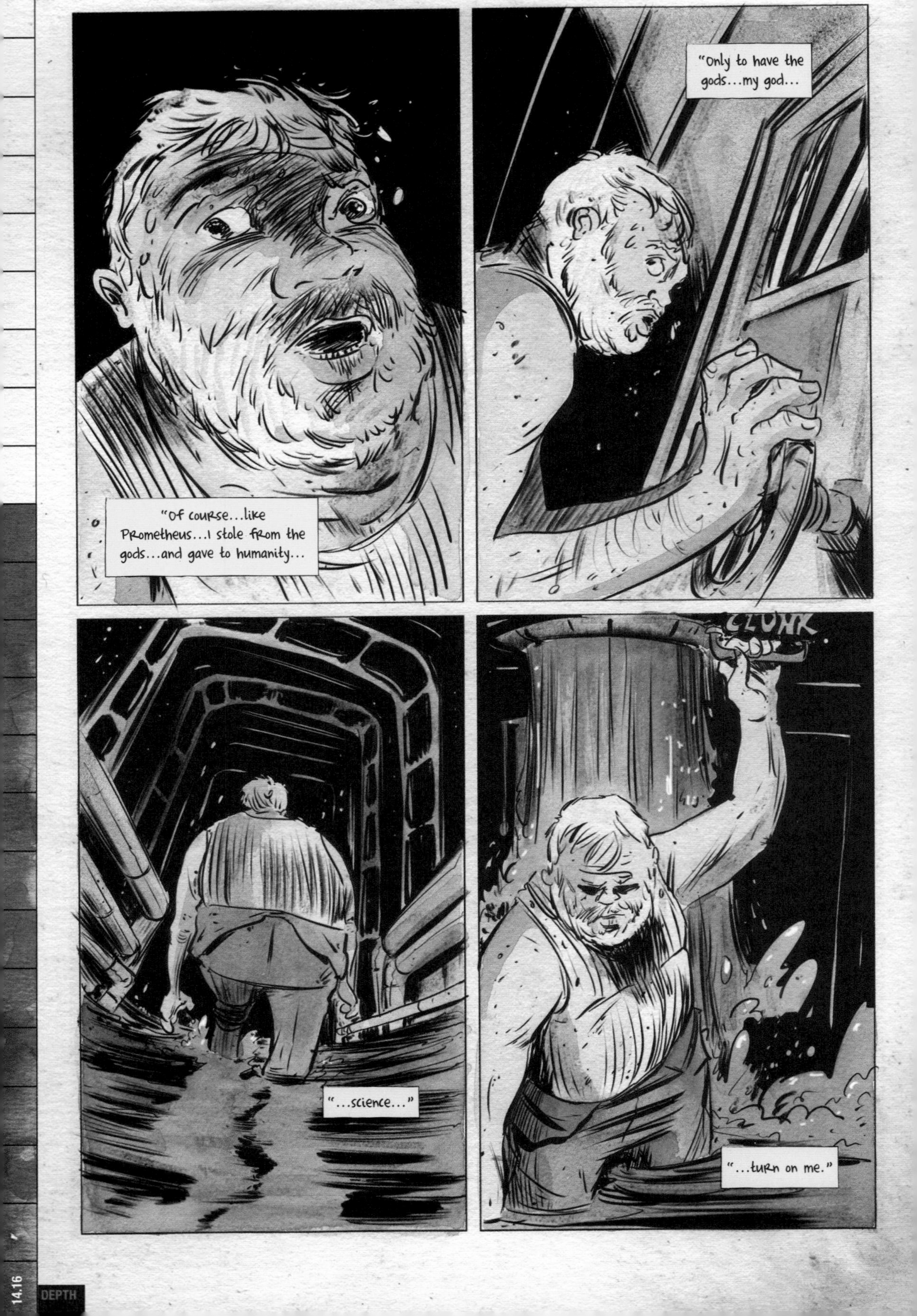
"Of course...like Prometheus...I stole from the gods...and gave to humanity...
"Only to have the gods...my god...
"...science..."
CLONK
"...turn on me."

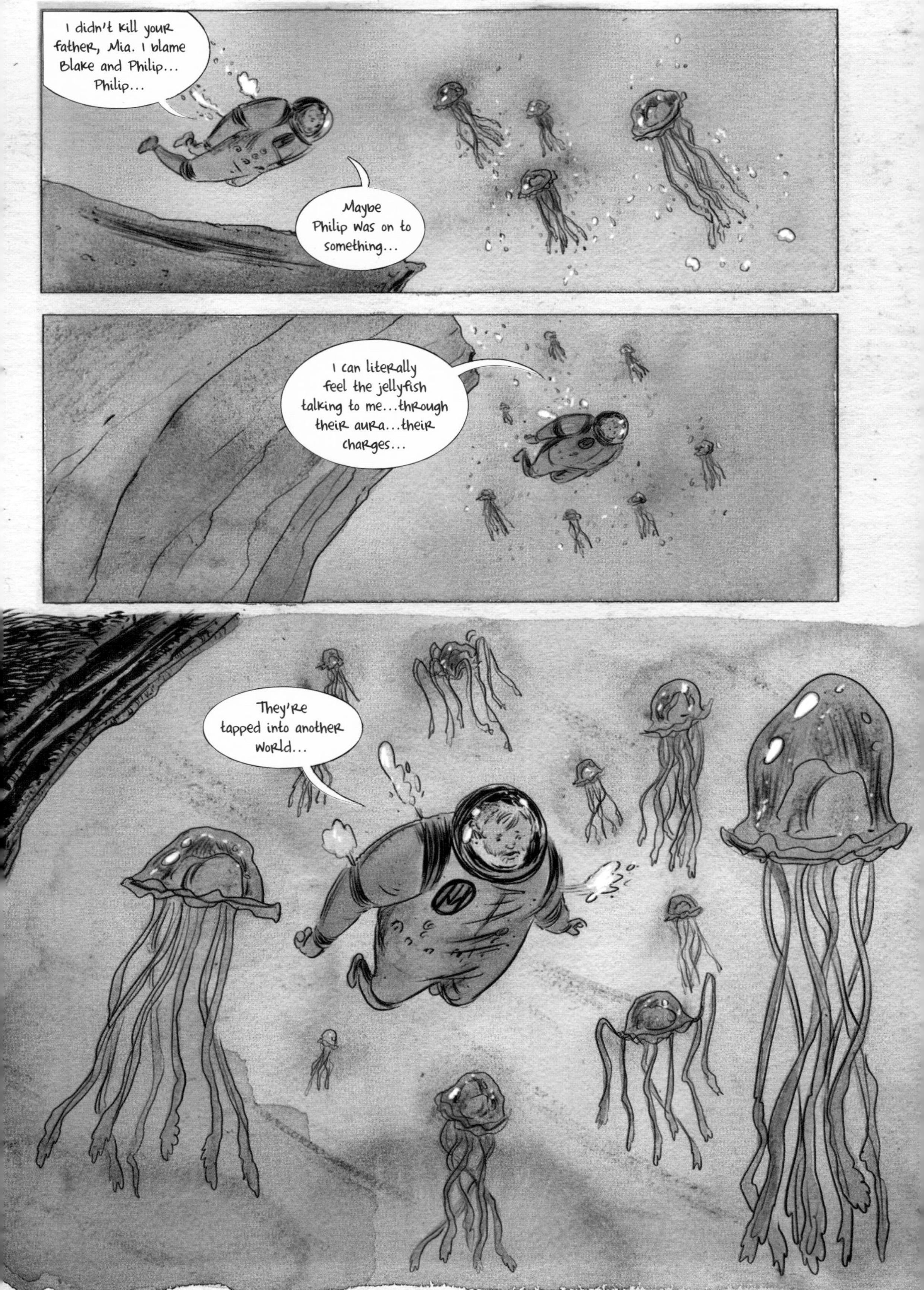
I didn't kill your father, Mia. I blame Blake and Philip... Philip...
Maybe Philip was on to something...
I can literally feel the jellyfish talking to me...through their aura...their charges...
They're tapped into another world...

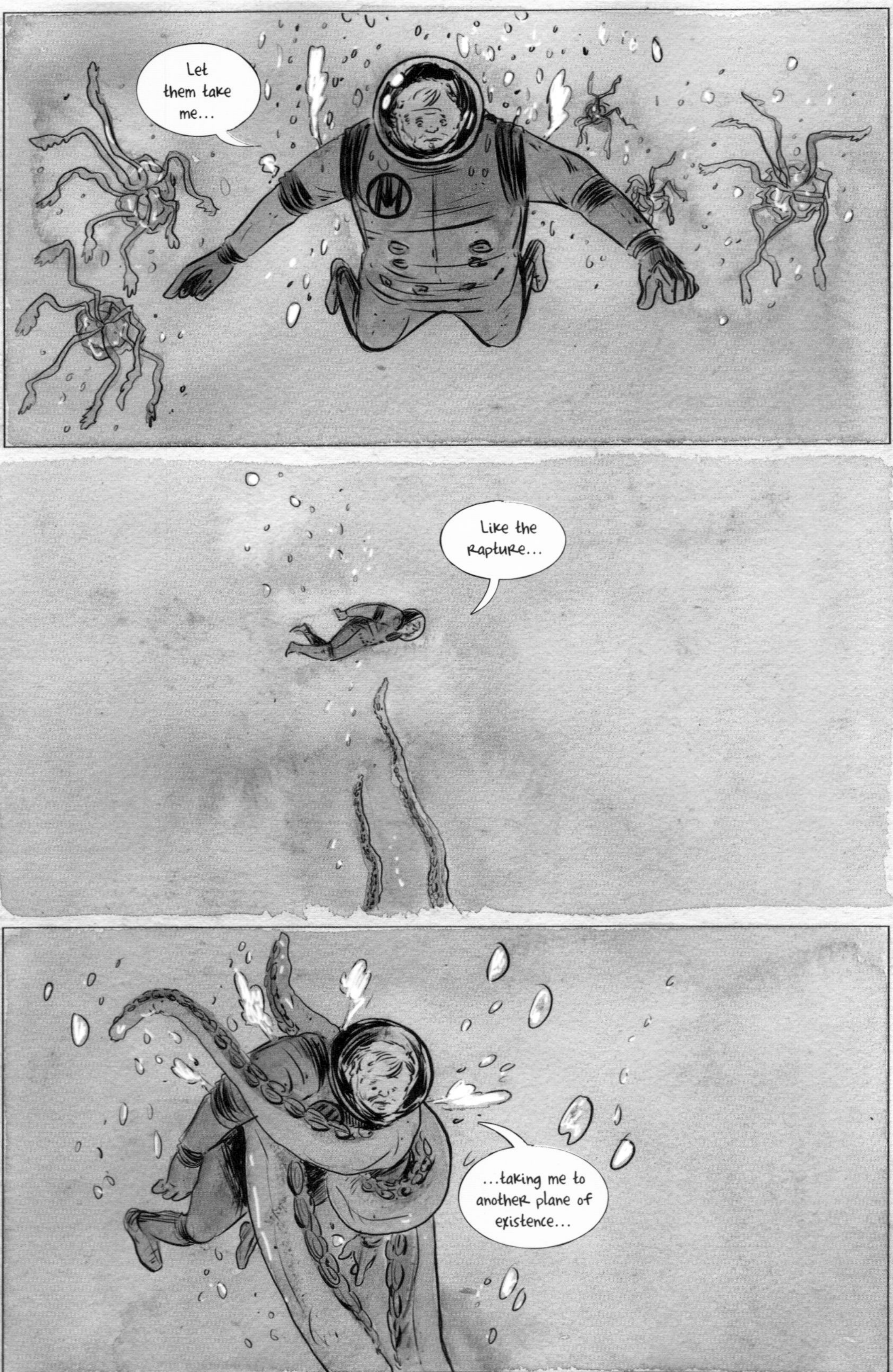
Let them take me...
Like the rapture...
...taking me to another plane of existence...

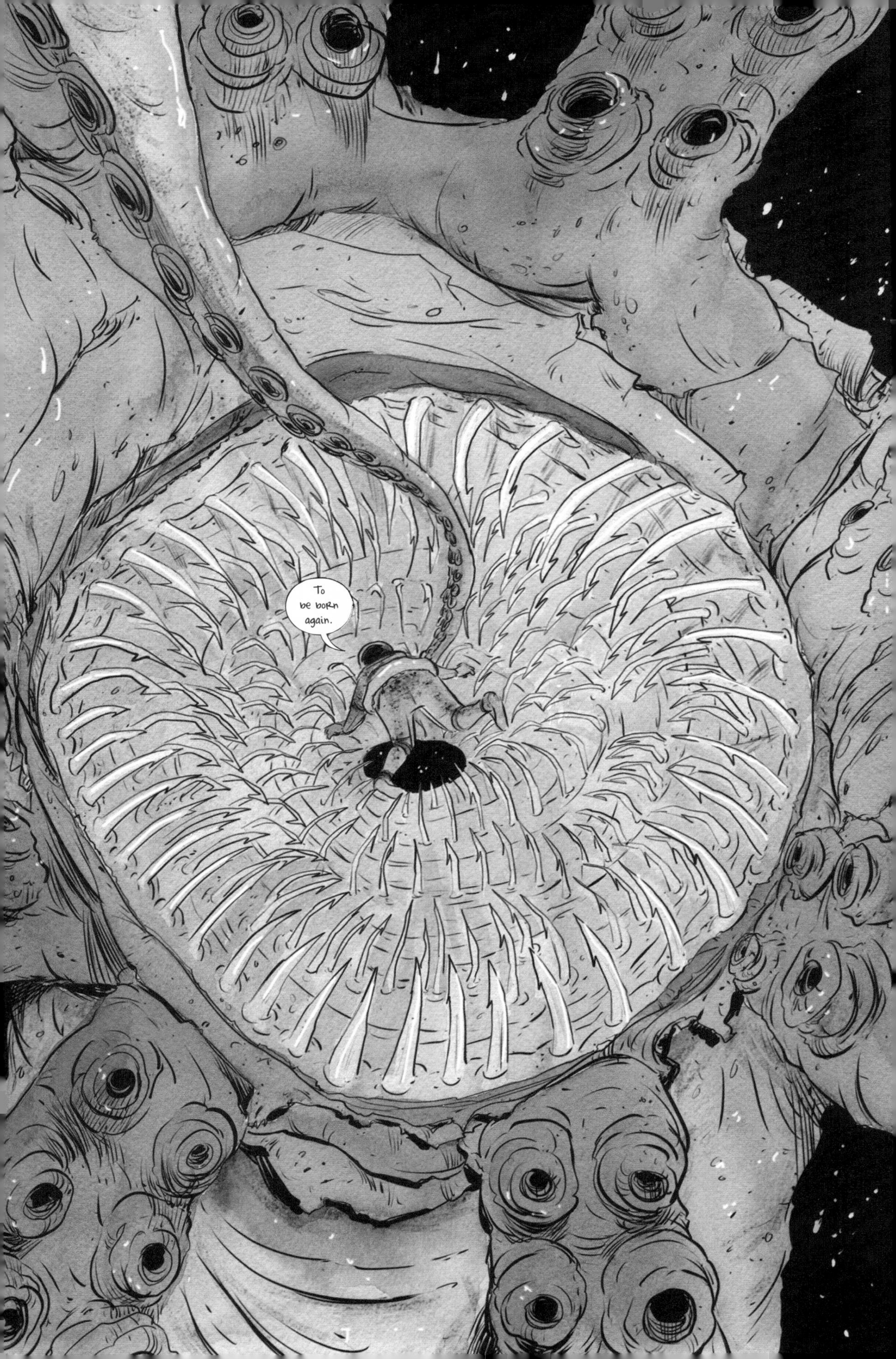
To be born again.

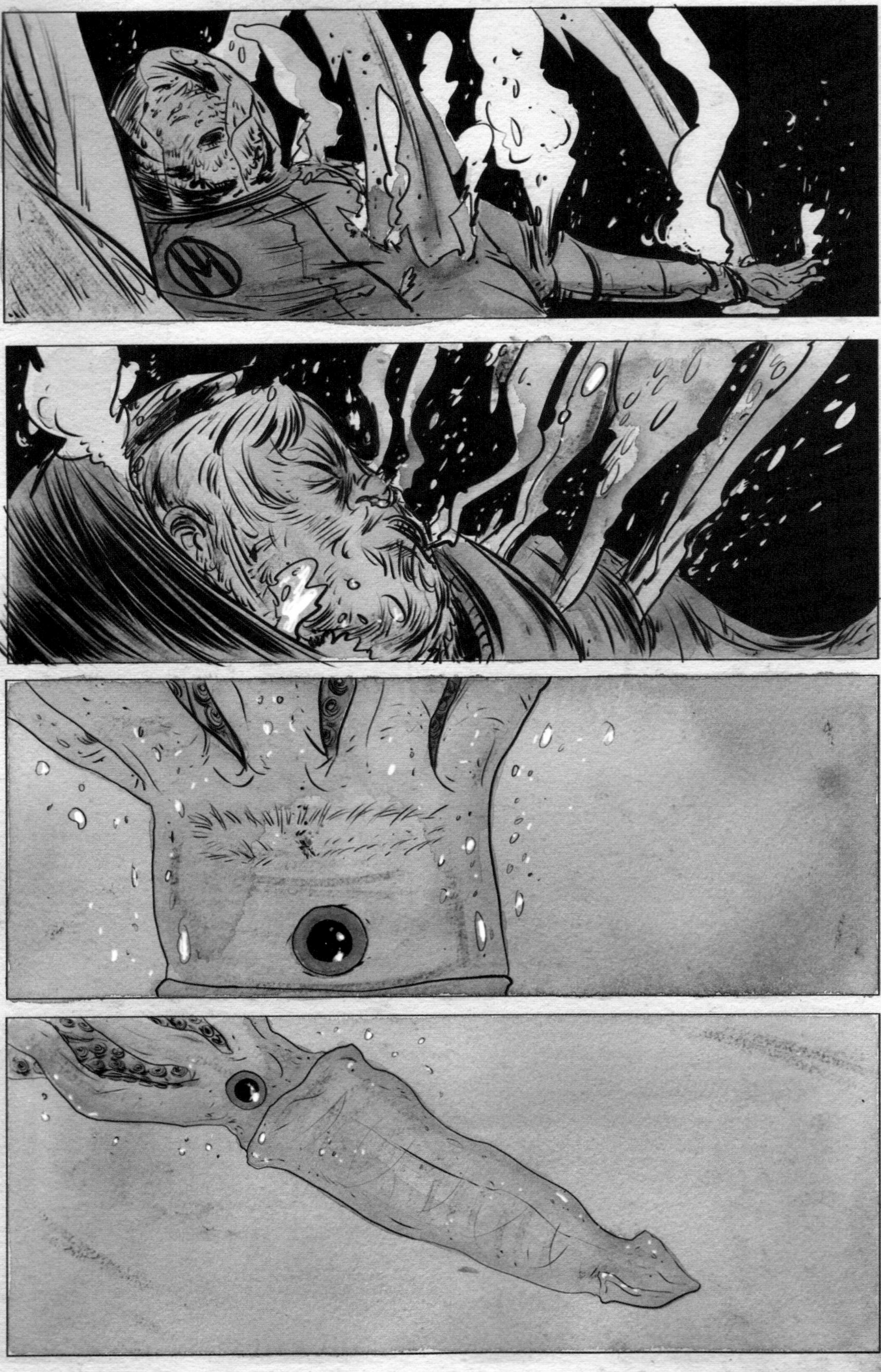

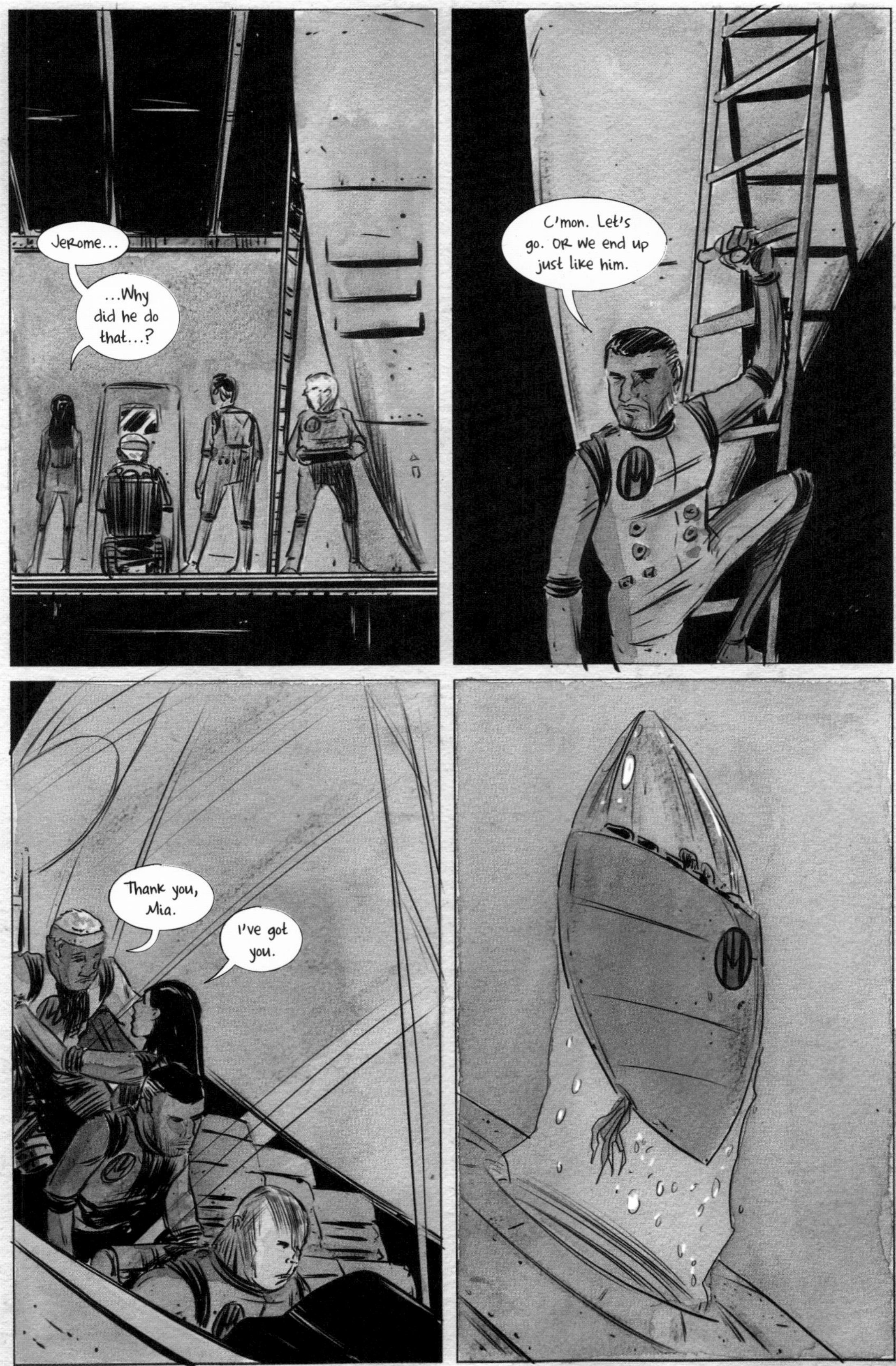
Jerome...
...Why did he do that...?
C'mon. Let's go. Or we end up just like him.
Thank you, Mia.
I've got you.

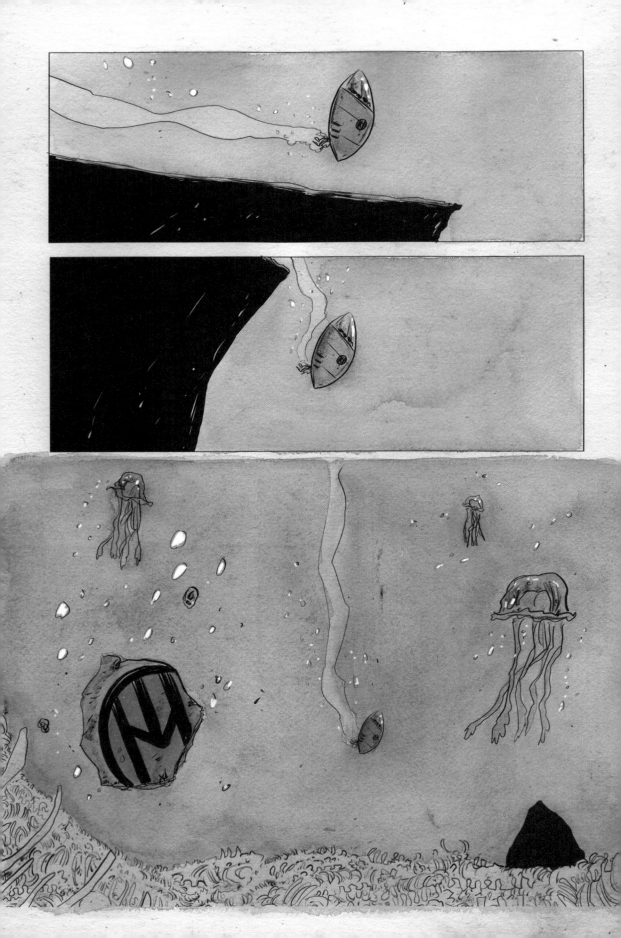

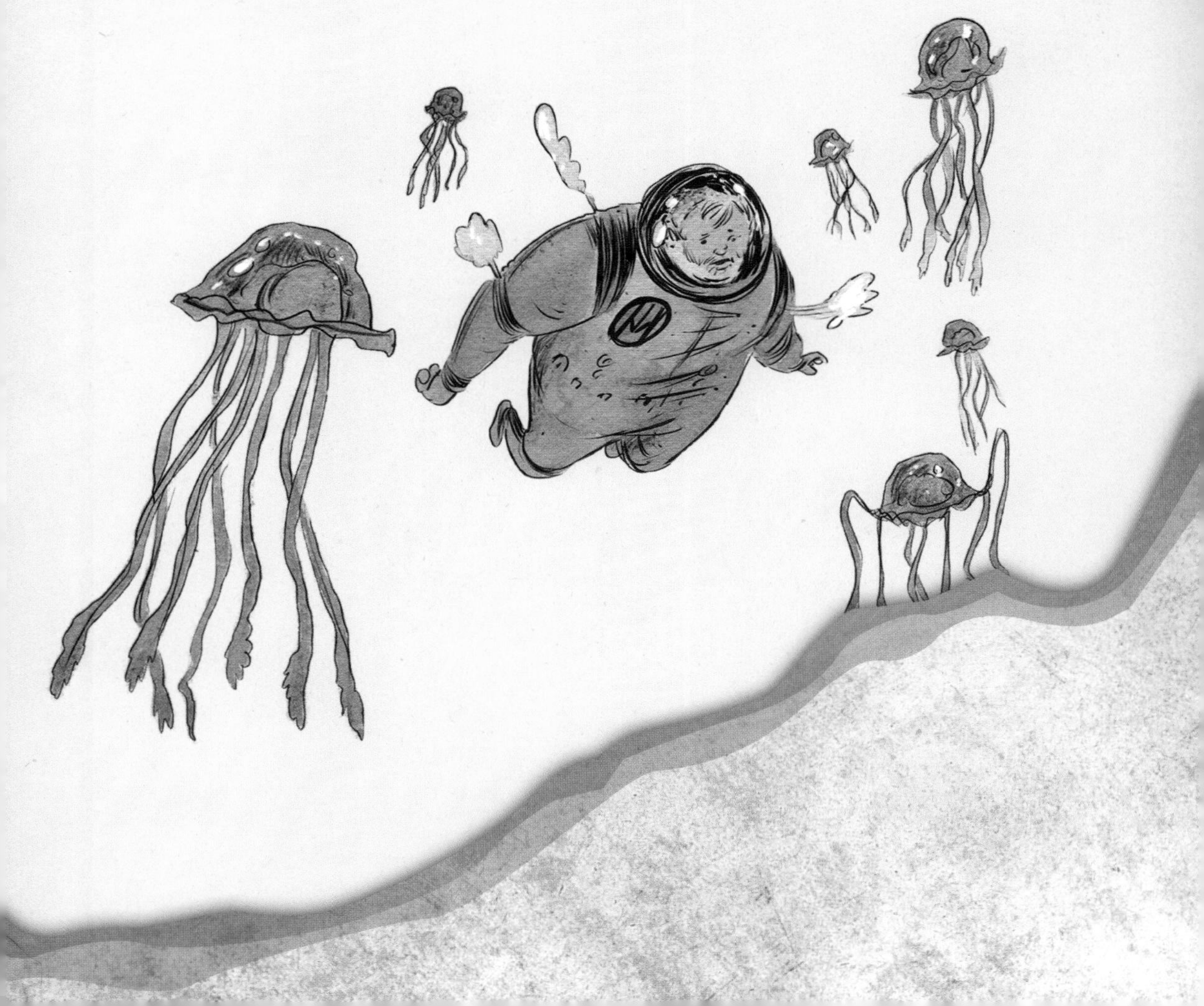

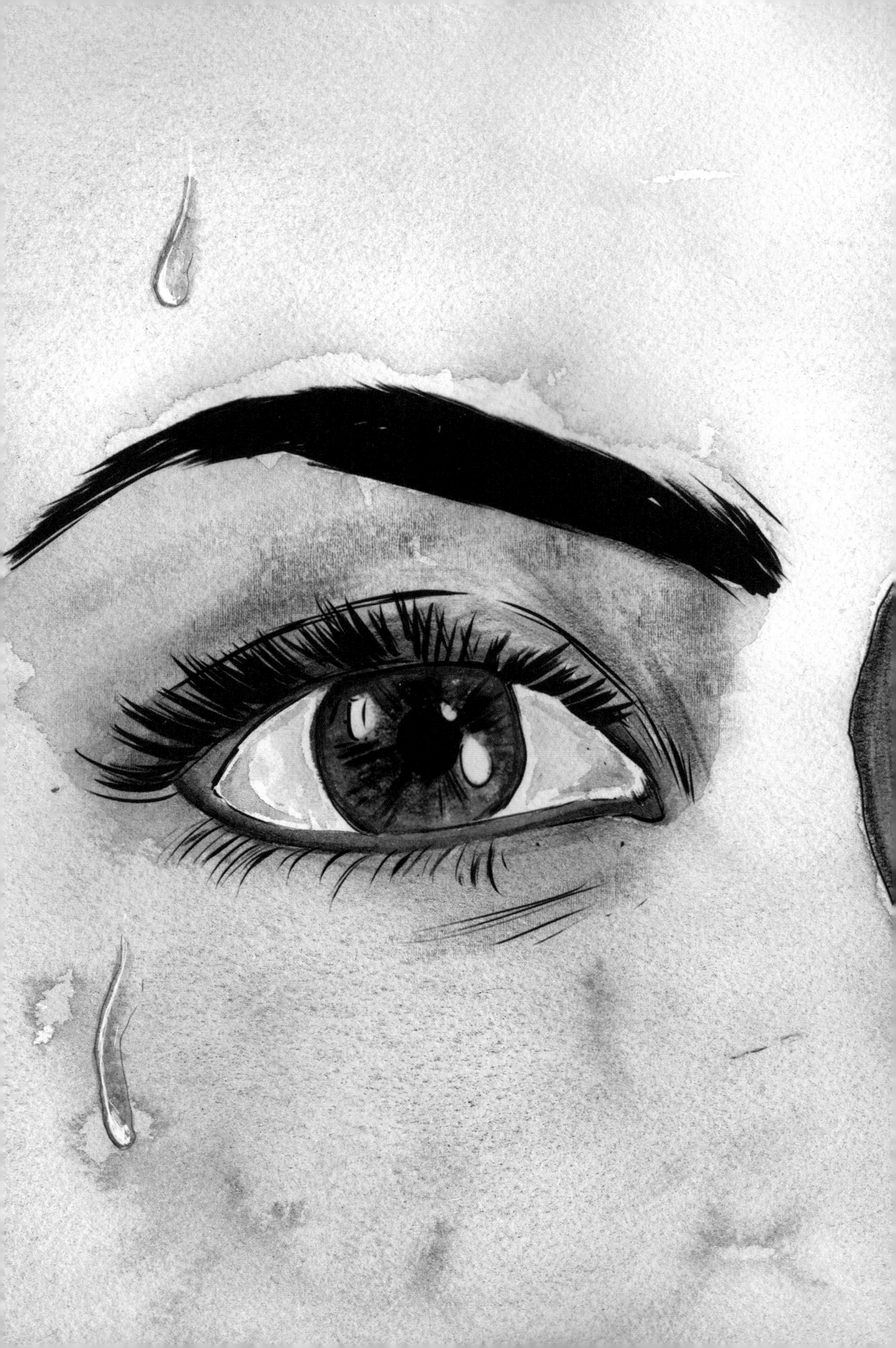

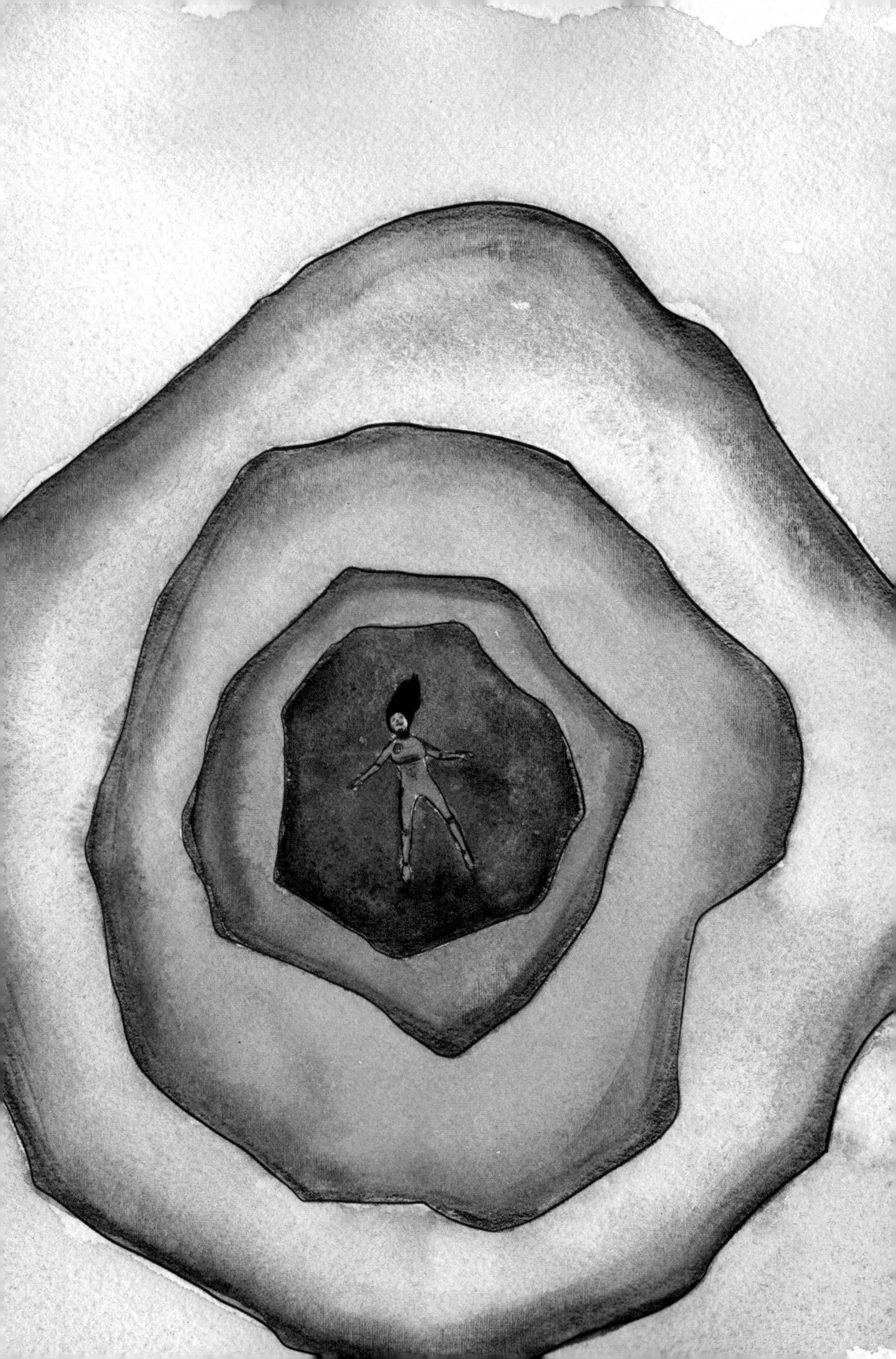

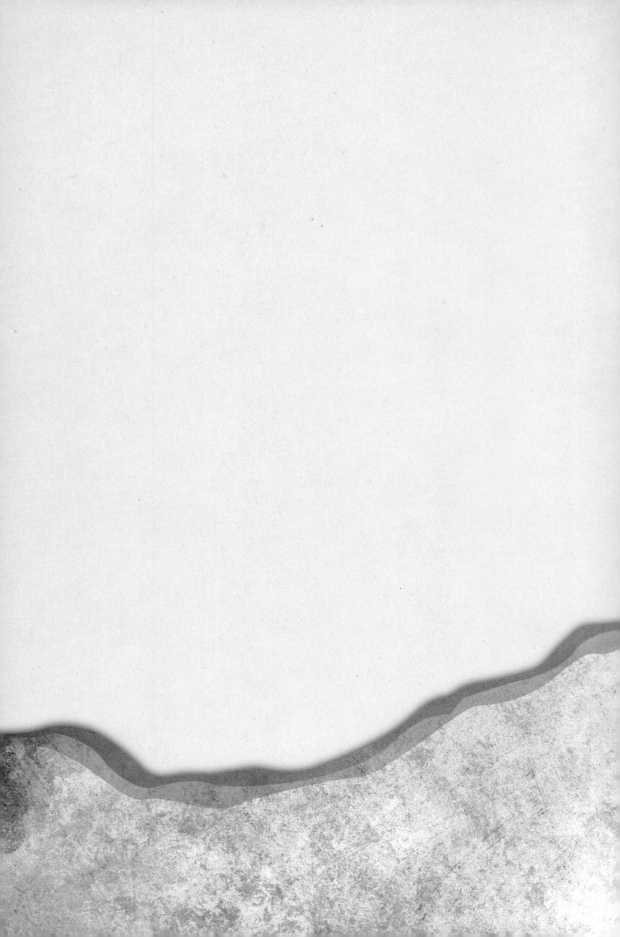

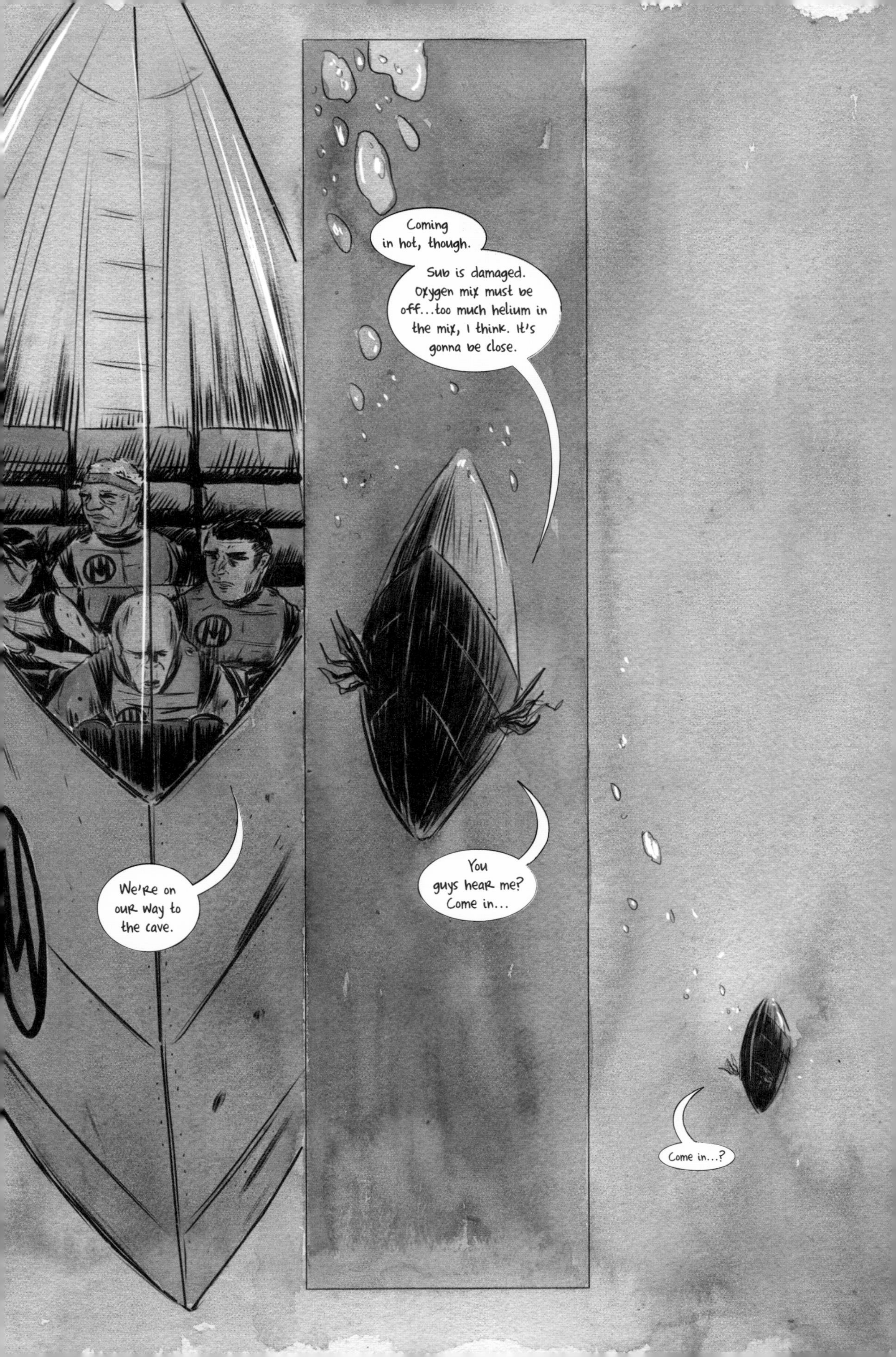
We're on our way to the cave.
Coming in hot, though.
Sub is damaged. Oxygen mix must be off...too much helium in the mix, I think. It's gonna be close.
You guys hear me? Come in...
Come in...?

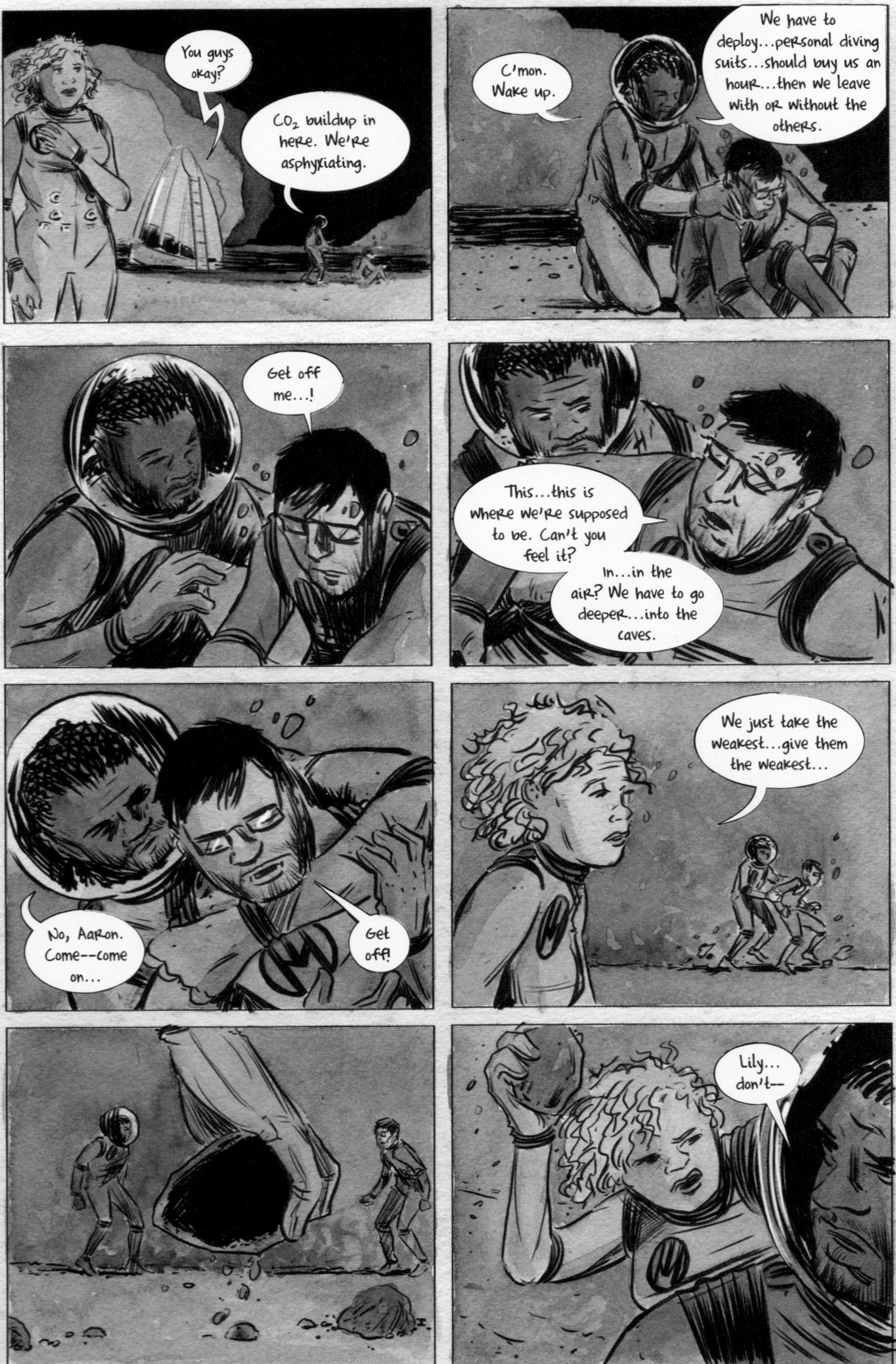
You guys okay?
CO_2 buildup in here. We're asphyxiating.
C'mon. Wake up.
We have to deploy...personal diving suits...should buy us an hour...then we leave with or without the others.
Get off me...!
This...this is where we're supposed to be. Can't you feel it?
In...in the air? We have to go deeper...into the caves.
No, Aaron. Come--come on...
Get off!
We just take the weakest...give them the weakest...
Lily... don't--

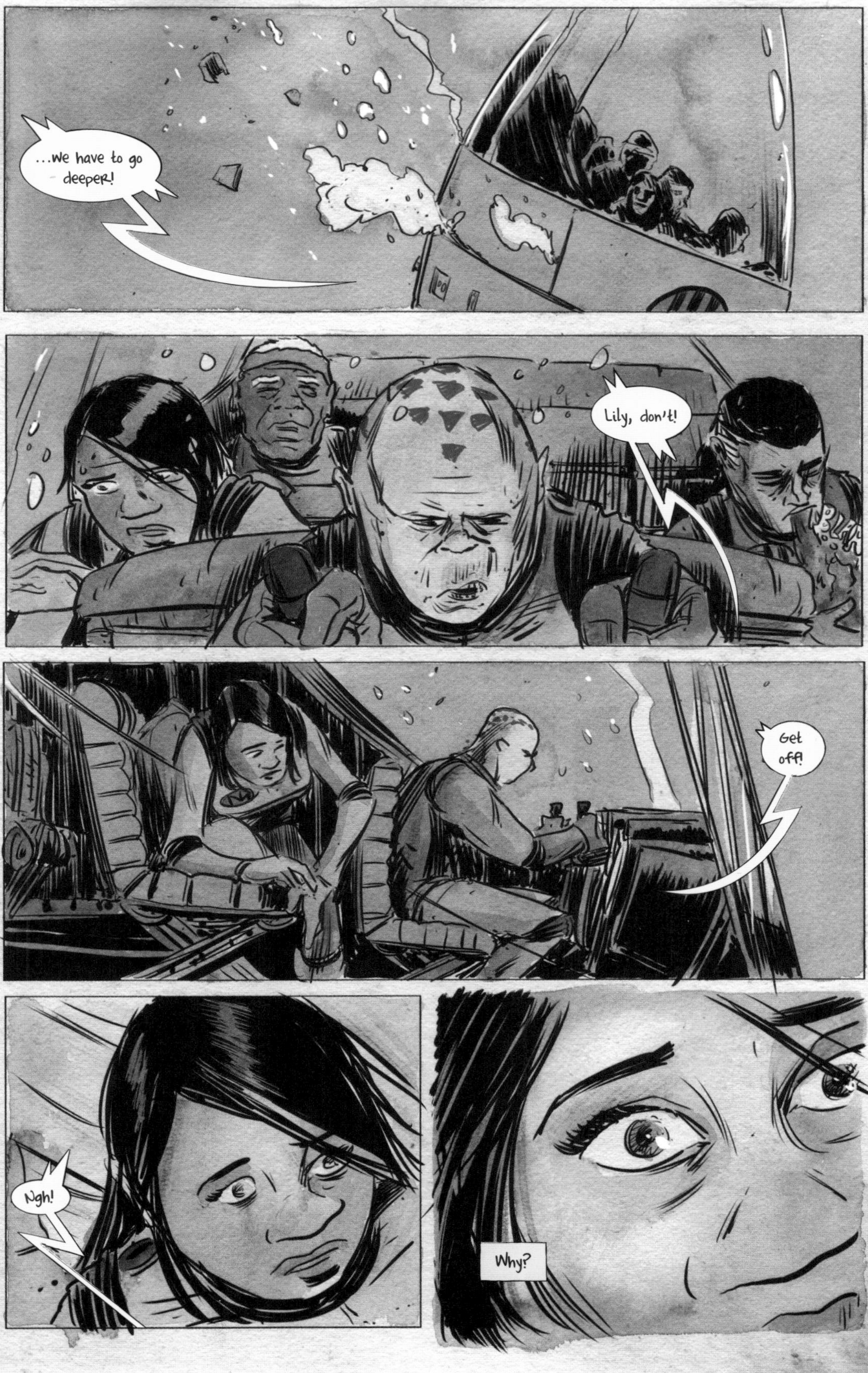
...We have to go deeper!
Lily, don't!
BLAH
Get off!
Ngh!
Why?

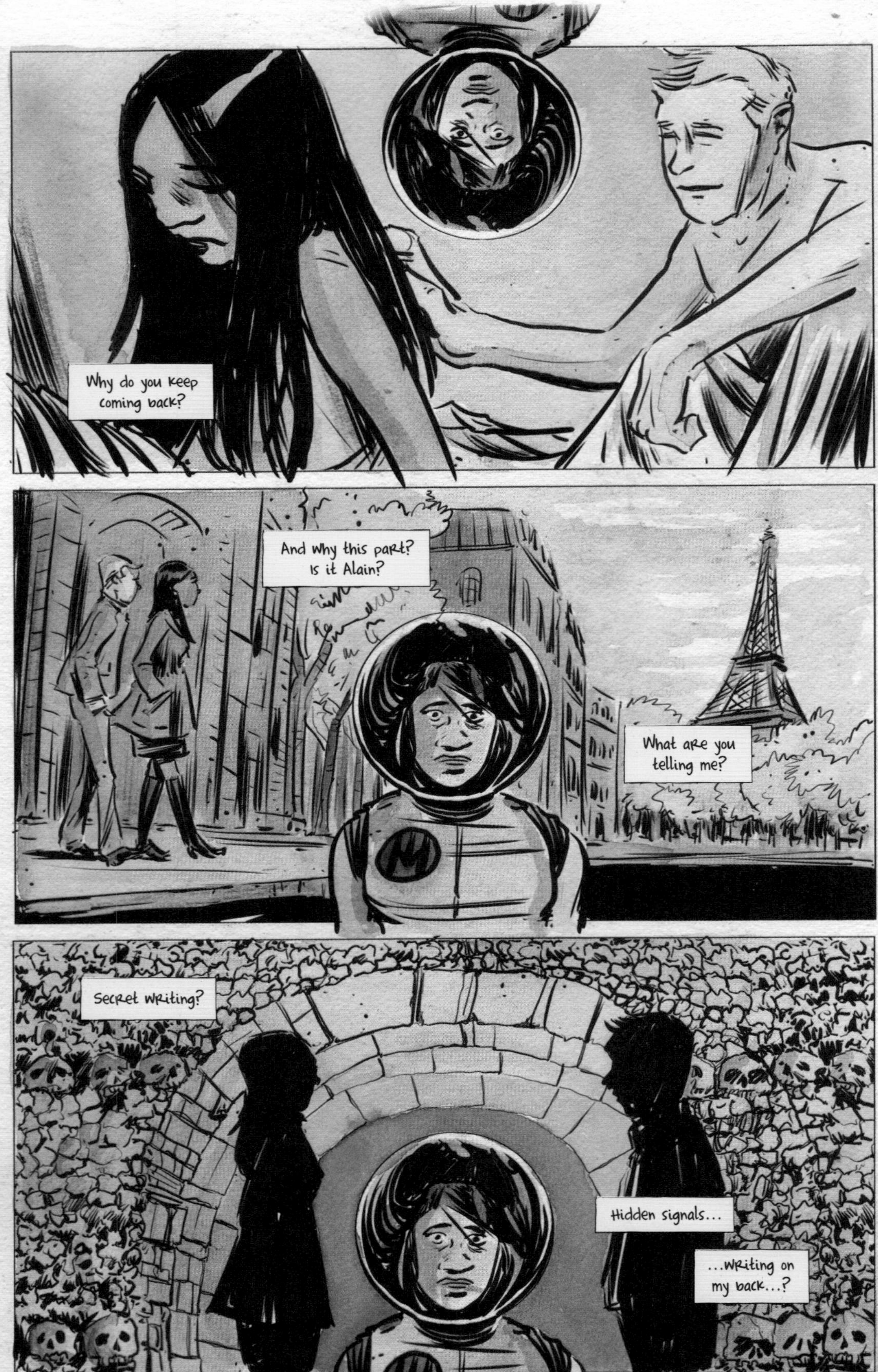

Why do you keep coming back?
And why this part? Is it Alain?
What are you telling me?
Secret writing?
Hidden signals...
...writing on my back...?

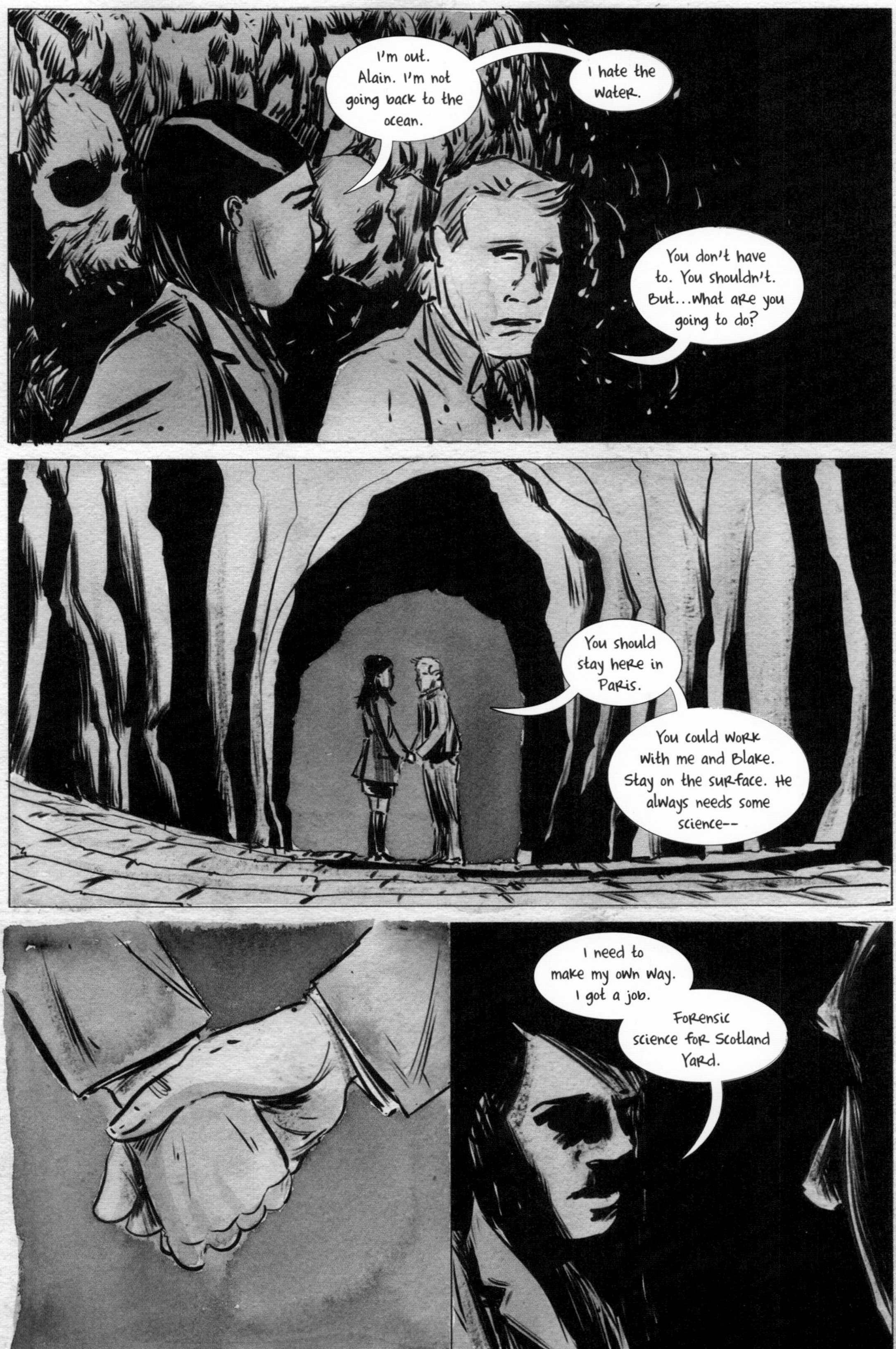
I'm out. Alain. I'm not going back to the ocean.
I hate the water.
You don't have to. You shouldn't. But...what are you going to do?
You should stay here in Paris.
You could work with me and Blake. Stay on the surface. He always needs some science--
I need to make my own way. I got a job.
Forensic science for Scotland Yard.

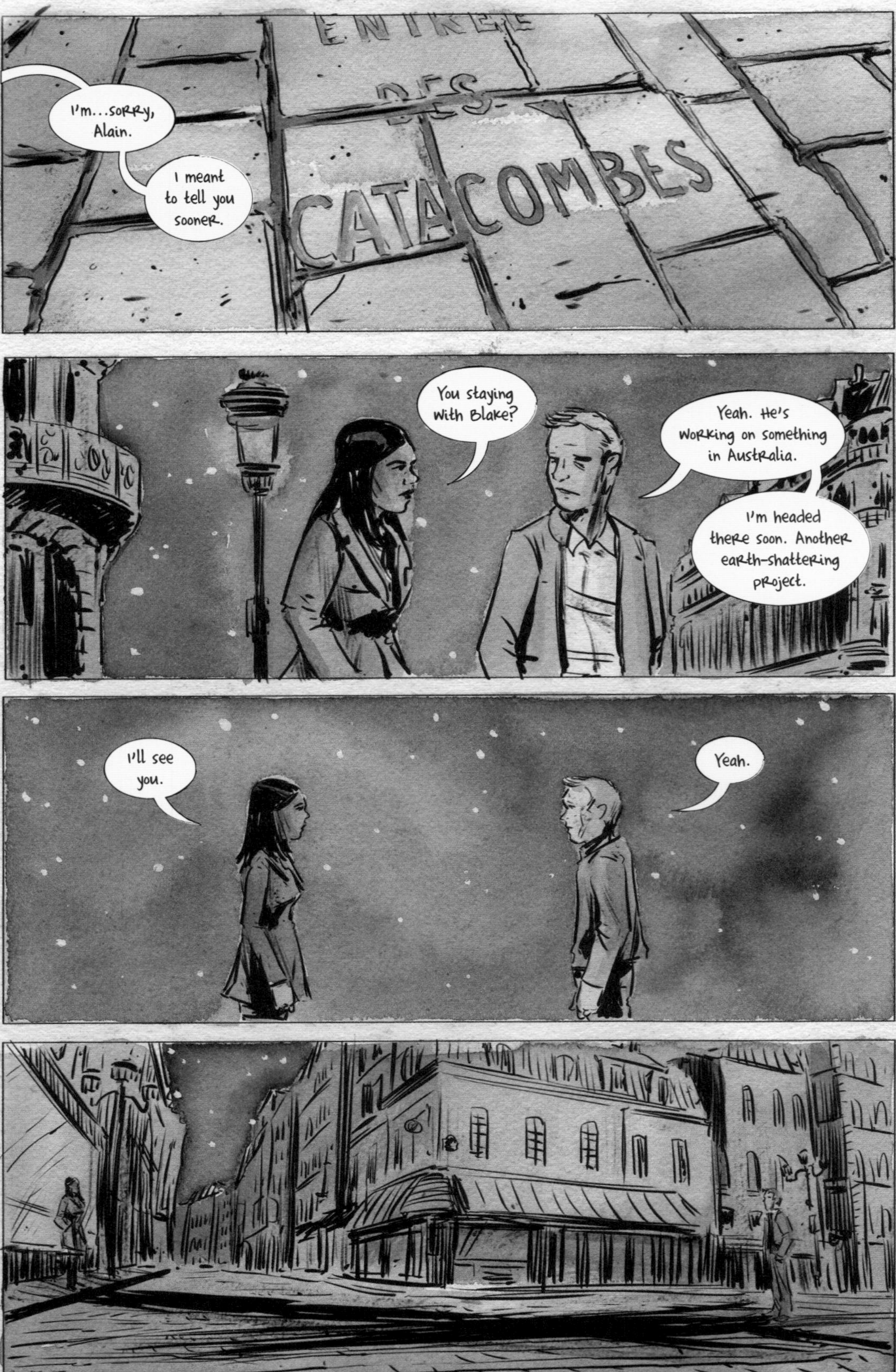
ENTRÉE DES CATACOMBES
I'm...sorry, Alain.
I meant to tell you sooner.
You staying with Blake?
Yeah. He's working on something in Australia.
I'm headed there soon. Another earth-shattering project.
I'll see you.
Yeah.

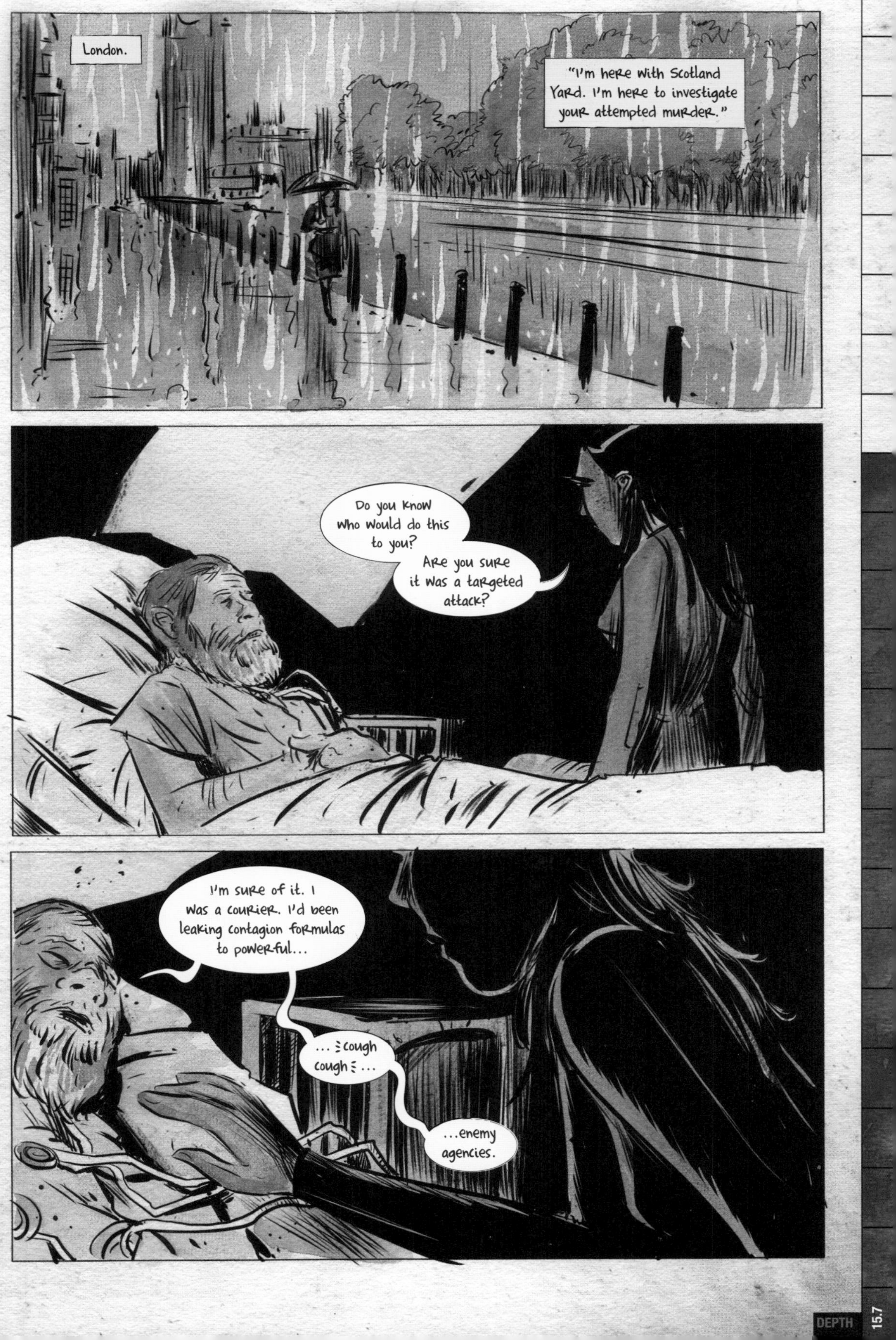
London.
"I'm here with Scotland Yard. I'm here to investigate your attempted murder."
Do you know who would do this to you?
Are you sure it was a targeted attack?
I'm sure of it. I was a courier. I'd been leaking contagion formulas to powerful...
... cough cough ...
...enemy agencies.

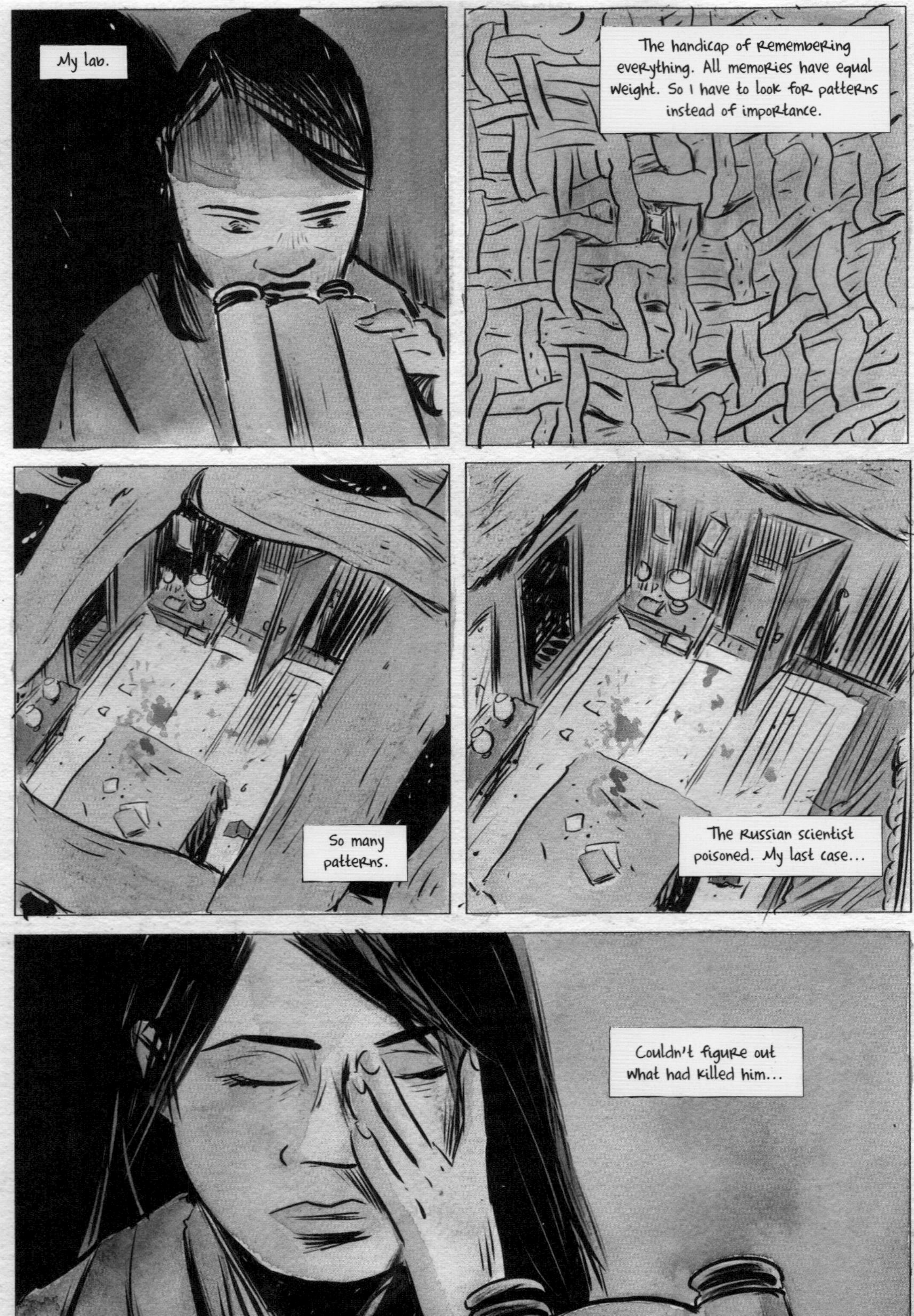
My lab.
The handicap of remembering everything. All memories have equal weight. So I have to look for patterns instead of importance.
So many patterns.
The Russian scientist poisoned. My last case...
Couldn't figure out what had killed him...

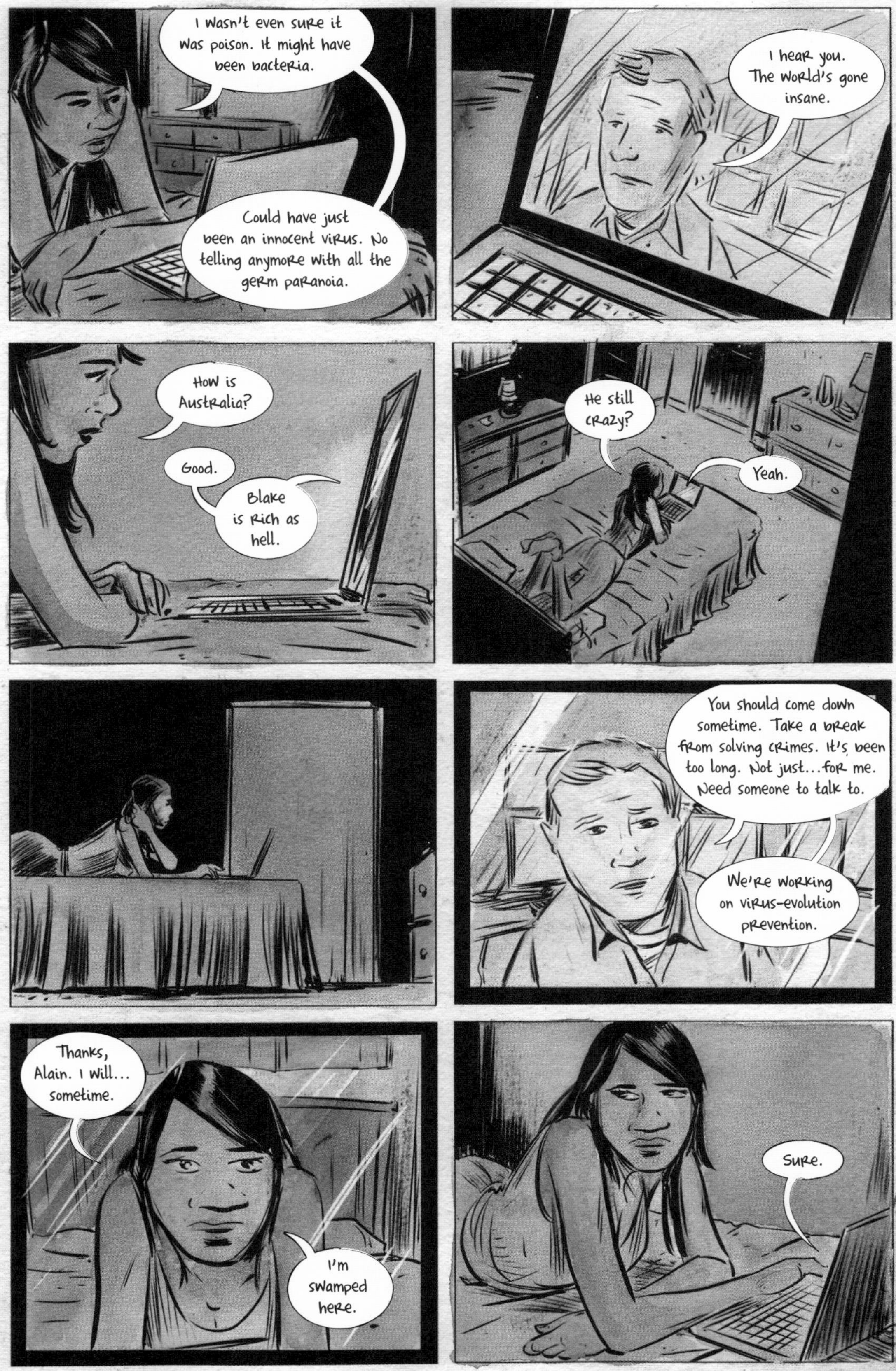
I Wasn't even sure it Was poison. It might have been bacteria.
Could have just been an innocent virus. No telling anymore with all the germ paranoia.
I hear you. The World's gone insane.
How is Australia?
Good.
Blake is rich as hell.
He still crazy?
Yeah.
You should come down sometime. Take a break from solving crimes. It's been too long. Not just...for me. Need someone to talk to.
We're working on virus-evolution prevention.
Thanks, Alain. I will... sometime.
I'm swamped here.
Sure.

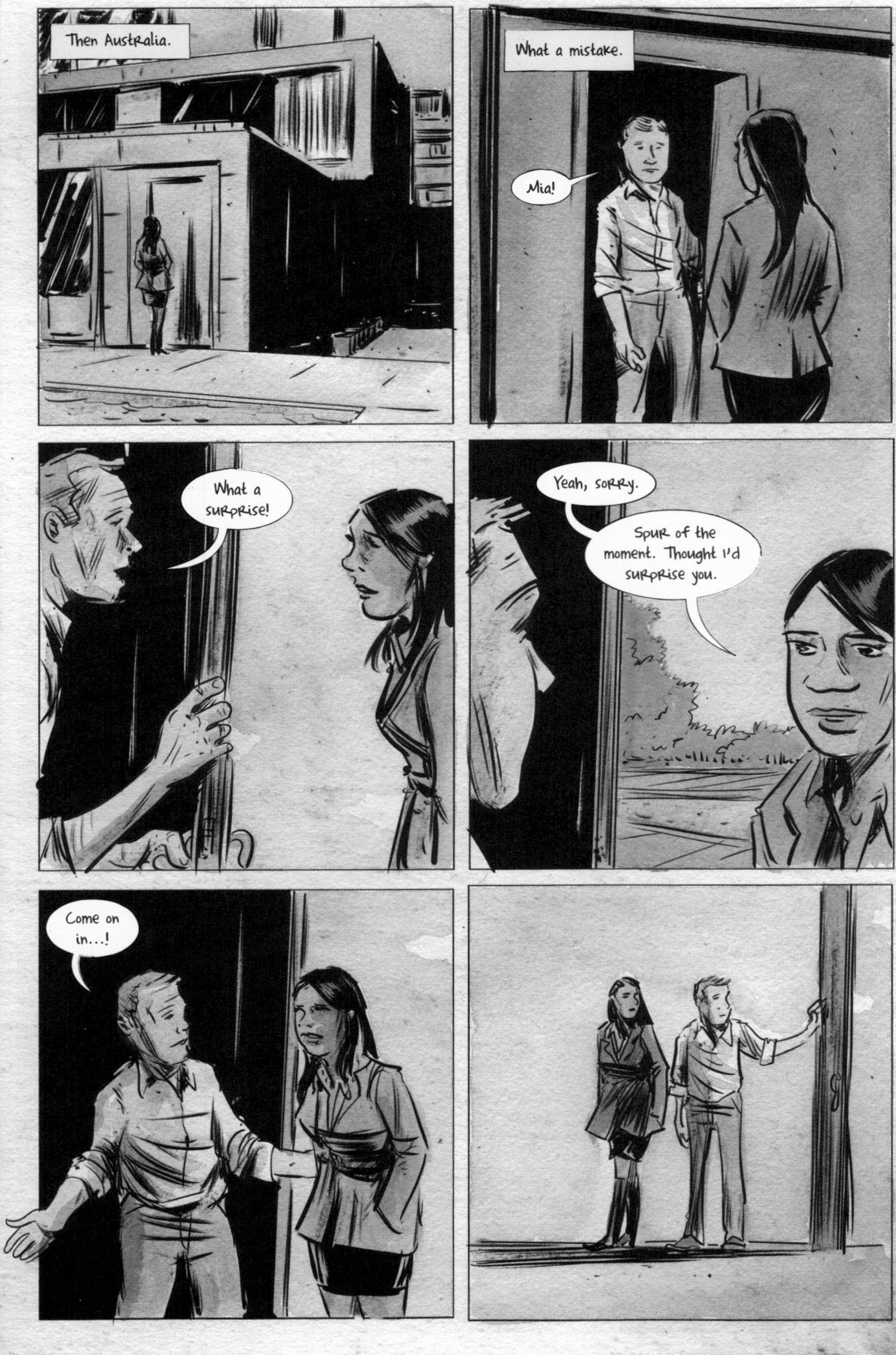
Then Australia.
What a mistake.
Mia!
What a surprise!
Yeah, sorry.
Spur of the moment. Thought I'd surprise you.
Come on in...!

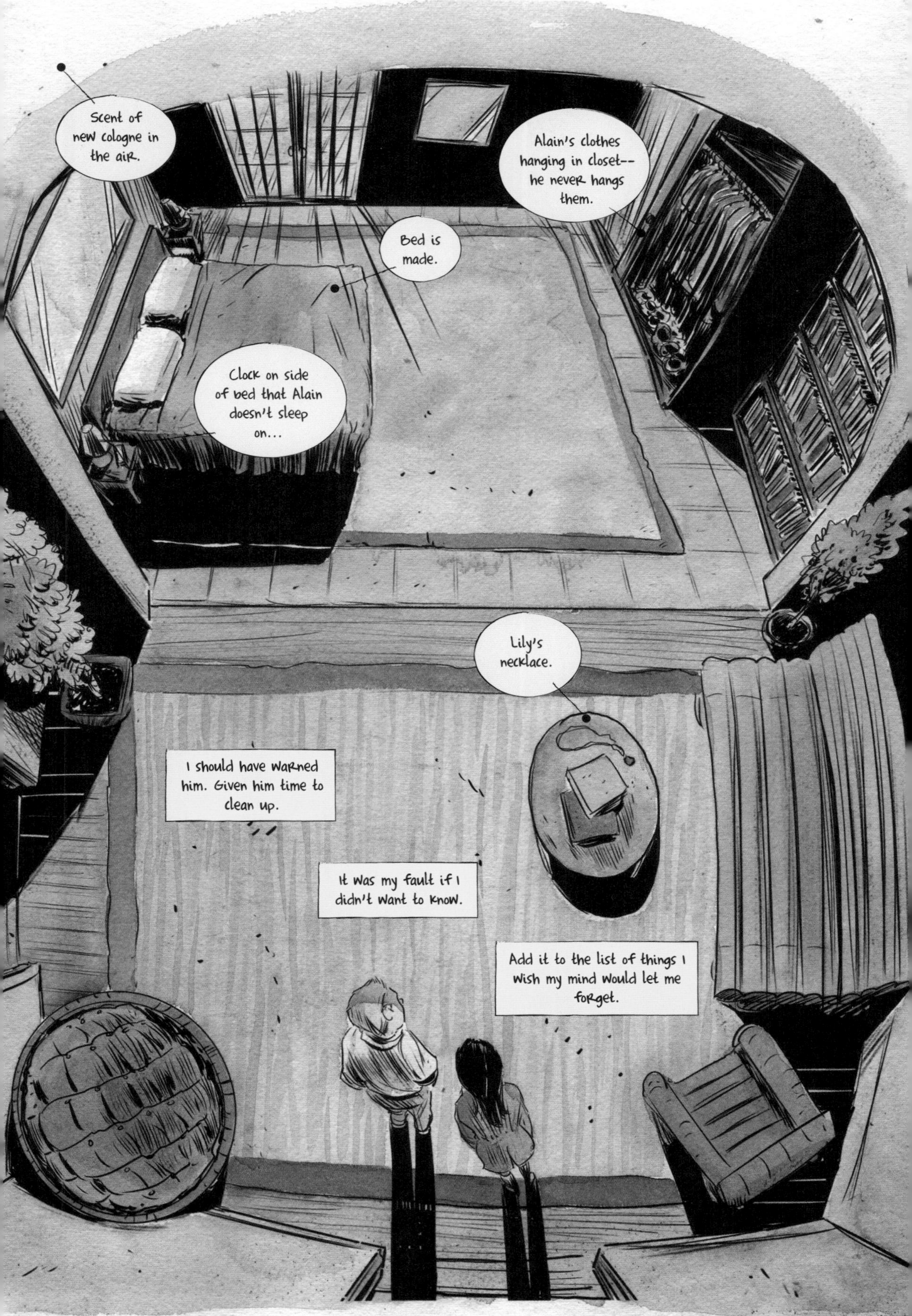
Scent of new cologne in the air.
Alain's clothes hanging in closet-- he never hangs them.
Bed is made.
Clock on side of bed that Alain doesn't sleep on...
Lily's necklace.
I should have warned him. Given him time to clean up.
It was my fault if I didn't want to know.
Add it to the list of things I wish my mind would let me forget.

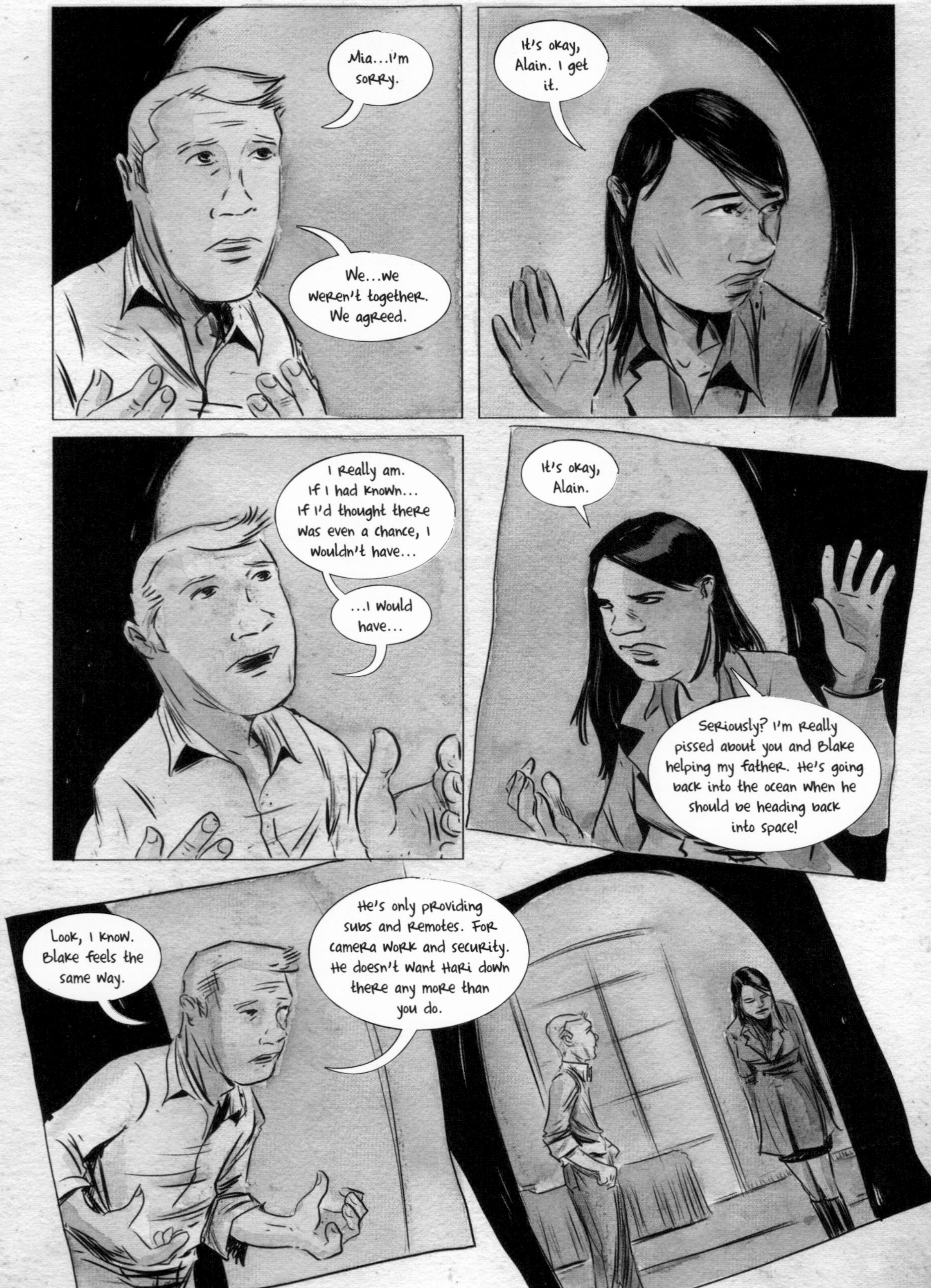
Mia...I'm sorry.
We...we weren't together. We agreed.
It's okay, Alain. I get it.
I really am. If I had known... If I'd thought there was even a chance, I wouldn't have...
...I would have...
It's okay, Alain.
Seriously? I'm really pissed about you and Blake helping my father. He's going back into the ocean when he should be heading back into space!
Look, I know. Blake feels the same way.
He's only providing subs and remotes. For camera work and security. He doesn't want Hari down there any more than you do.

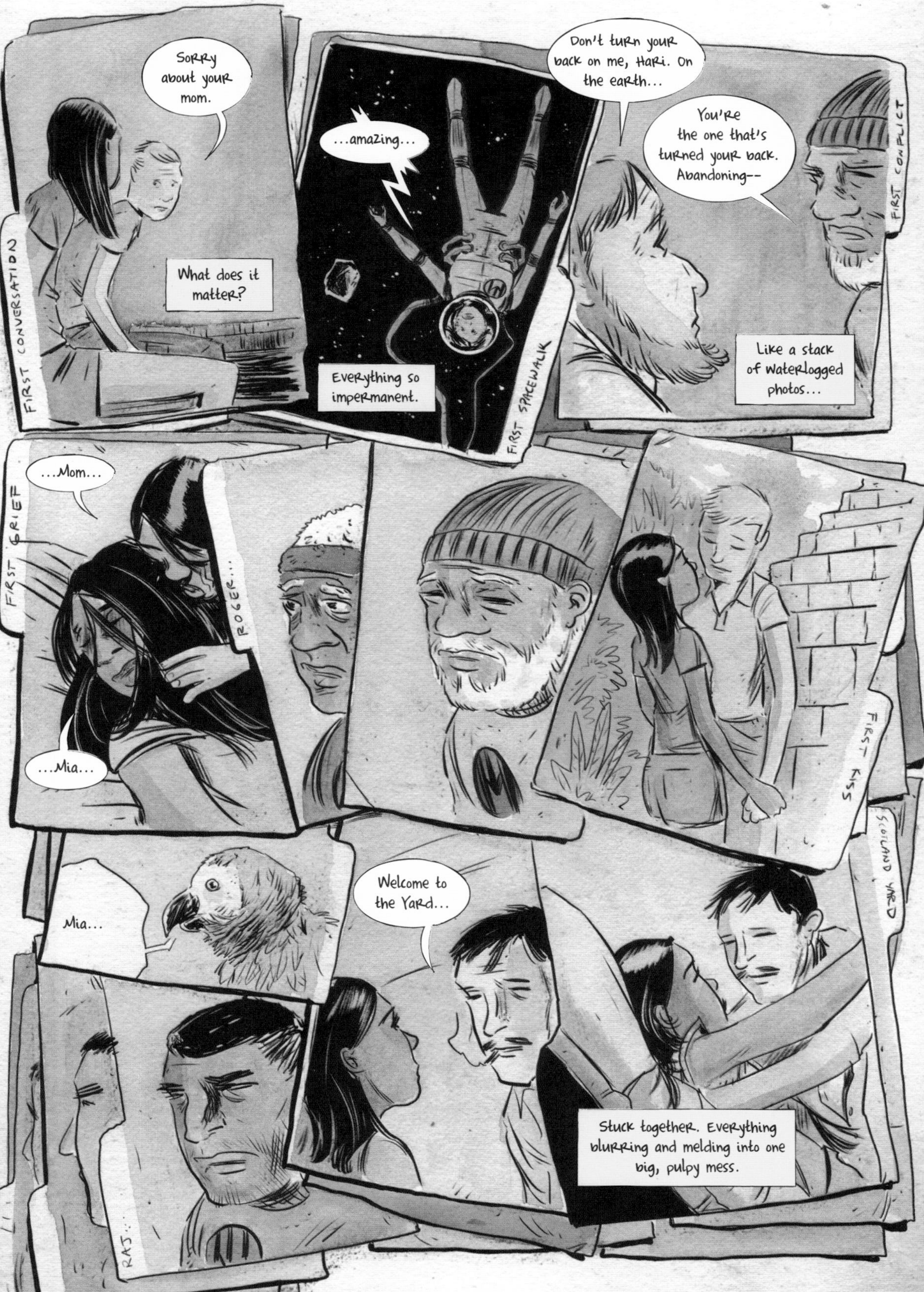

Sorry about your mom.
What does it matter?
FIRST CONVERSATION
...amazing...
Everything so impermanent.
FIRST SPACEWALK
Don't turn your back on me, Hari. On the earth...
You're the one that's turned your back. Abandoning--
FIRST CONFLICT
Like a stack of waterlogged photos...
...Mom...
FIRST GRIEF
...Mia...
ROGER...
FIRST KISS
Mia...
Welcome to the Yard...
SCOTLAND YARD
Stuck together. Everything blurring and melding into one big, pulpy mess.
RAJ...

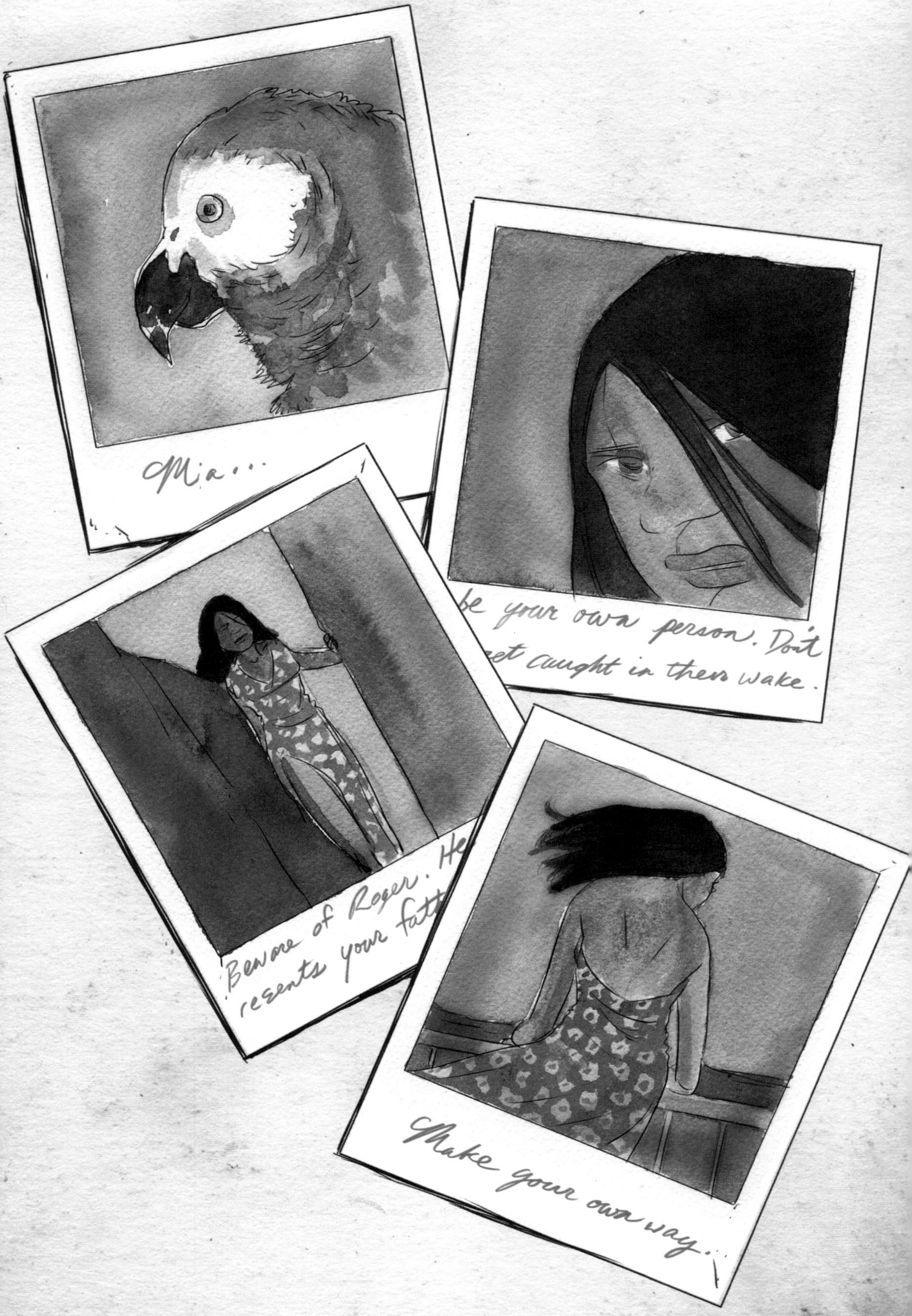
Mia...
be your own person. Don't
et caught in their wake.
Beware of Roger. He
resents your fath
Make your own way...

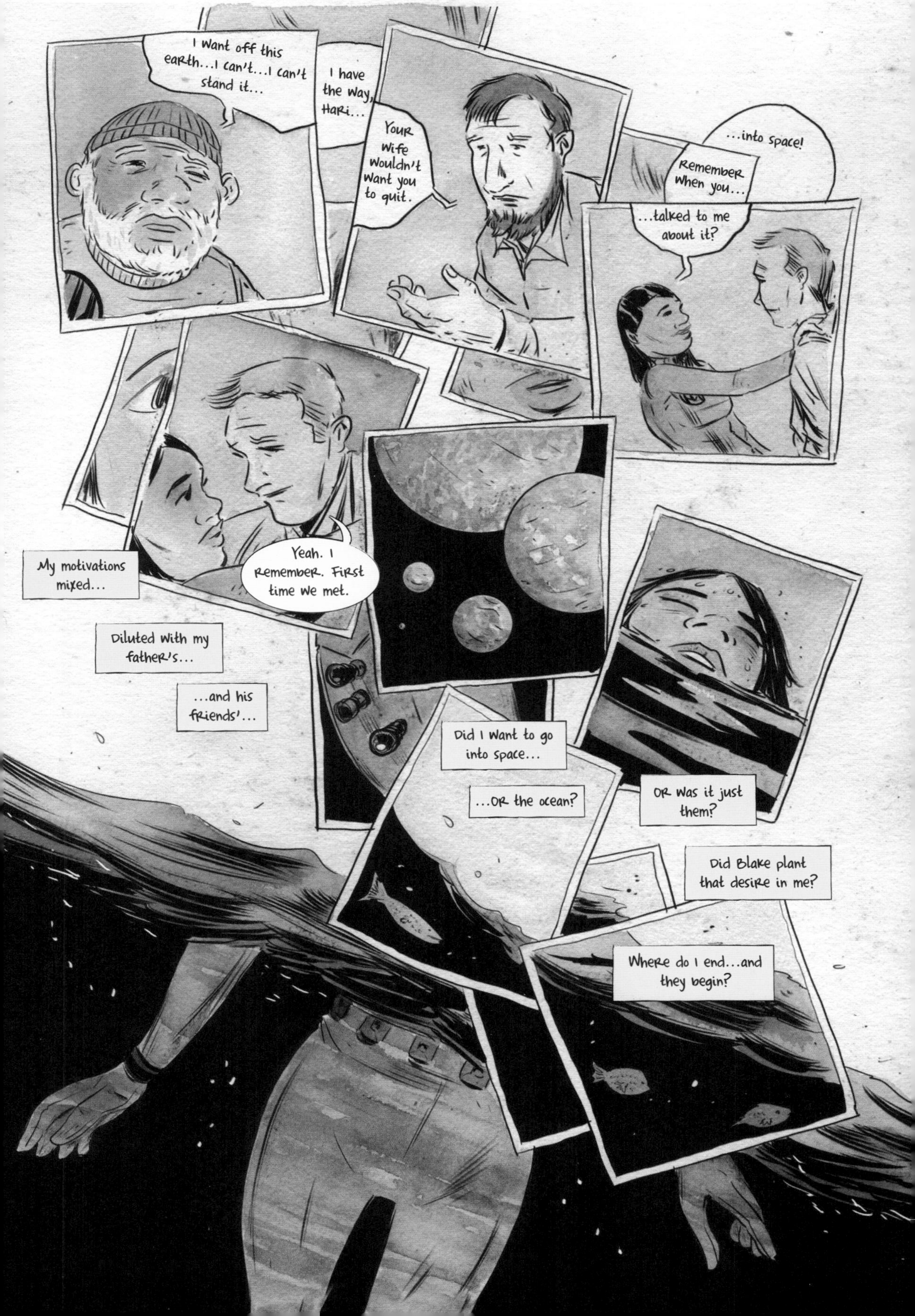
I want off this earth...I can't...I can't stand it...
I have the way, Hari...
Your wife wouldn't want you to quit.
...into space!
Remember when you...
...talked to me about it?
Yeah. I remember. First time we met.
My motivations mixed...
Diluted with my father's...
...and his friends'...
Did I want to go into space...
...or the ocean?
Or was it just them?
Did Blake plant that desire in me?
Where do I end...and they begin?

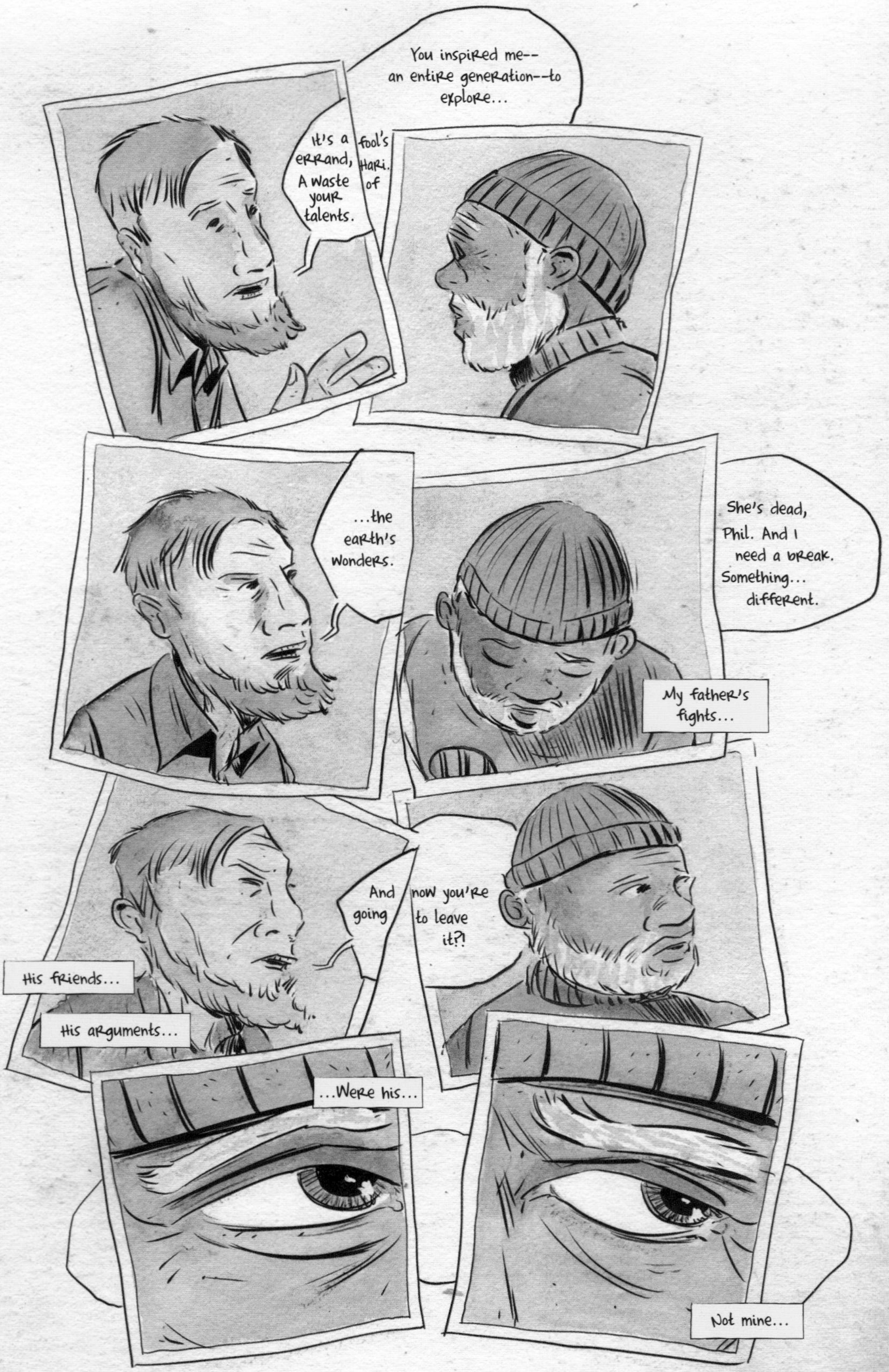

You inspired me-- an entire generation--to explore...
It's a fool's errand, Hari. A waste of your talents.
...the earth's wonders.
She's dead, Phil. And I need a break. Something... different.
My father's fights...
And now you're going to leave it?!
His friends...
His arguments...
...Were his...
Not mine...

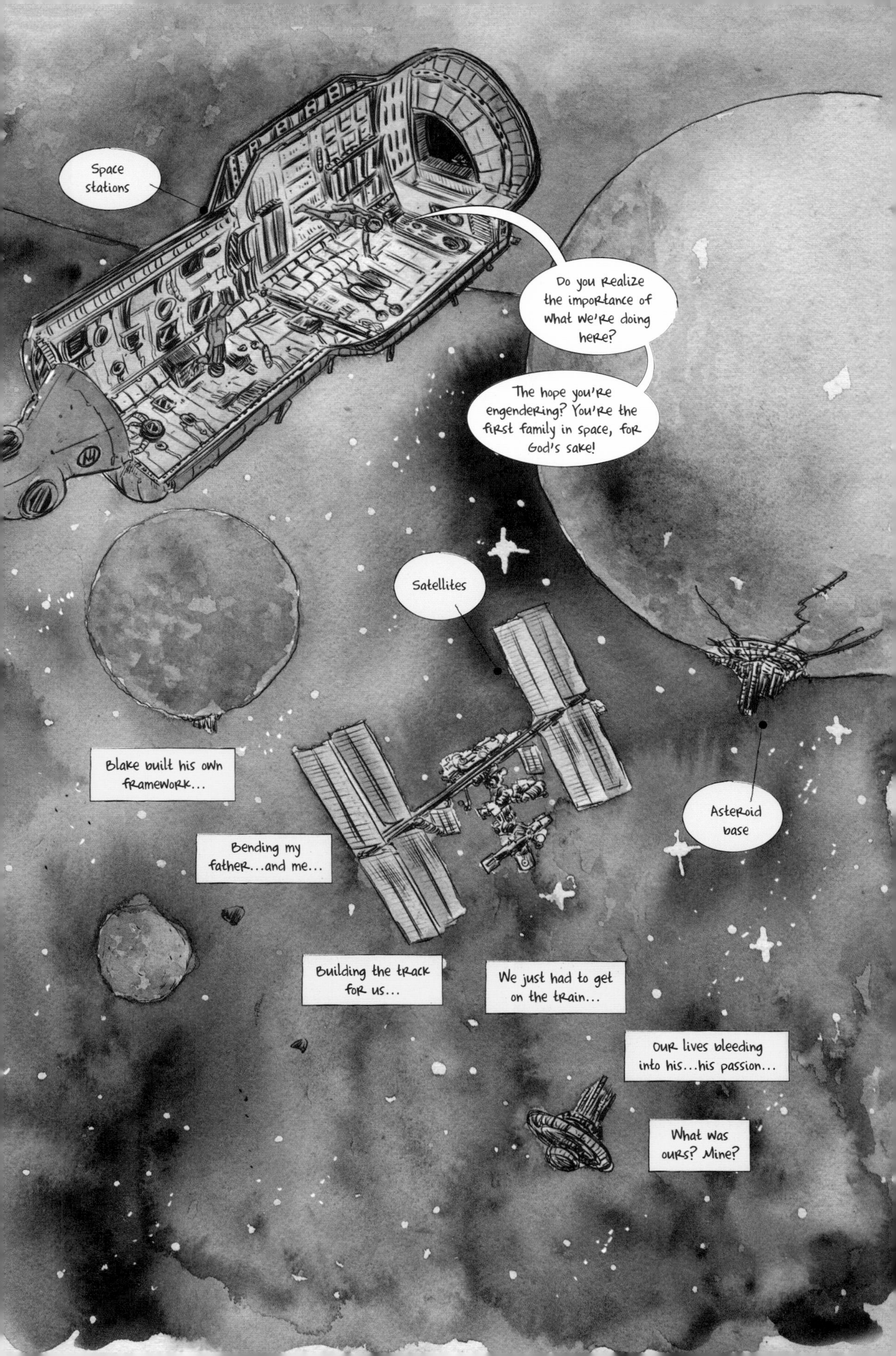
Space stations
Do you realize the importance of what we're doing here?
The hope you're engendering? You're the first family in space, for God's sake!
Satellites
Asteroid base
Blake built his own framework...
Bending my father...and me...
Building the track for us...
We just had to get on the train...
Our lives bleeding into his...his passion...
What was ours? Mine?

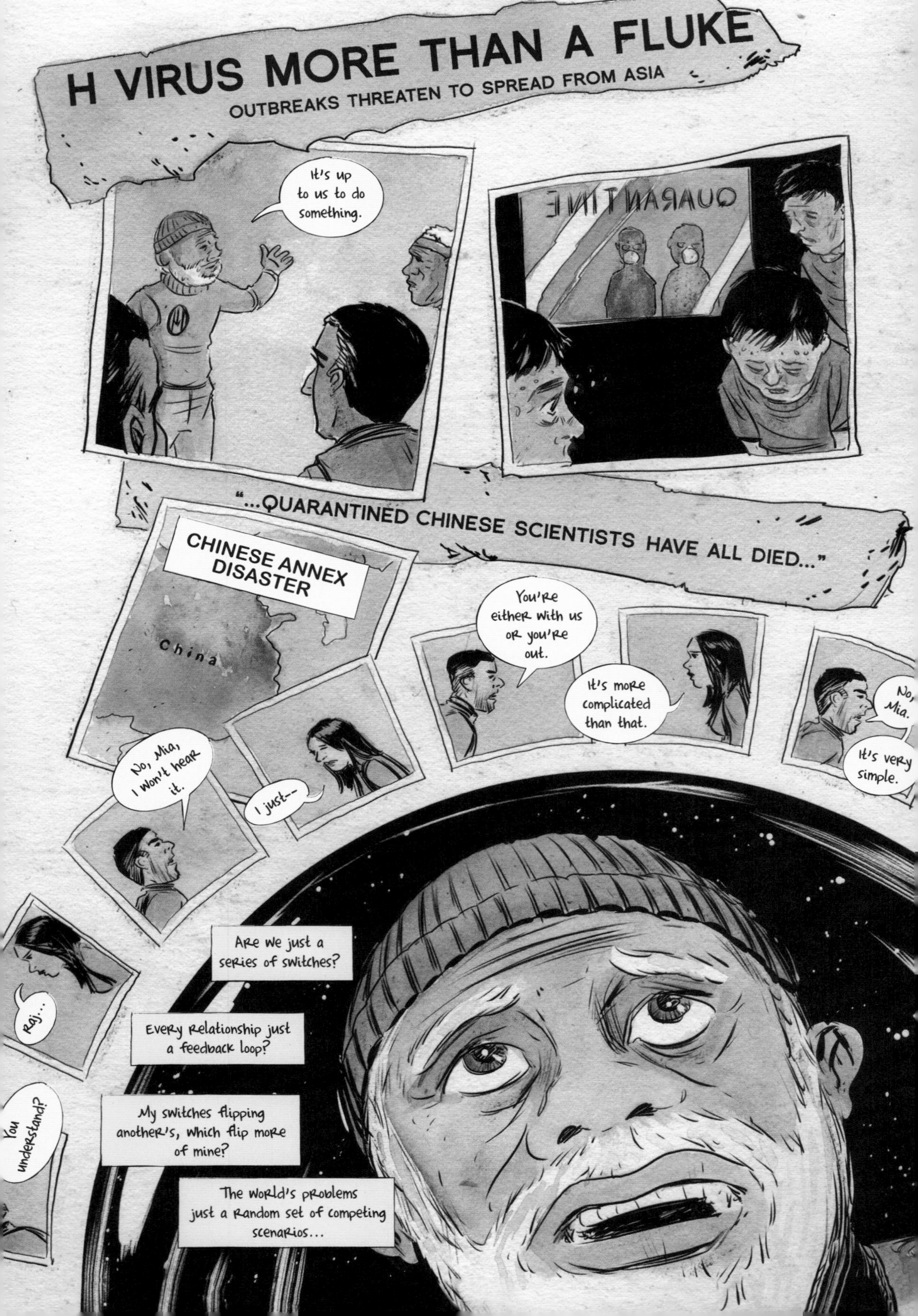
H VIRUS MORE THAN A FLUKE
OUTBREAKS THREATEN TO SPREAD FROM ASIA
It's up to us to do something.
QUARANTINE
"...QUARANTINED CHINESE SCIENTISTS HAVE ALL DIED..."
CHINESE ANNEX DISASTER
China
You're either with us or you're out.
It's more complicated than that.
No, Mia.
It's very simple.
No, Mia, I won't hear it.
I just--
Are we just a series of switches?
Every relationship just a feedback loop?
My switches flipping another's, which flip more of mine?
The world's problems just a random set of competing scenarios...
Raj...
You understand?

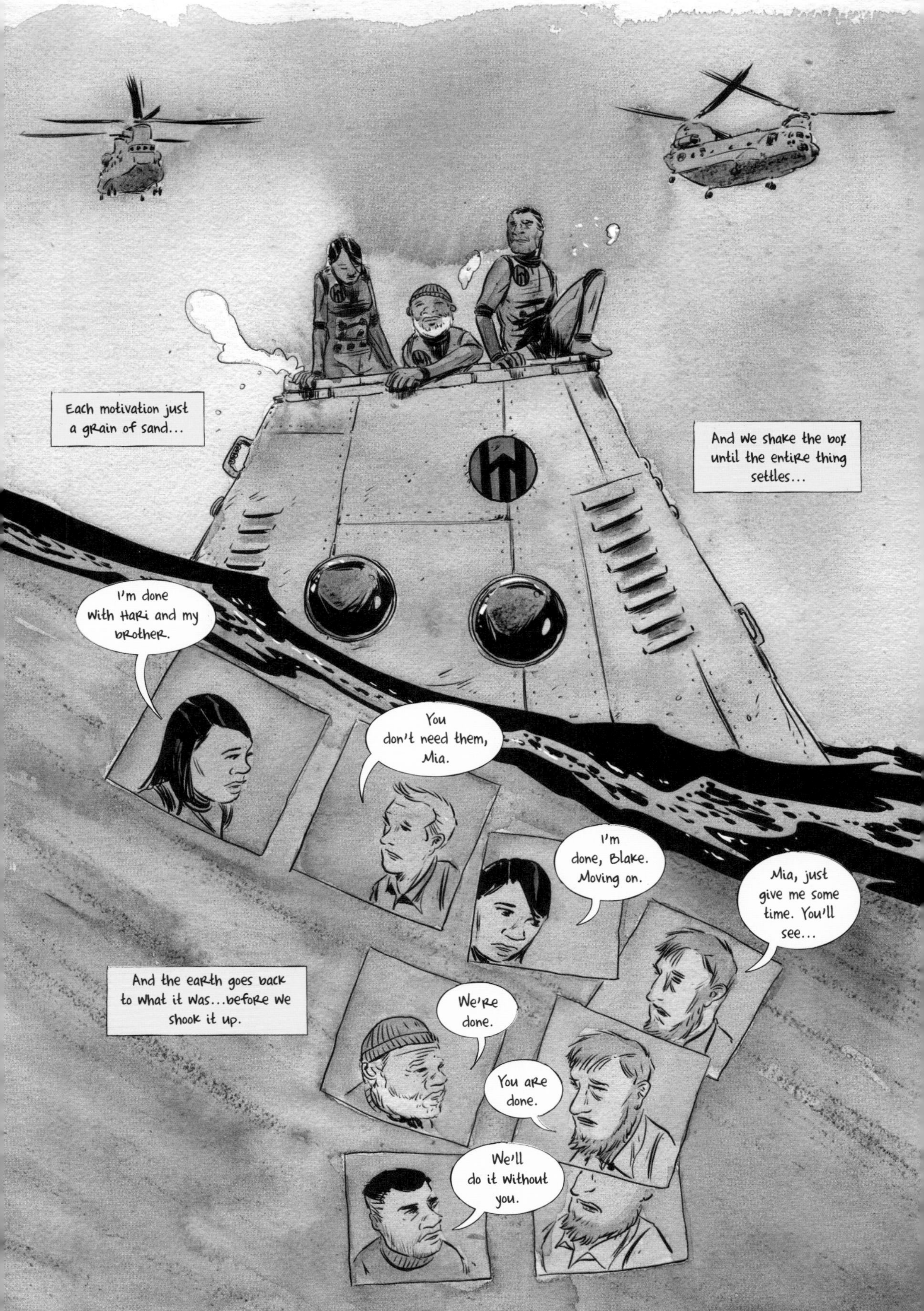
Each motivation just a grain of sand...
And we shake the box until the entire thing settles...
I'm done with Hari and my brother.
You don't need them, Mia.
I'm done, Blake. Moving on.
Mia, just give me some time. You'll see...
And the earth goes back to what it was...before we shook it up.
We're done.
You are done.
We'll do it without you.

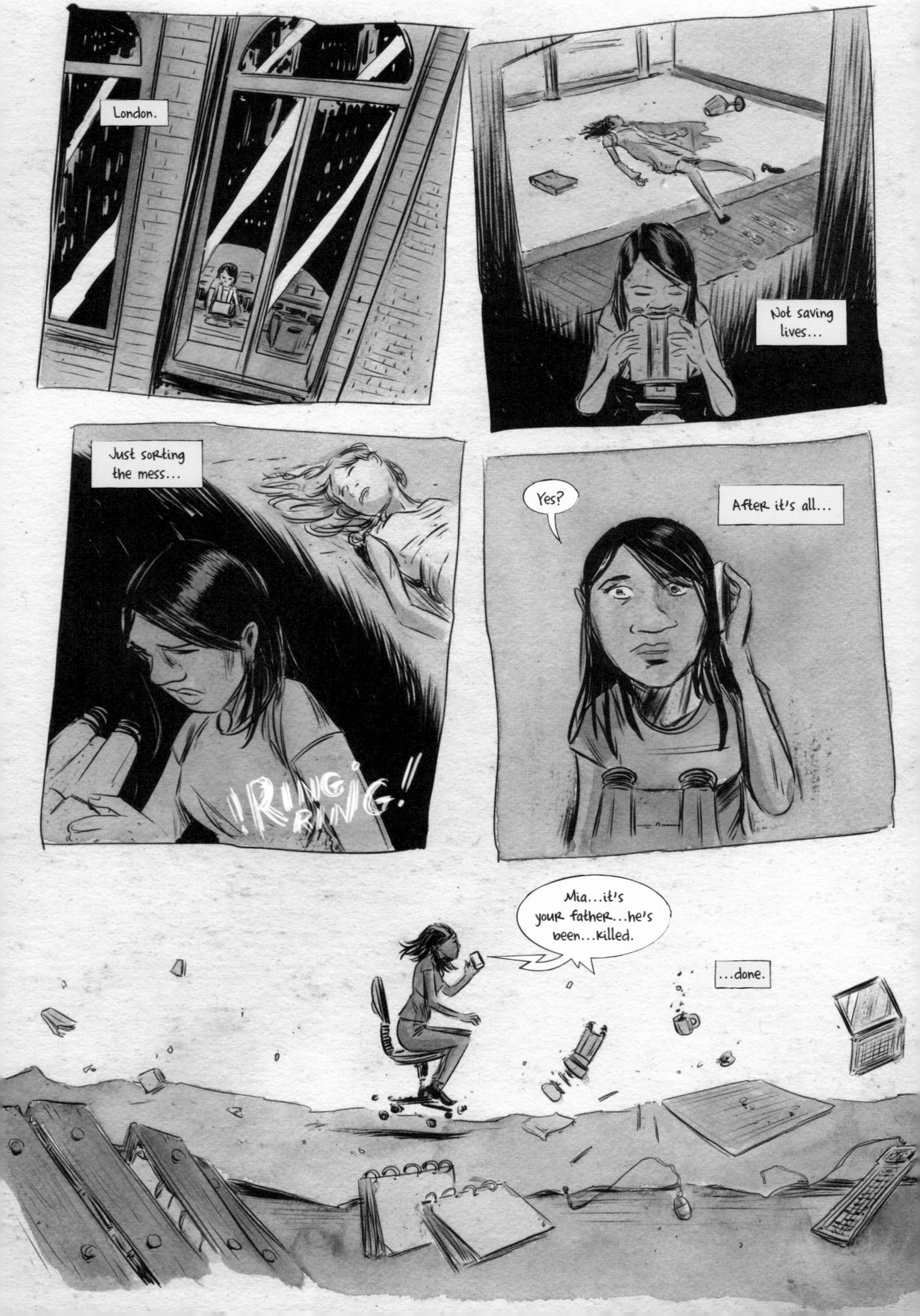
London.
Not saving lives...
Just sorting the mess...
!!RING RING!!
Yes?
After it's all...
Mia...it's your father...he's been...killed.
...done.

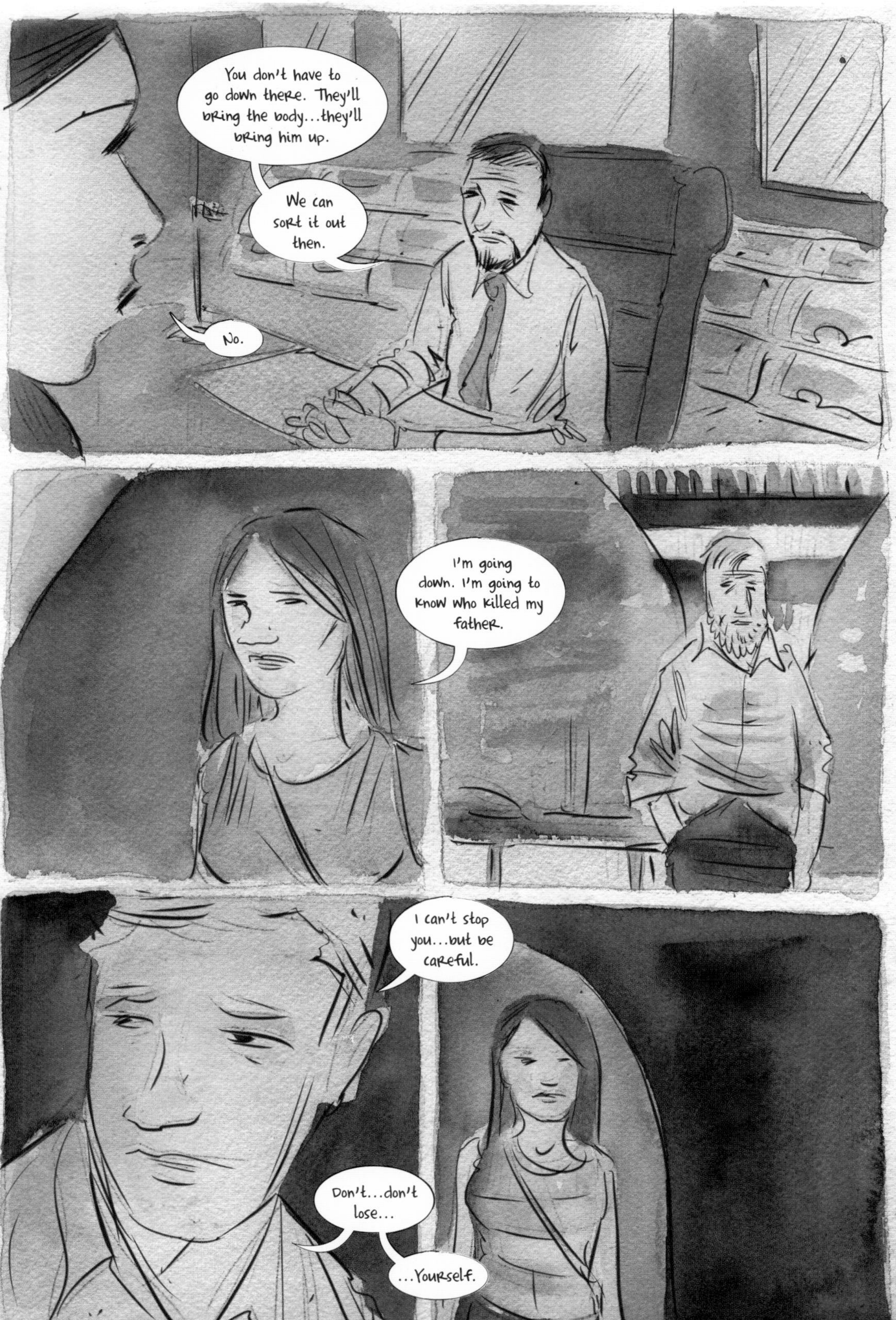
You don't have to go down there. They'll bring the body...they'll bring him up.
We can sort it out then.
No.
I'm going down. I'm going to know who killed my father.
I can't stop you...but be careful.
Don't...don't lose...
...Yourself.

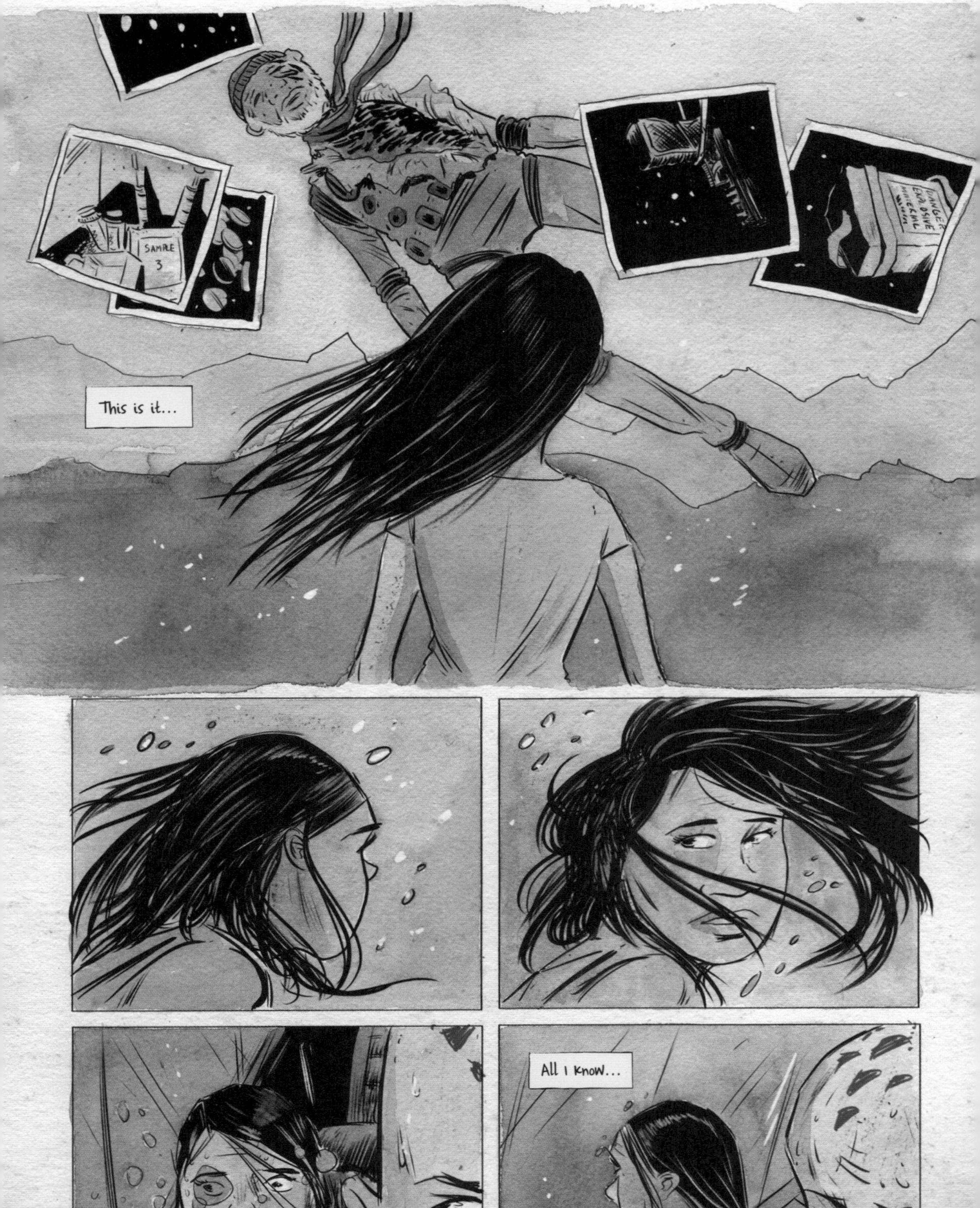
SAMPLE
3
This is it...
All I know...

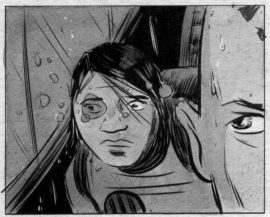

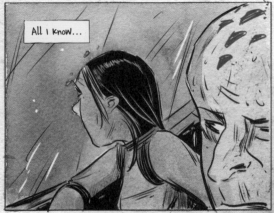

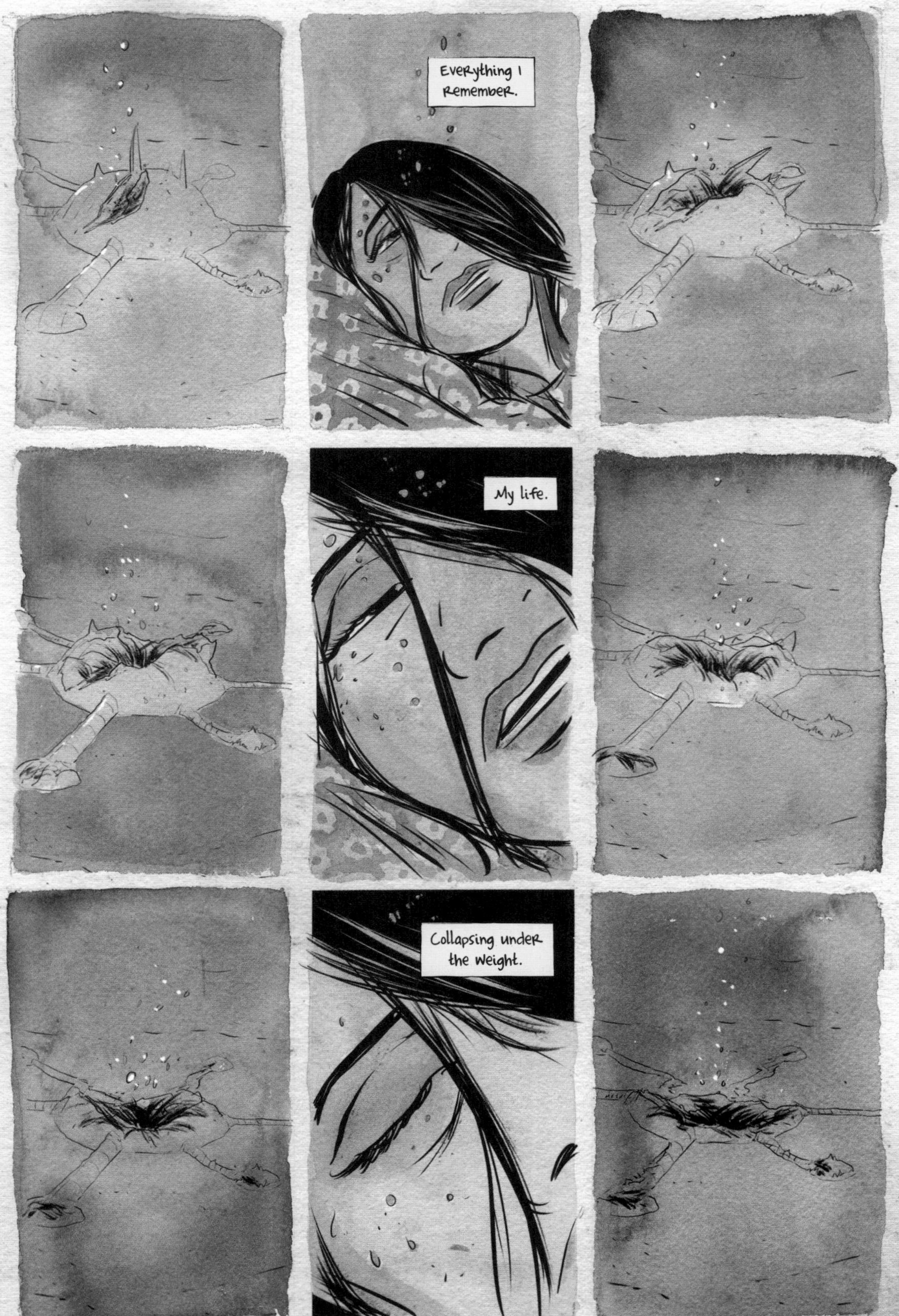
Everything I remember.
My life.
Collapsing under the weight.

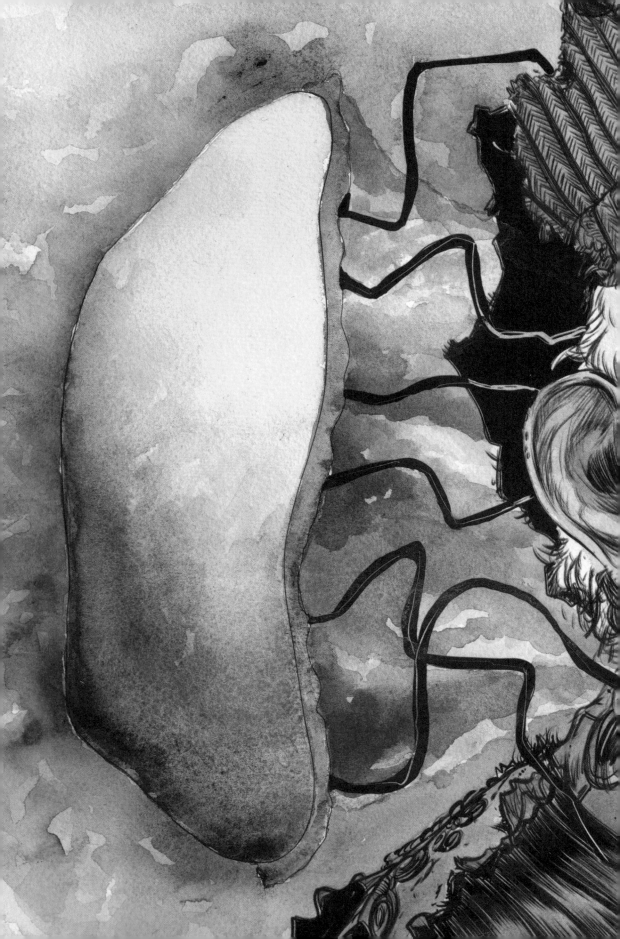

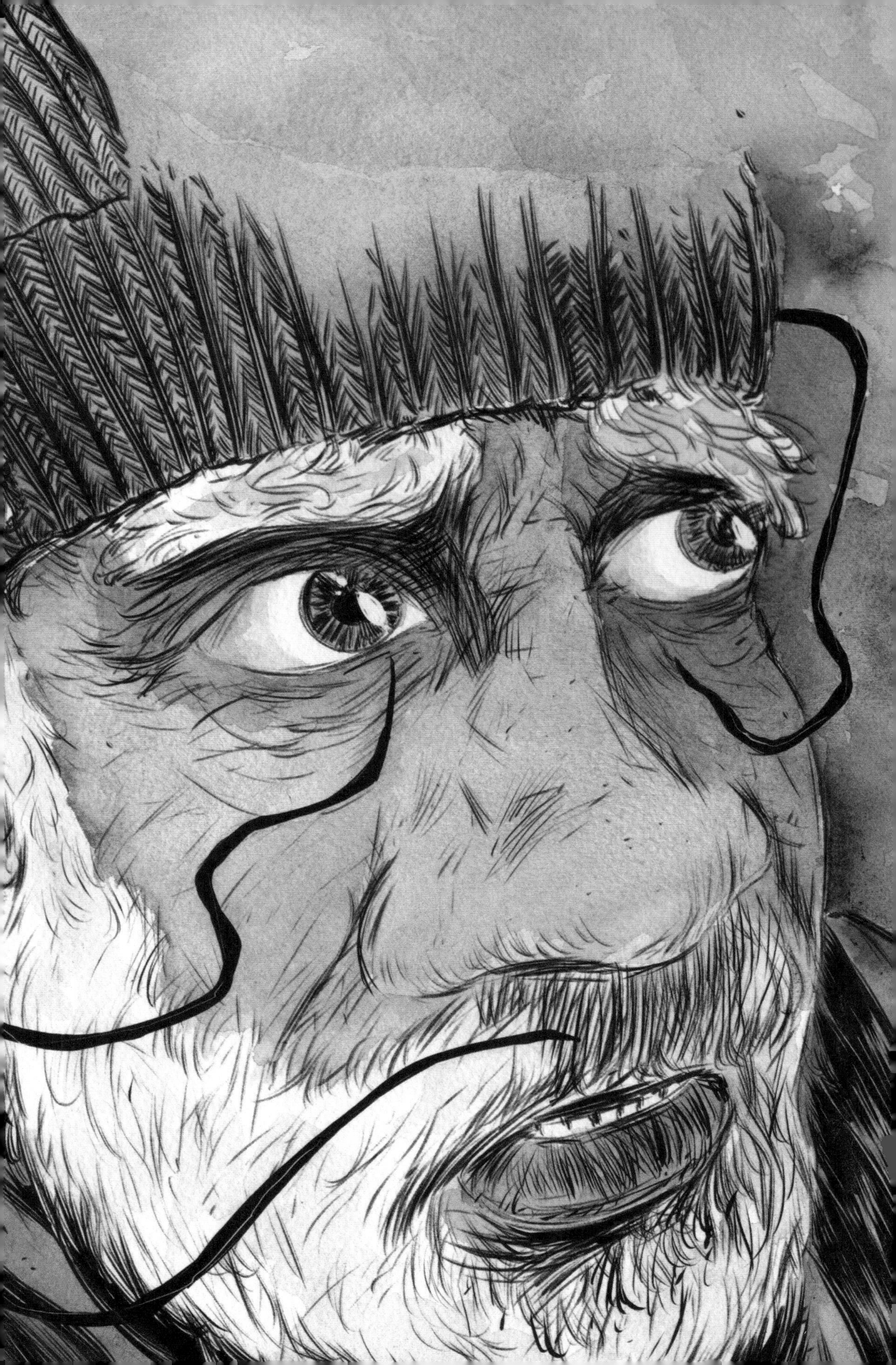

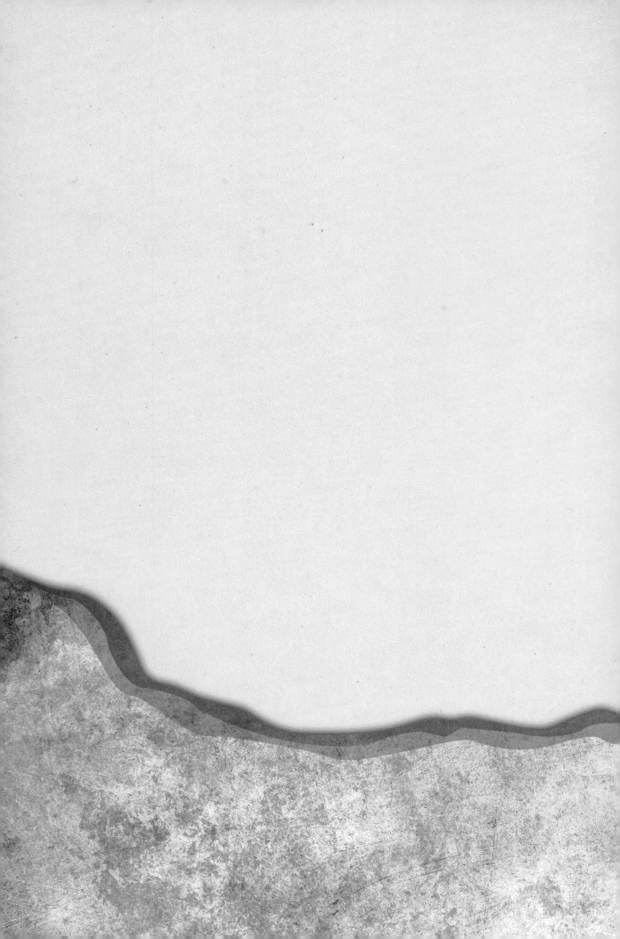

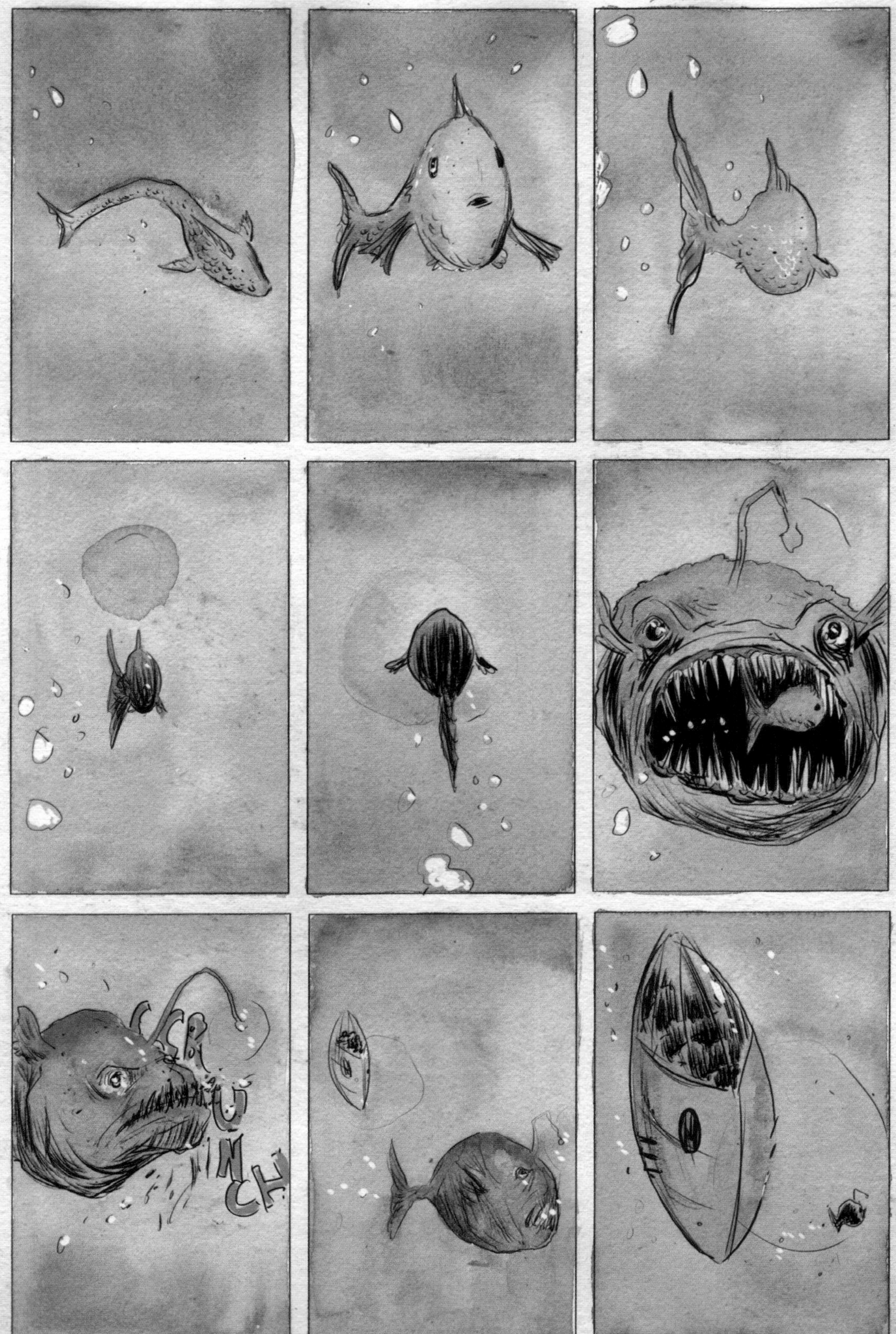
CRUNCH

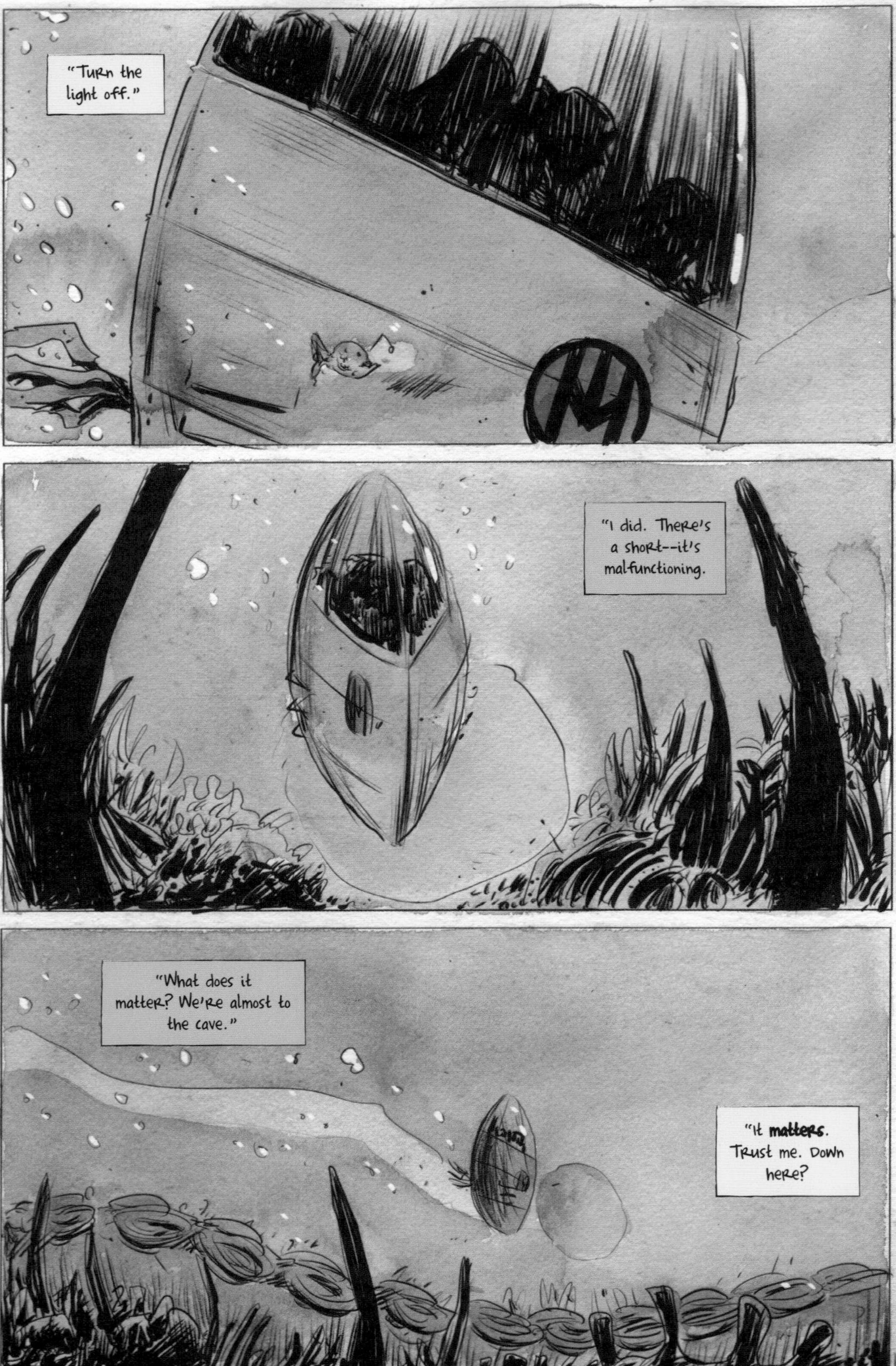
"Turn the light off."
"I did. There's a short--it's malfunctioning.
"What does it matter? We're almost to the cave."
"It **matters**. Trust me. Down here?

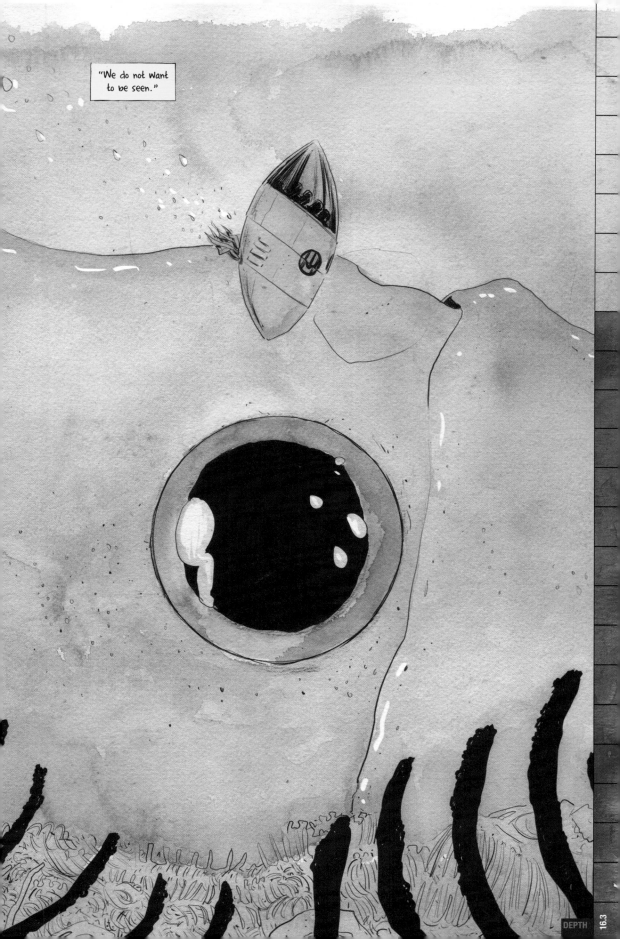

"We do not want to be seen."

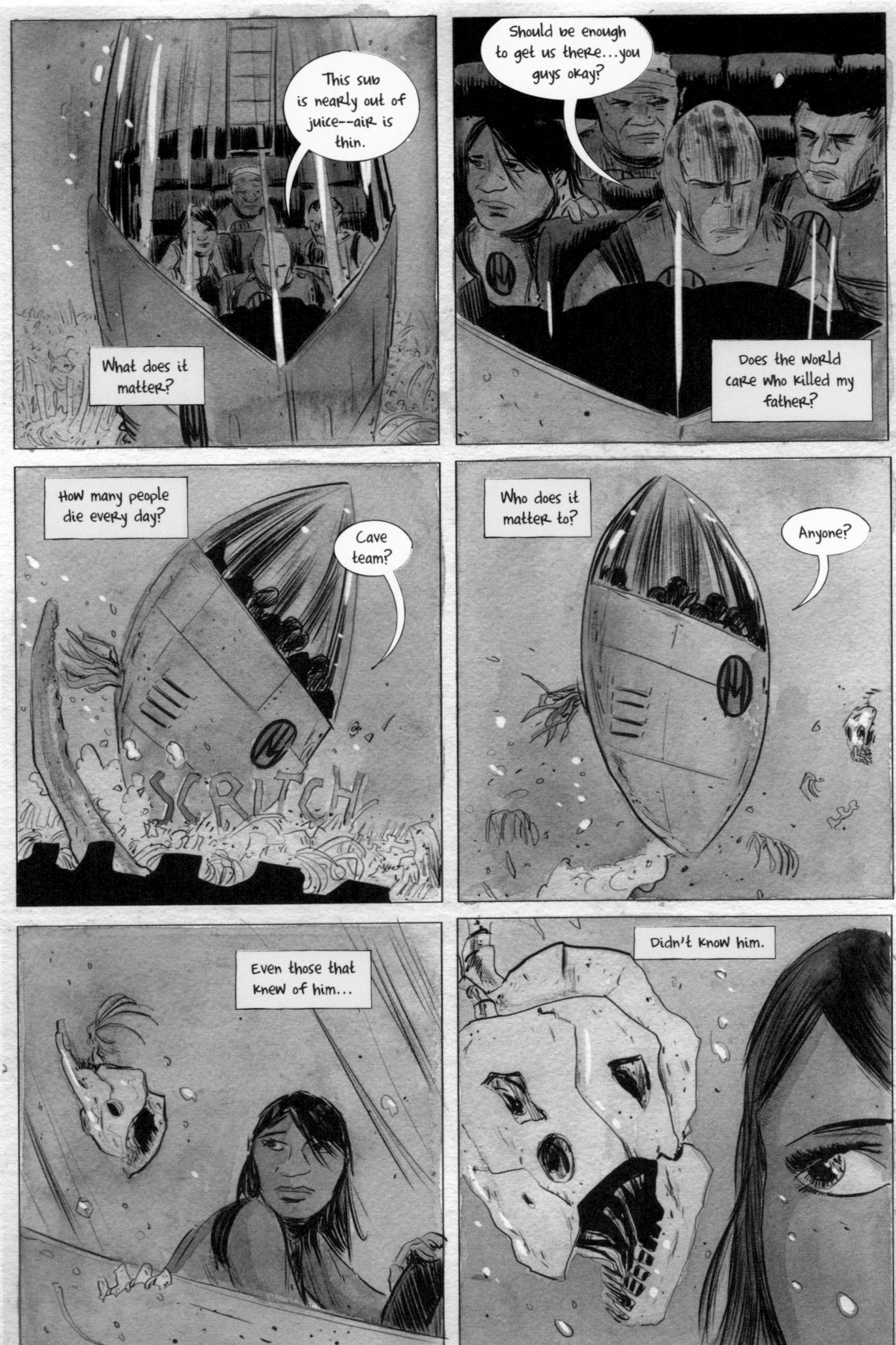
This sub is nearly out of juice--air is thin.
What does it matter?
Should be enough to get us there...you guys okay?
Does the world care who killed my father?
How many people die every day?
Cave team?
SCRITCH
Who does it matter to?
Anyone?
Even those that knew of him...
Didn't know him.

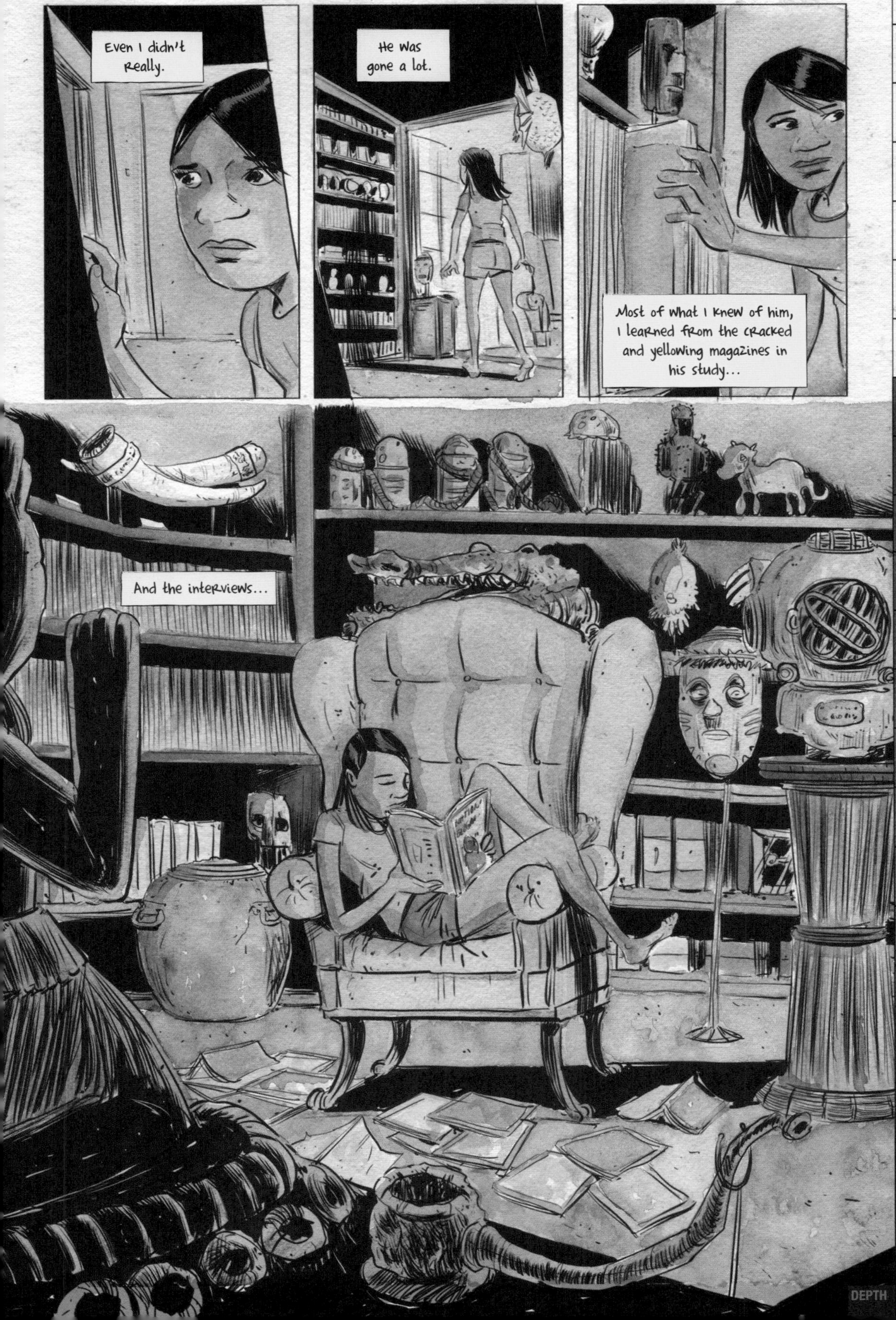
Even I didn't really.
He was gone a lot.
Most of what I knew of him, I learned from the cracked and yellowing magazines in his study...
And the interviews...

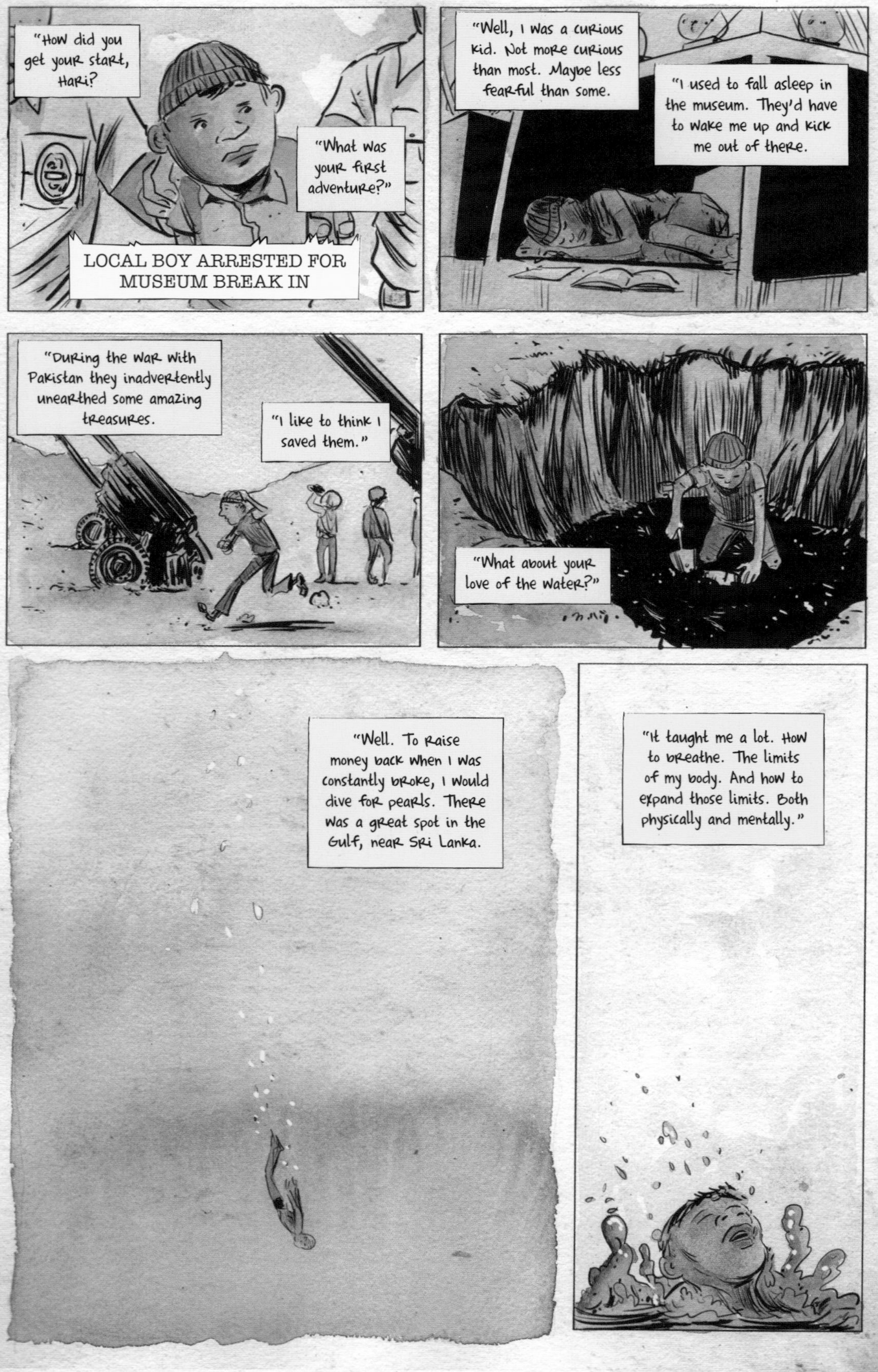
"How did you get your start, Hari?
"What was your first adventure?"
LOCAL BOY ARRESTED FOR MUSEUM BREAK IN
"Well, I was a curious kid. Not more curious than most. Maybe less fearful than some.
"I used to fall asleep in the museum. They'd have to wake me up and kick me out of there.
"During the war with Pakistan they inadvertently unearthed some amazing treasures.
"I like to think I saved them."
"What about your love of the water?"
"Well. To raise money back when I was constantly broke, I would dive for pearls. There was a great spot in the Gulf, near Sri Lanka.
"It taught me a lot. How to breathe. The limits of my body. And how to expand those limits. Both physically and mentally."

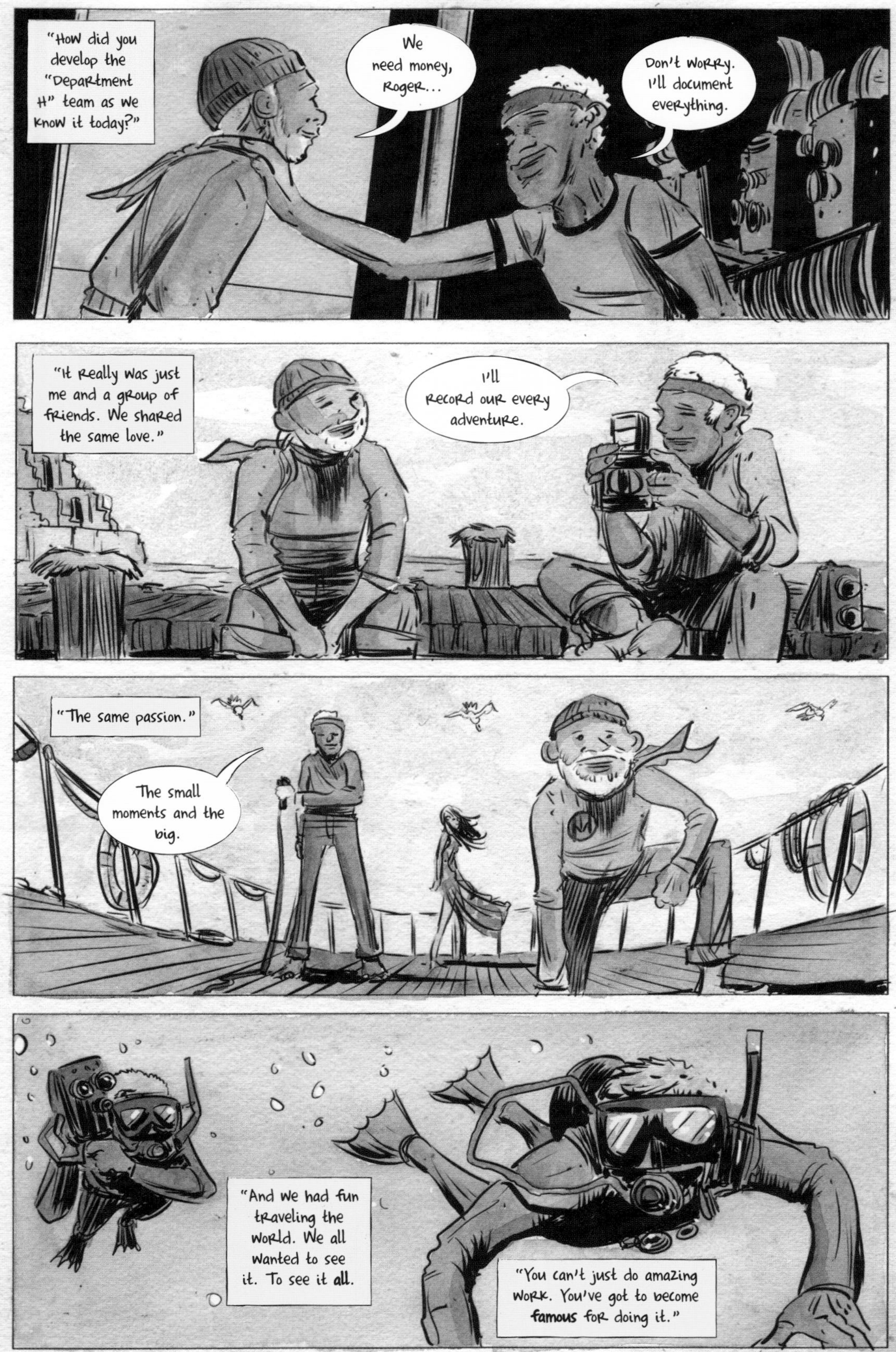
"How did you develop the "Department H" team as we know it today?"
We need money, Roger...
Don't worry. I'll document everything.
"It really was just me and a group of friends. We shared the same love."
I'll record our every adventure.
"The same passion."
The small moments and the big.
"And we had fun traveling the world. We all wanted to see it. To see it **all**.
"You can't just do amazing work. You've got to become **famous** for doing it."

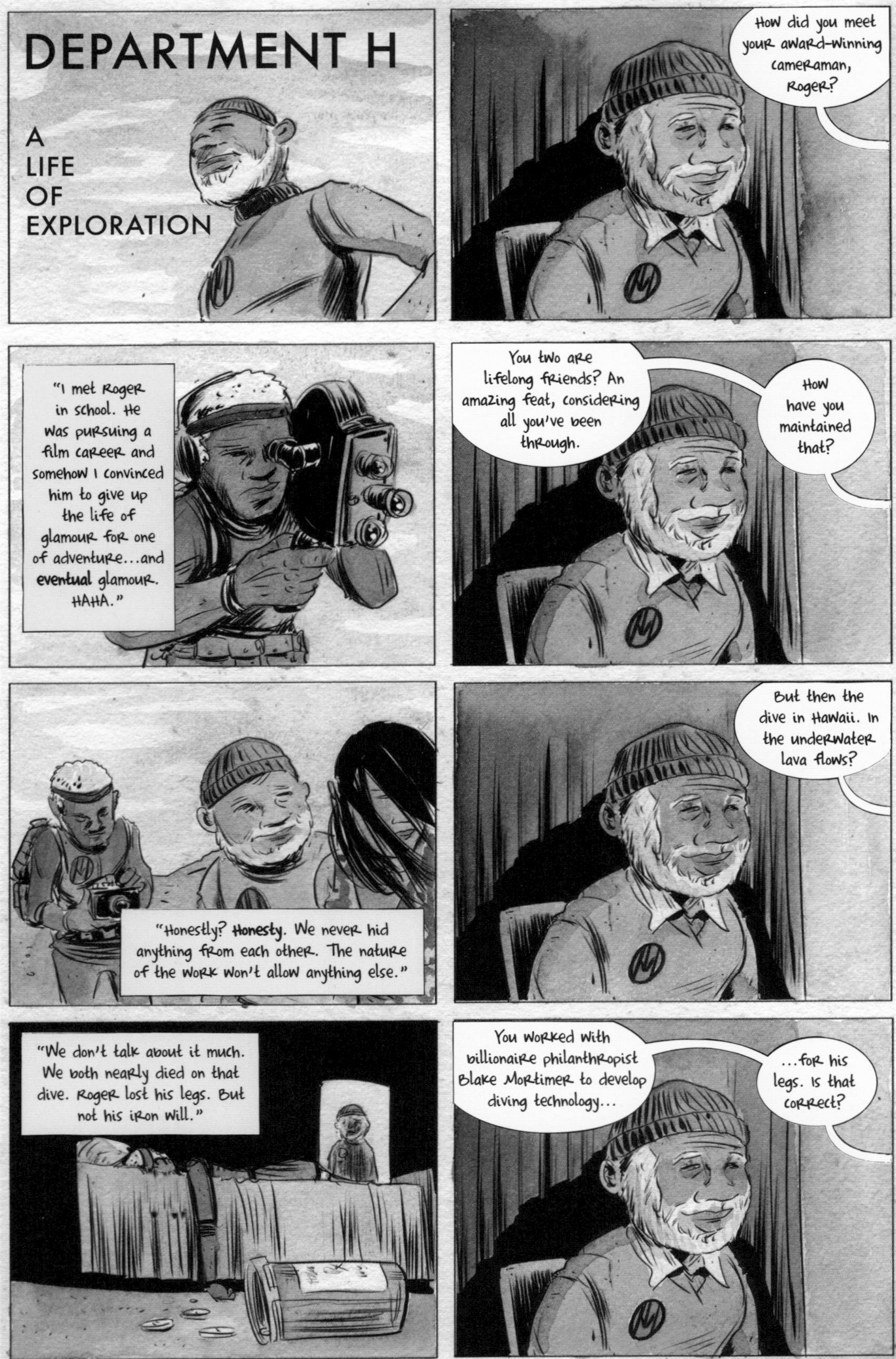
DEPARTMENT H
A LIFE OF EXPLORATION
How did you meet your award-winning cameraman, Roger?
"I met Roger in school. He was pursuing a film career and somehow I convinced him to give up the life of glamour for one of adventure...and **eventual** glamour. HAHA."
You two are lifelong friends? An amazing feat, considering all you've been through.
How have you maintained that?
"Honestly? **Honesty**. We never hid anything from each other. The nature of the work won't allow anything else."
But then the dive in Hawaii. In the underwater lava flows?
"We don't talk about it much. We both nearly died on that dive. Roger lost his legs. But not his iron will."
You worked with billionaire philanthropist Blake Mortimer to develop diving technology...
...for his legs. Is that correct?

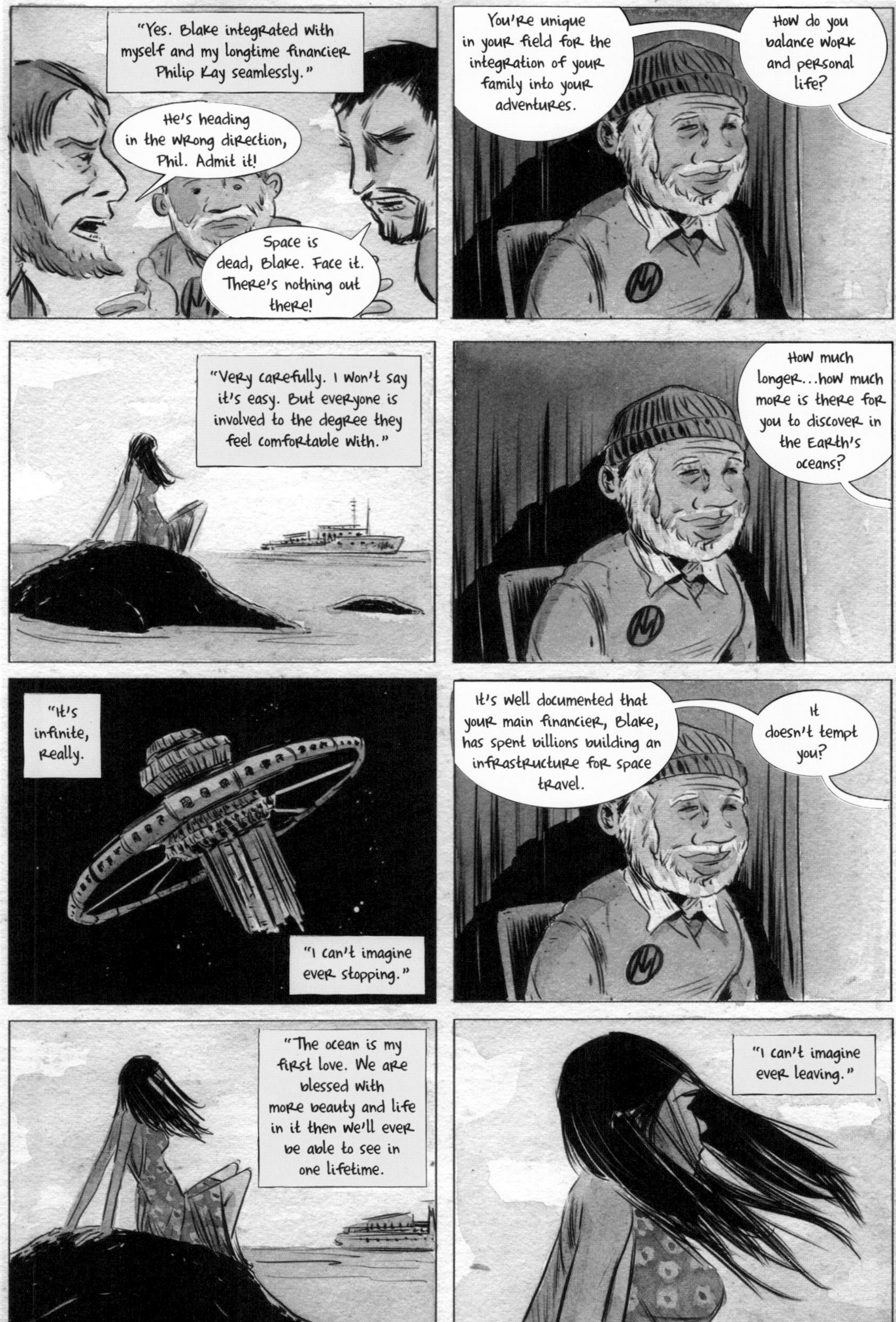
"Yes. Blake integrated with myself and my longtime financier Philip Kay seamlessly."
He's heading in the wrong direction, Phil. Admit it!
Space is dead, Blake. Face it. There's nothing out there!
You're unique in your field for the integration of your family into your adventures.
How do you balance work and personal life?
"Very carefully. I won't say it's easy. But everyone is involved to the degree they feel comfortable with."
How much longer...how much more is there for you to discover in the Earth's oceans?
"It's infinite, really.
"I can't imagine ever stopping."
It's well documented that your main financier, Blake, has spent billions building an infrastructure for space travel.
It doesn't tempt you?
"The ocean is my first love. We are blessed with more beauty and life in it then we'll ever be able to see in one lifetime.
"I can't imagine ever leaving."

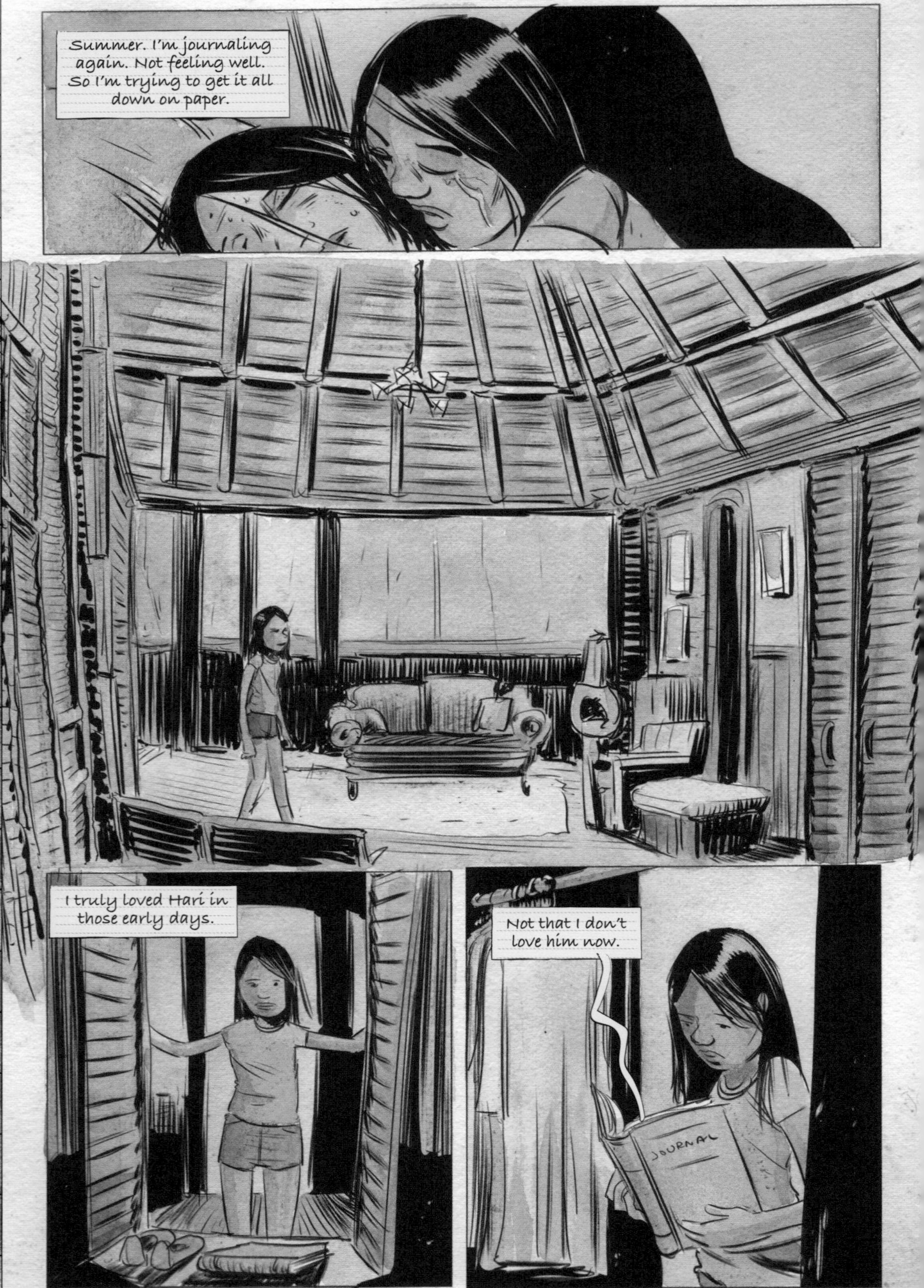
Summer. I'm journaling again. Not feeling well. So I'm trying to get it all down on paper.
I truly loved Hari in those early days.
Not that I don't love him now.
JOURNAL

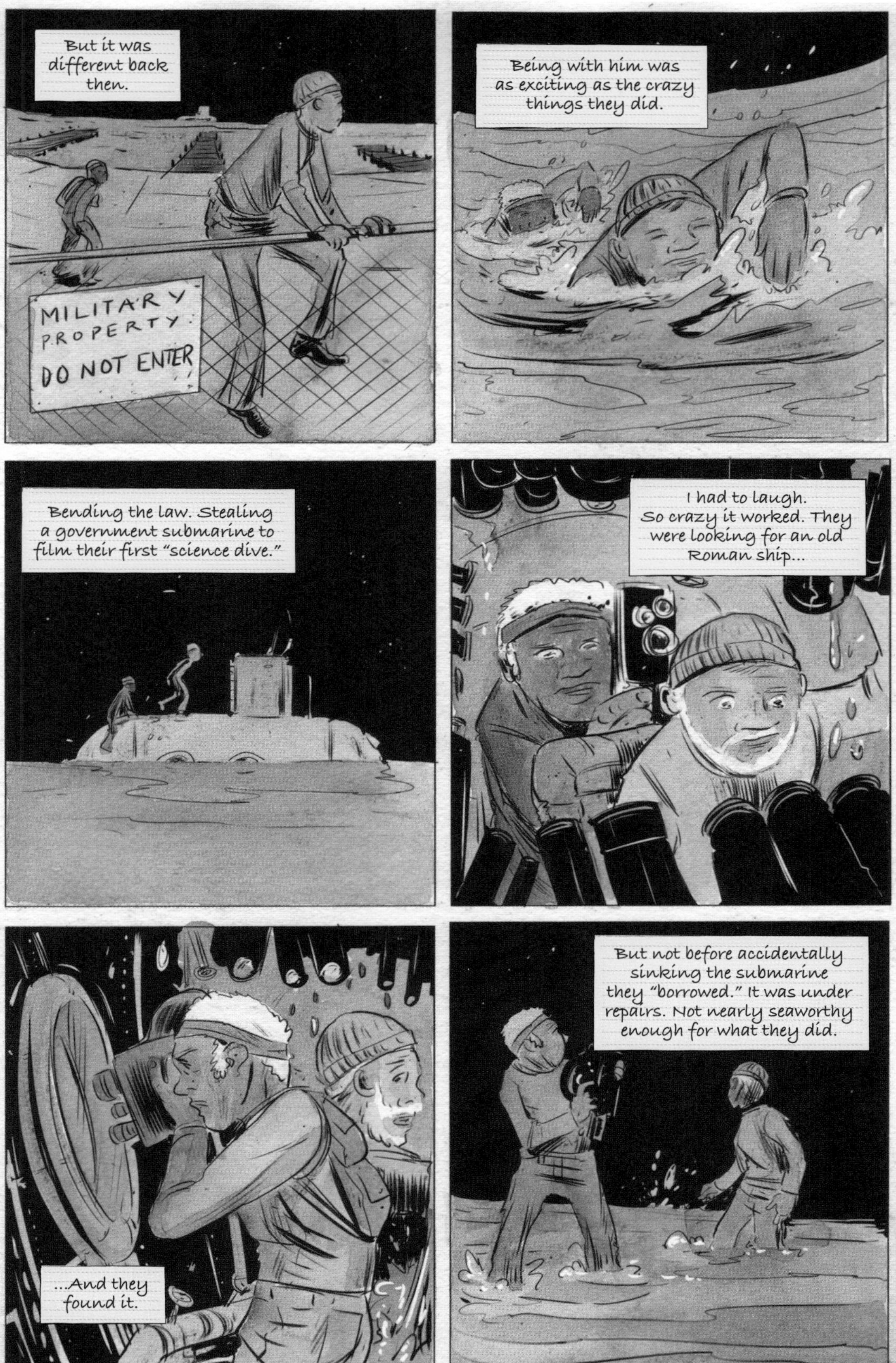
But it was different back then.
MILITARY PROPERTY
DO NOT ENTER
Being with him was as exciting as the crazy things they did.
Bending the law. Stealing a government submarine to film their first "science dive."
I had to laugh. So crazy it worked. They were looking for an old Roman ship...
...And they found it.
But not before accidentally sinking the submarine they "borrowed." It was under repairs. Not nearly seaworthy enough for what they did.

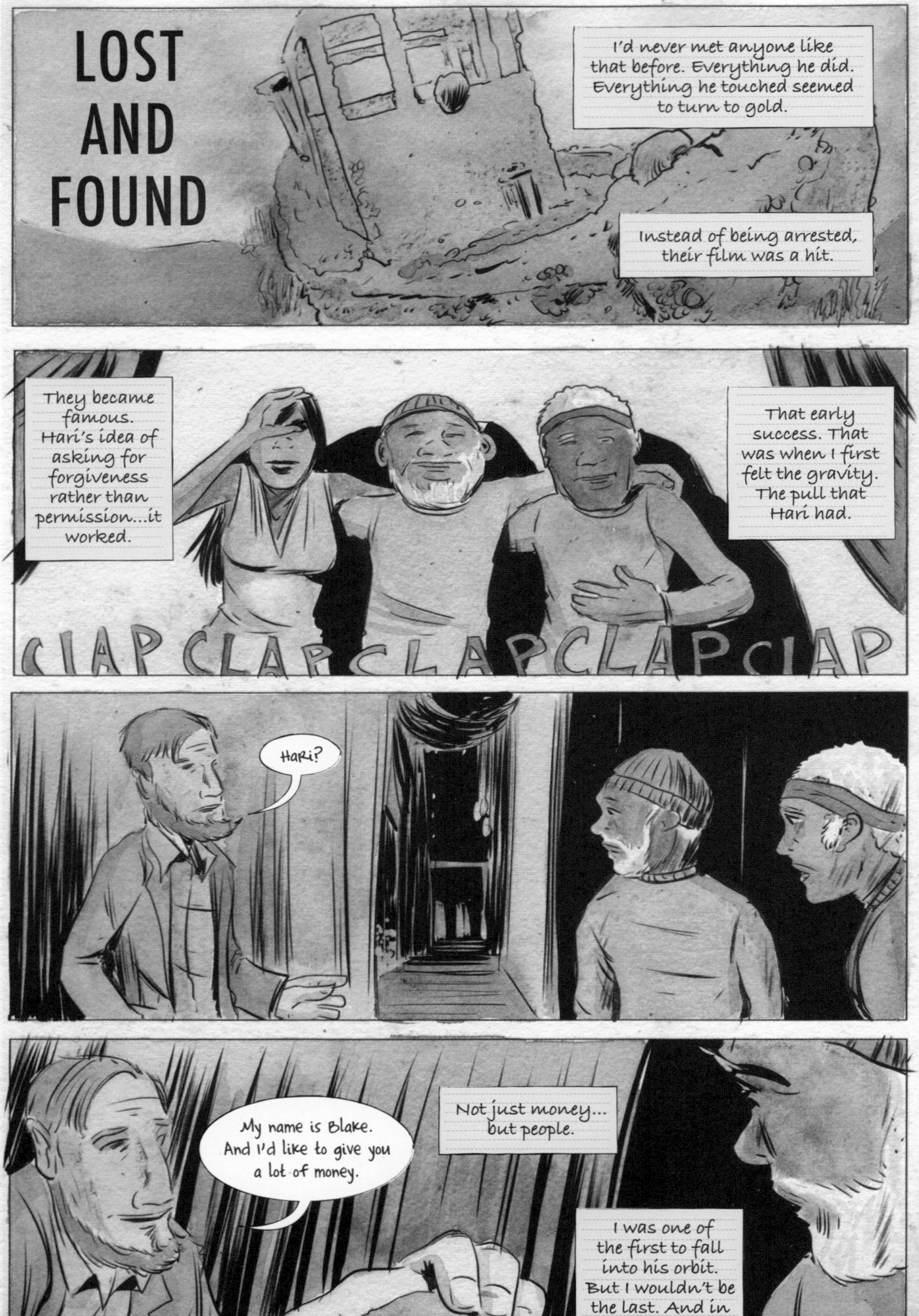
LOST AND FOUND
I'd never met anyone like that before. Everything he did. Everything he touched seemed to turn to gold.
Instead of being arrested, their film was a hit.
They became famous. Hari's idea of asking for forgiveness rather than permission...it worked.
That early success. That was when I first felt the gravity. The pull that Hari had.
CLAP CLAP CLAP CLAP
Hari?
My name is Blake. And I'd like to give you a lot of money.
Not just money... but people.
I was one of the first to fall into his orbit. But I wouldn't be the last. And in those early days, I didn't mind.

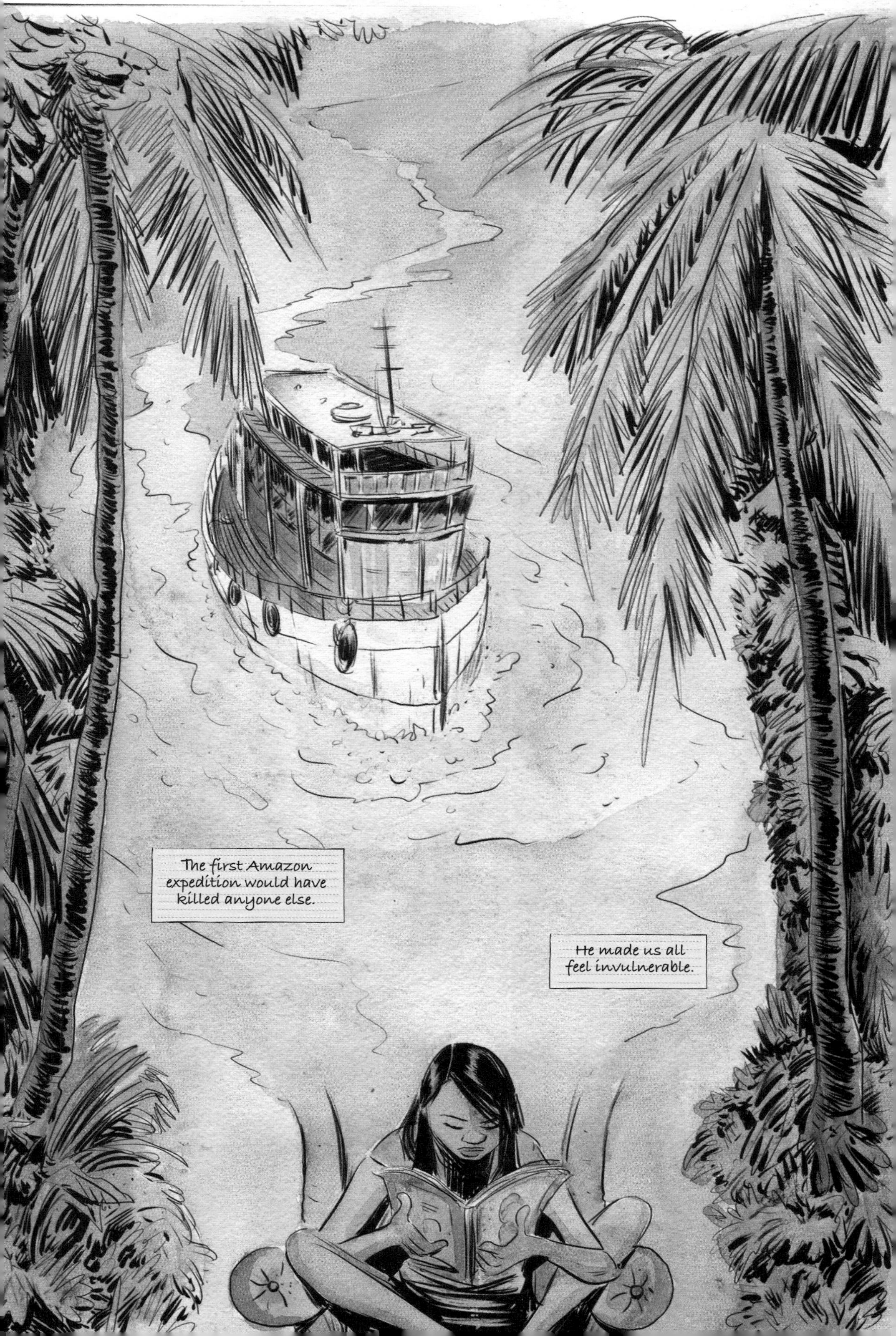
The first Amazon expedition would have killed anyone else.
He made us all feel invulnerable.

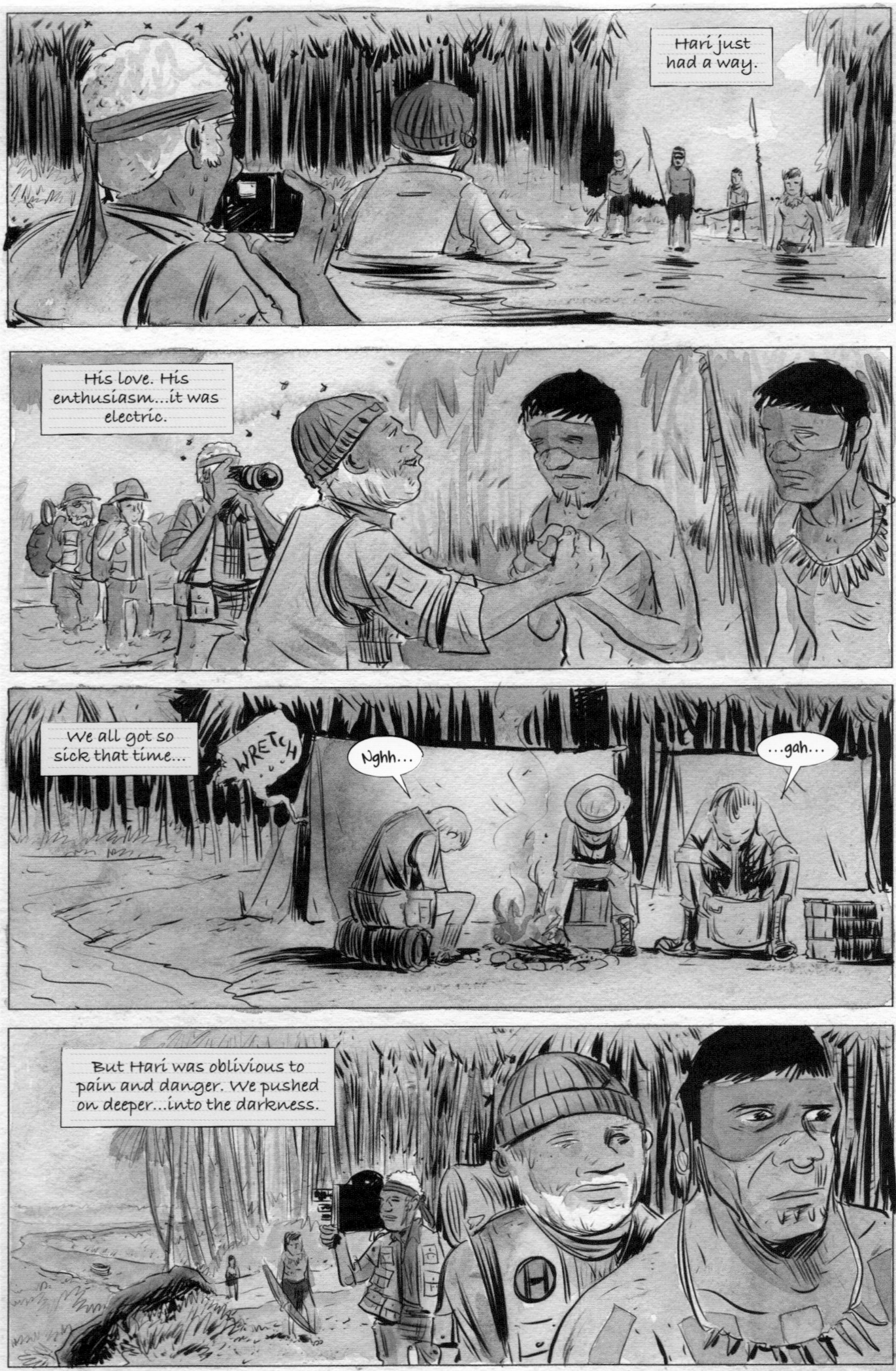
Hari just had a way.
His love. His enthusiasm...it was electric.
We all got so sick that time...
WRETCH
Nghh...
...gah...
But Hari was oblivious to pain and danger. We pushed on deeper...into the darkness.

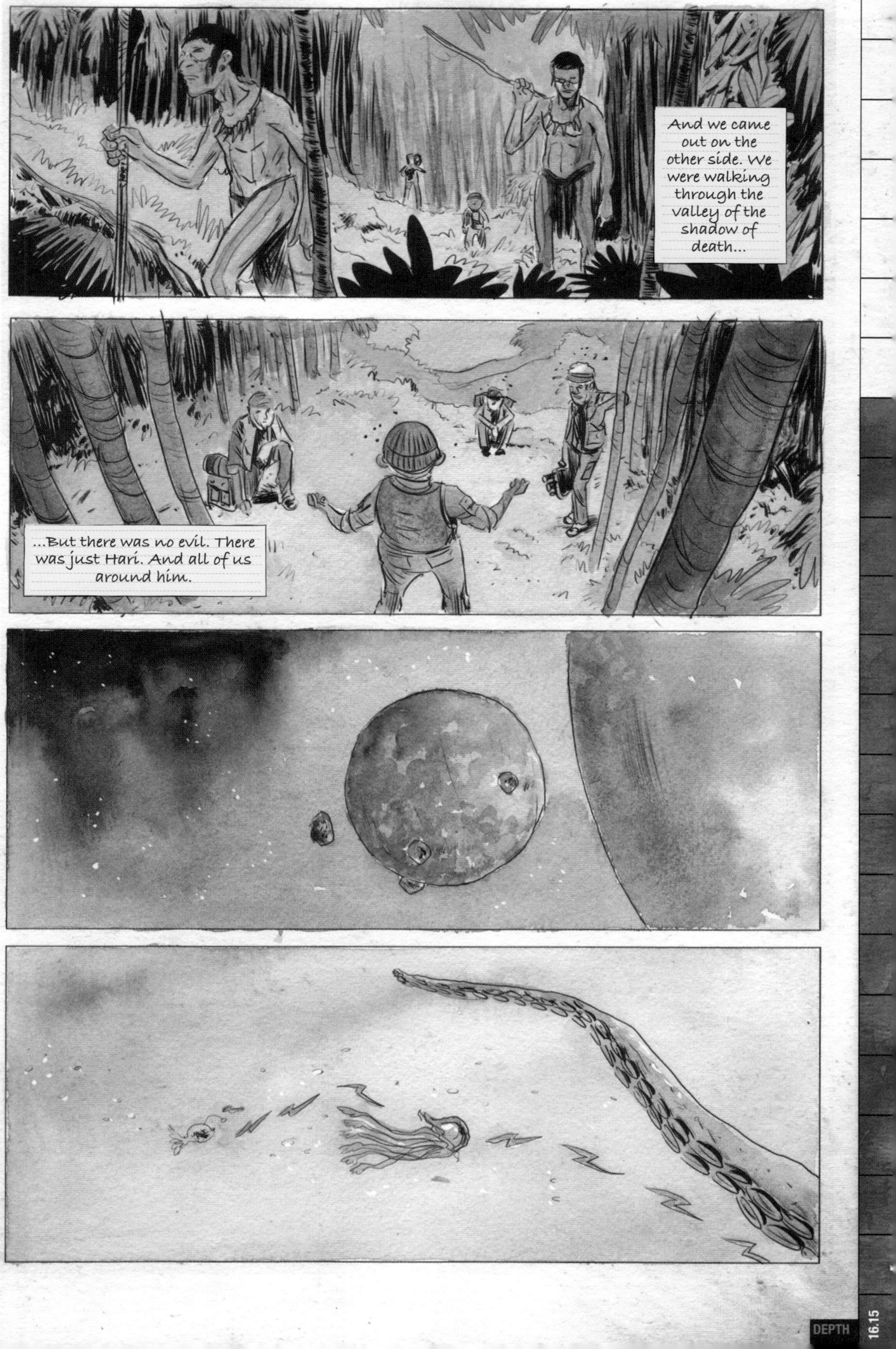
And we came out on the other side. We were walking through the valley of the shadow of death...
...But there was no evil. There was just Hari. And all of us around him.

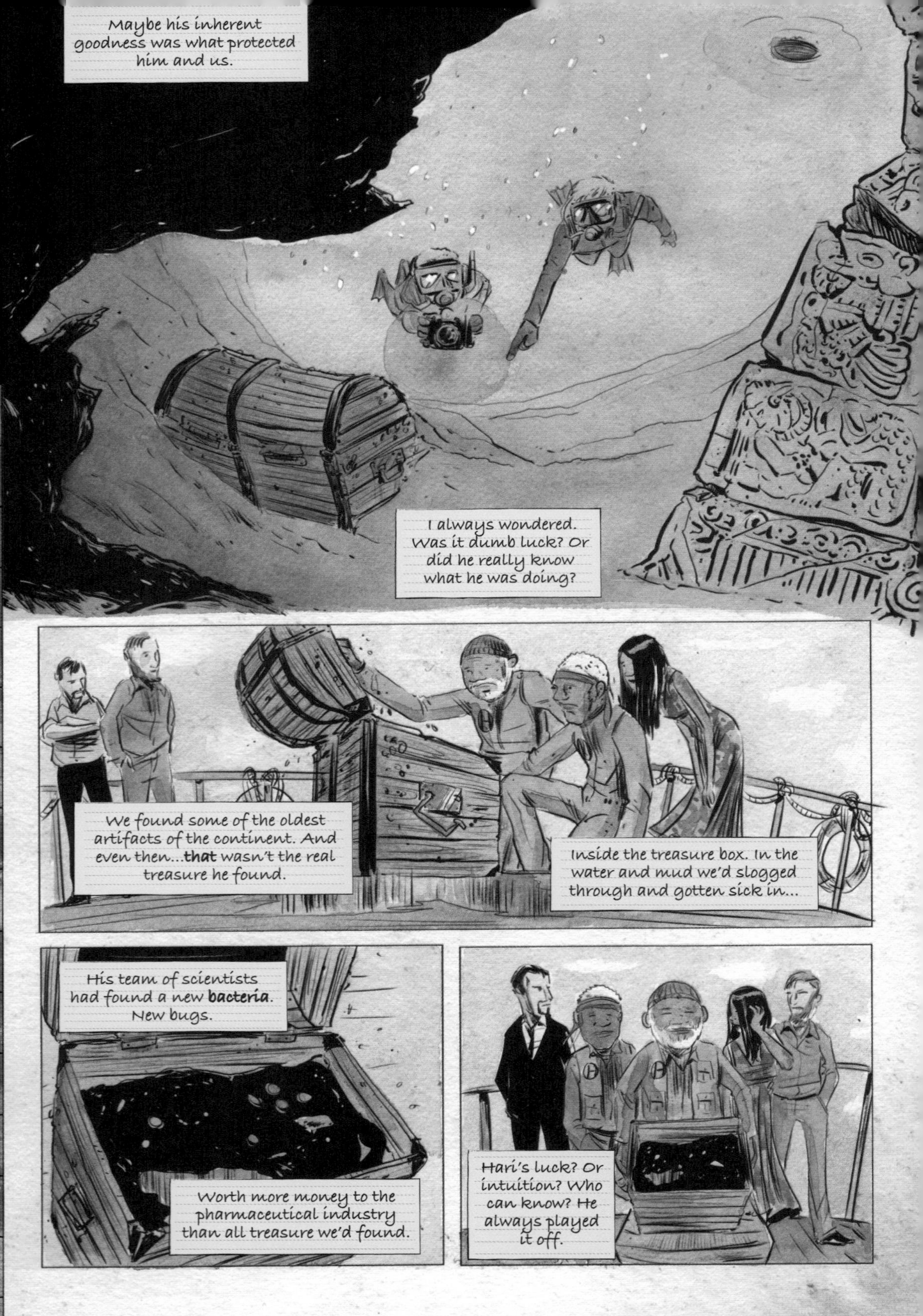

Maybe his inherent goodness was what protected him and us.
I always wondered. Was it dumb luck? Or did he really know what he was doing?
We found some of the oldest artifacts of the continent. And even then...**that** wasn't the real treasure he found.
Inside the treasure box. In the water and mud we'd slogged through and gotten sick in...
His team of scientists had found a new **bacteria**. New bugs.
Worth more money to the pharmaceutical industry than all treasure we'd found.
Hari's luck? Or intuition? Who can know? He always played it off.

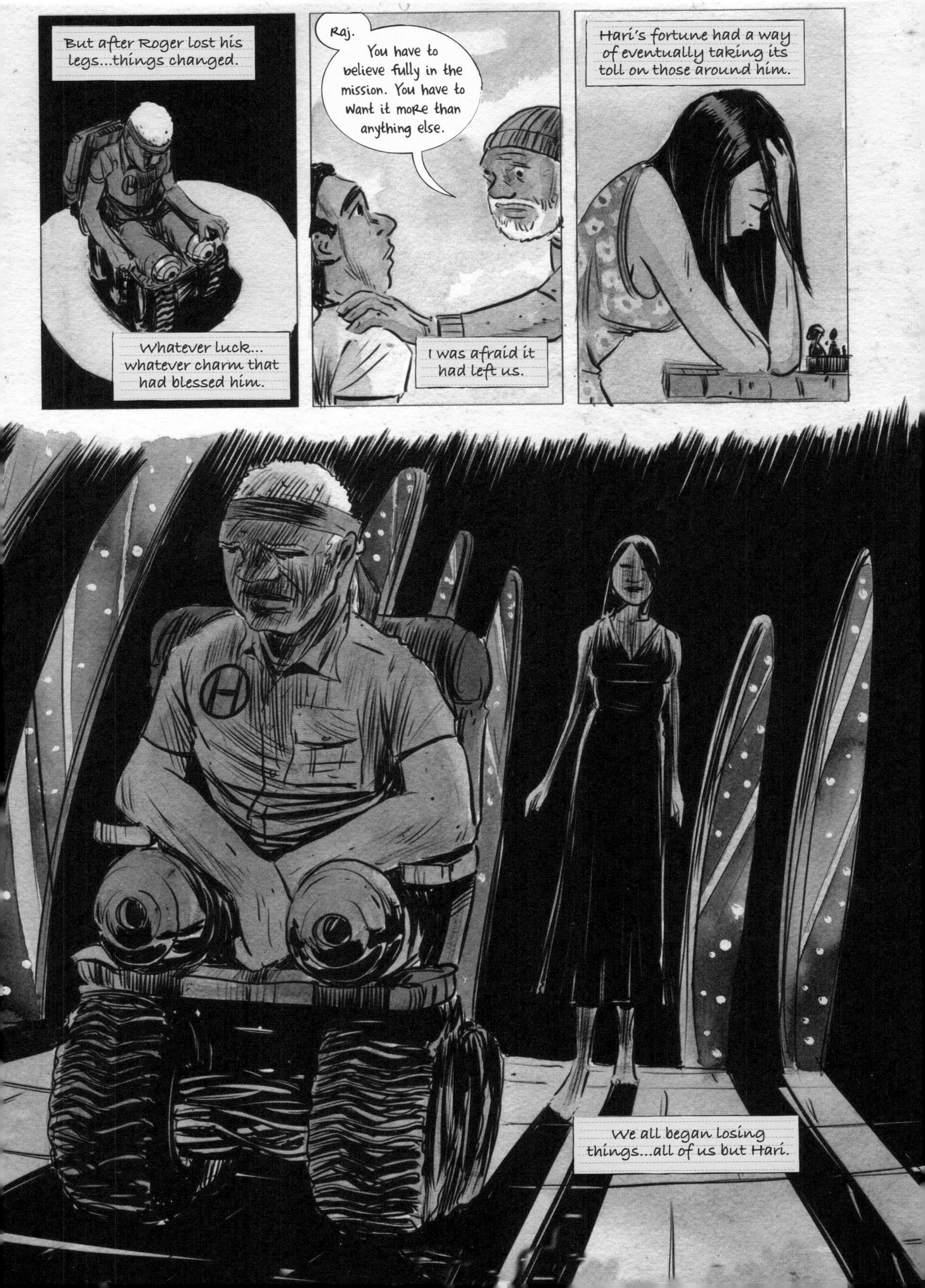
But after Roger lost his legs...things changed.
Whatever luck... whatever charm that had blessed him.
Raj.
You have to believe fully in the mission. You have to want it more than anything else.
I was afraid it had left us.
Hari's fortune had a way of eventually taking its toll on those around him.
We all began losing things...all of us but Hari.

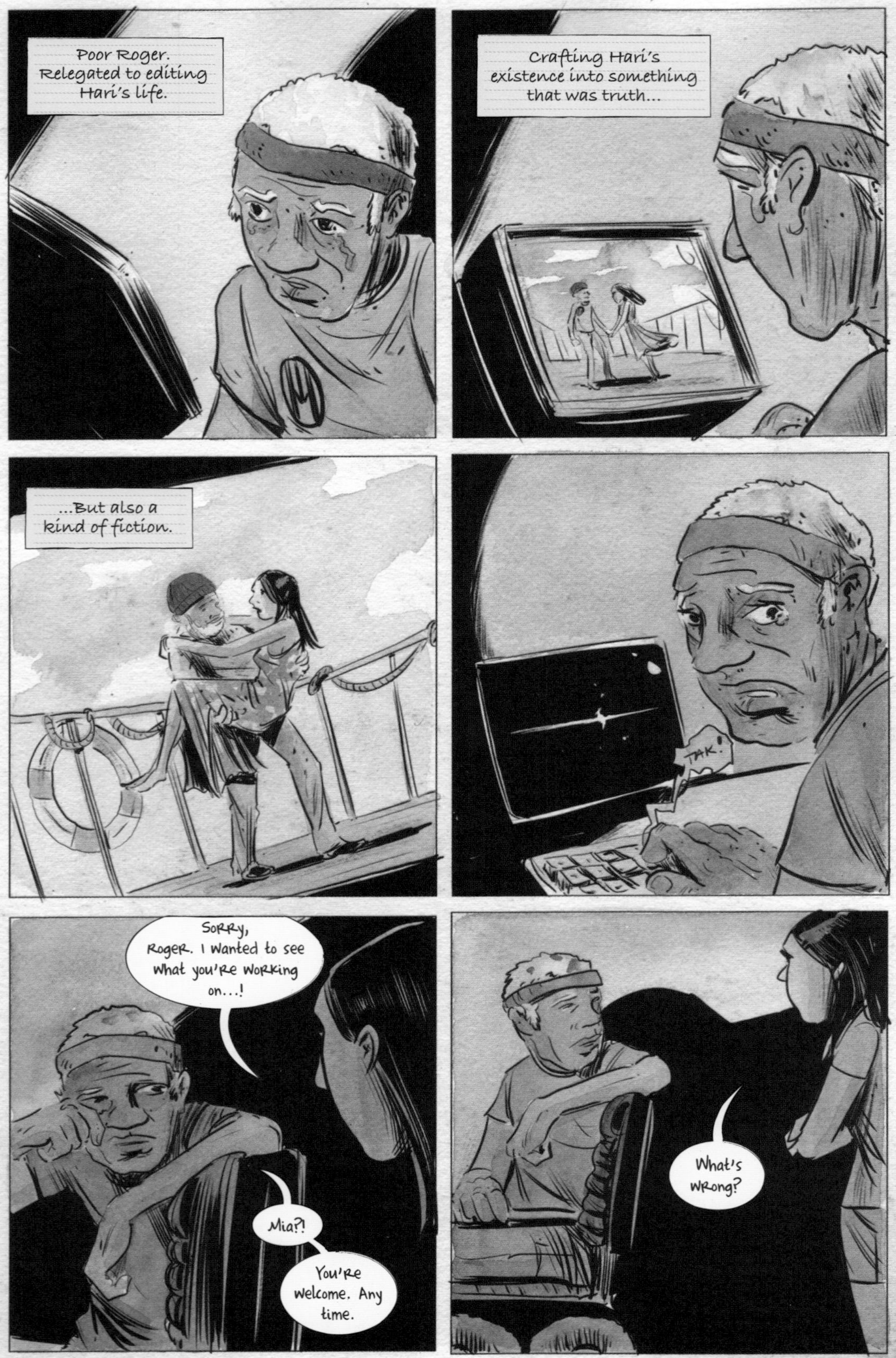
Poor Roger. Relegated to editing Hari's life.
Crafting Hari's existence into something that was truth...
...But also a kind of fiction.
TAK!
SORRY, ROGER. I WANTED TO SEE WHAT YOU'RE WORKING ON...!
MIA?!
YOU'RE WELCOME. ANY TIME.
WHAT'S WRONG?

Mia?

Nothing, nothing, you little sneak.

RUFFLE

Just...

Be your own person, Mia.

Have your own ideas.

If I can just take all the memories.

Don't be the moon in someone else's sky.

Collate them. Triangulate. Merge every point of view...

I want to be a sun, Roger. A star!

...With my own memories...

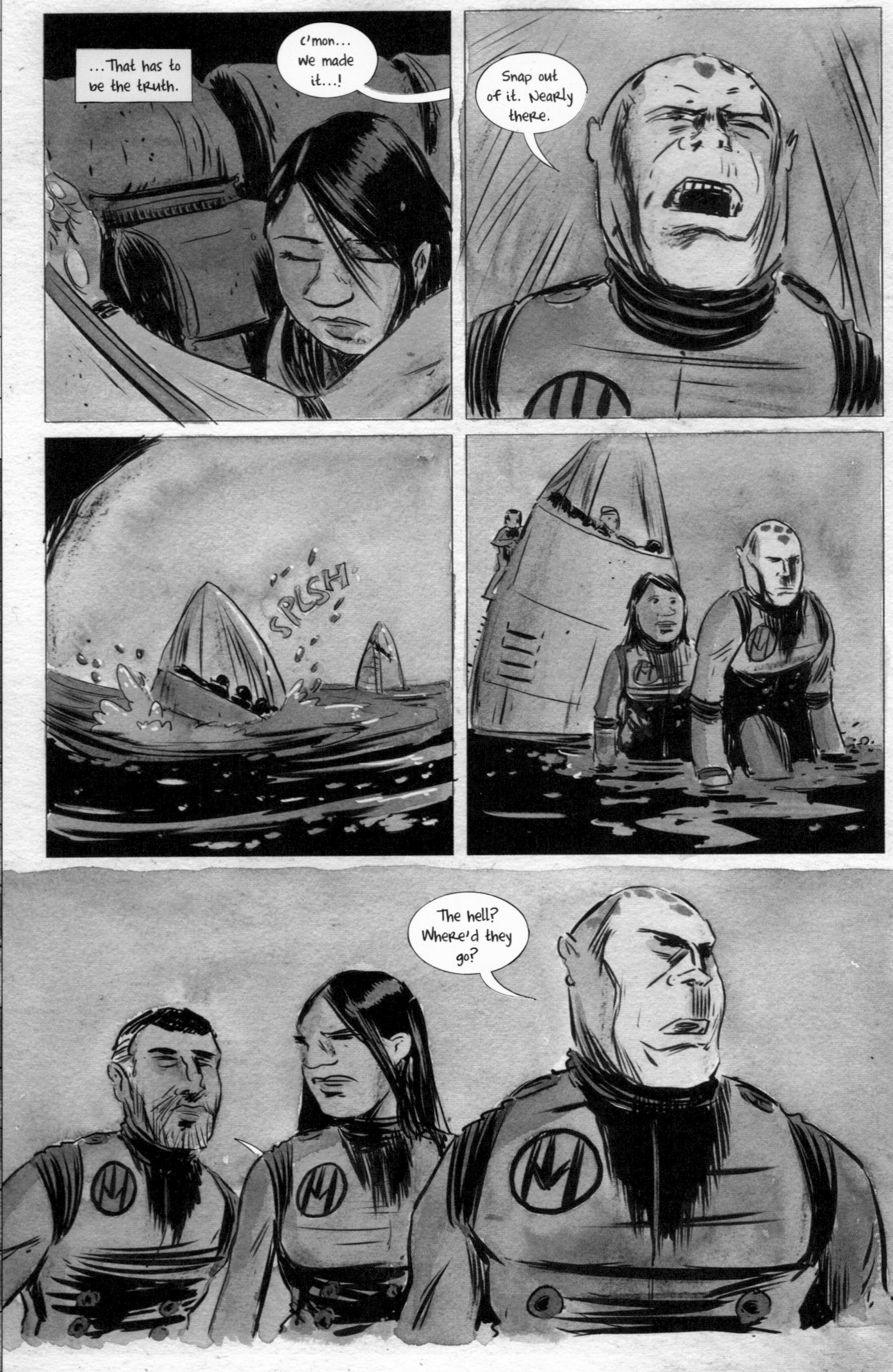
...That has to be the truth.
C'mon... we made it...!
Snap out of it. Nearly there.
SPLSH
The hell? Where'd they go?

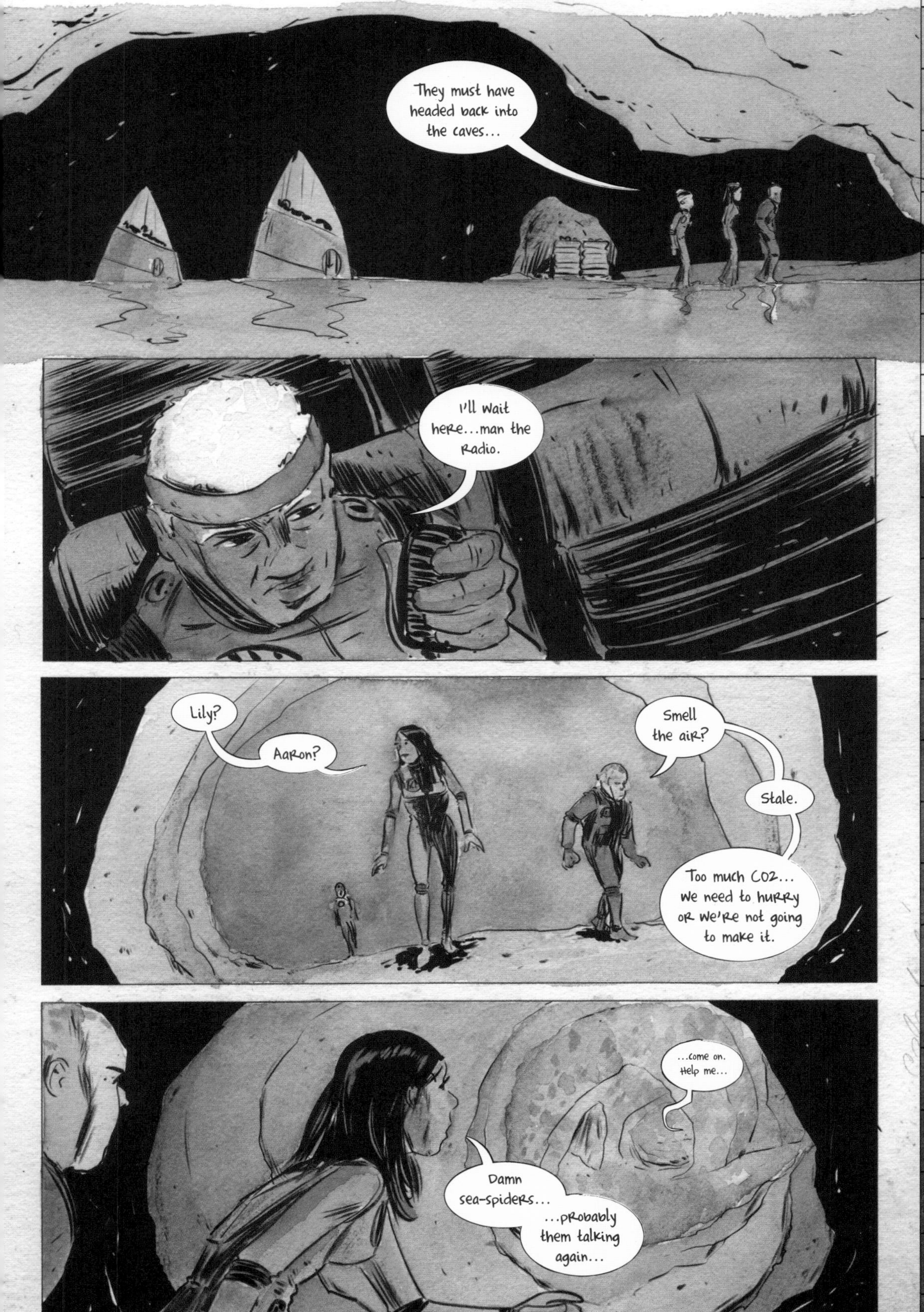
They must have headed back into the caves...
I'll wait here...man the Radio.
Lily?
Aaron?
Smell the air?
Stale.
Too much CO2... we need to hurry or we're not going to make it.
...come on. Help me...
Damn sea-spiders...
...probably them talking again...

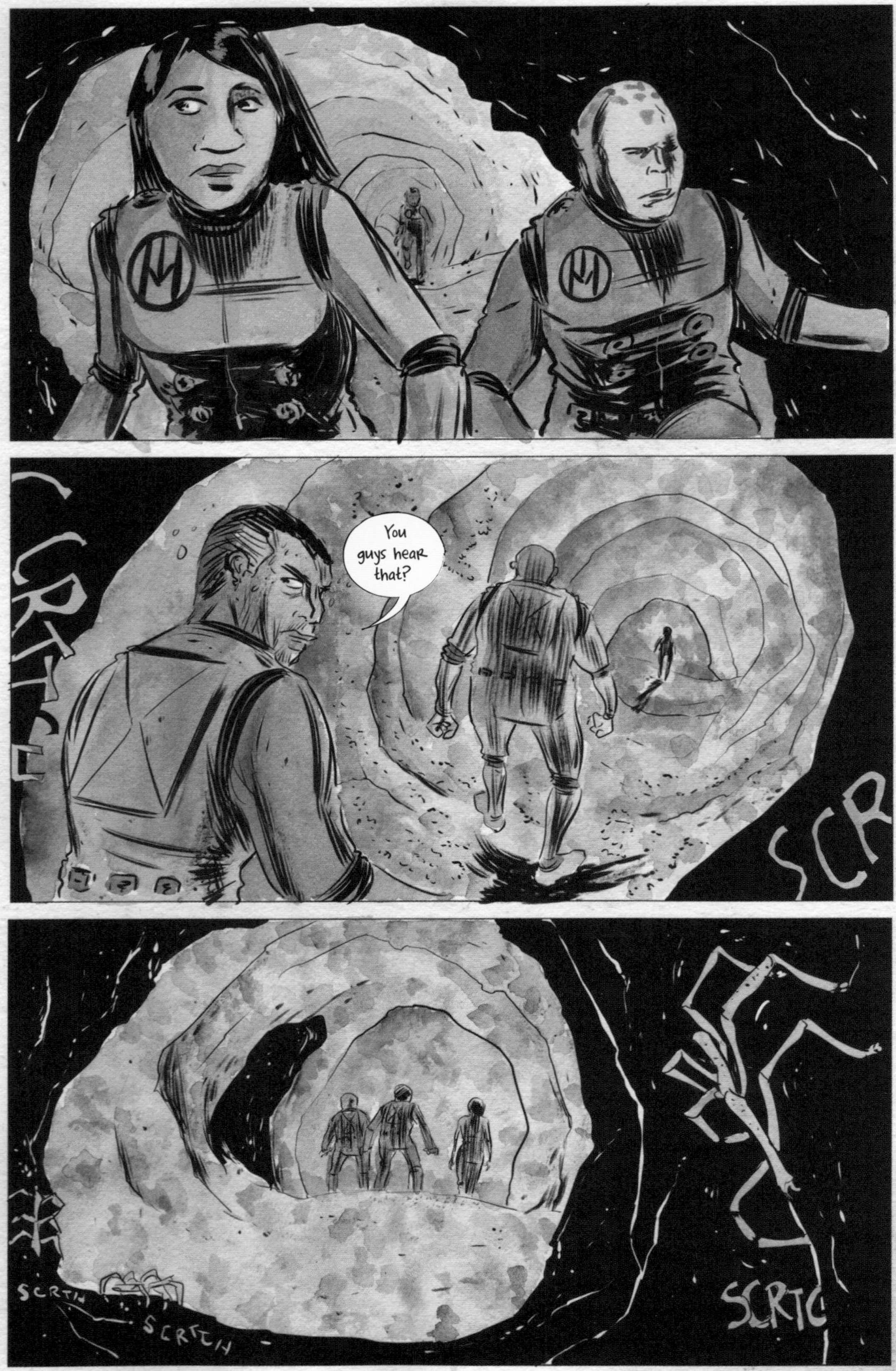

CRTCH
You guys hear that?
SCR
SCRTCH
SCRTCH
SCRTC

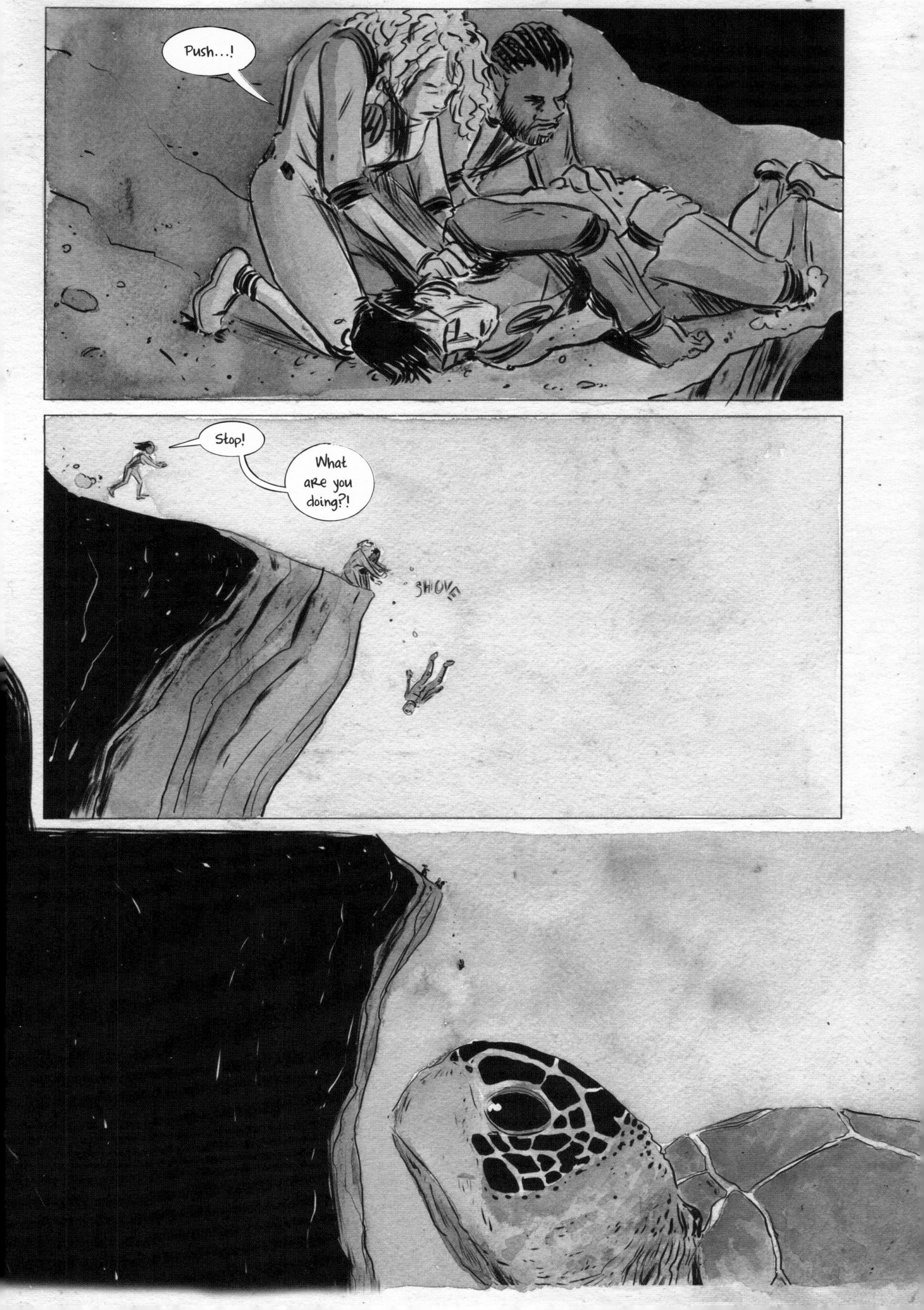
Push...!
Stop!
What are you doing?!
SHOVE

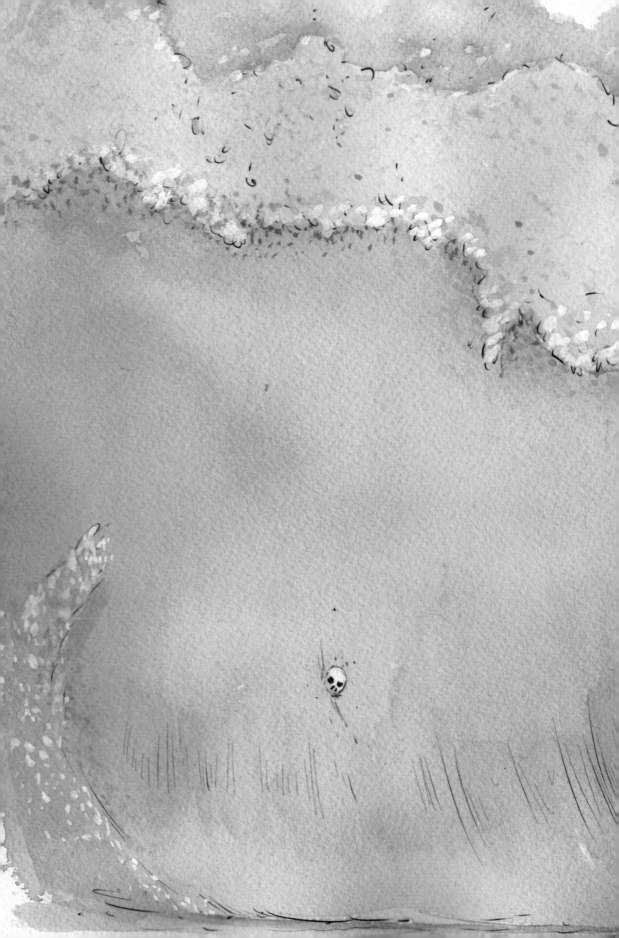

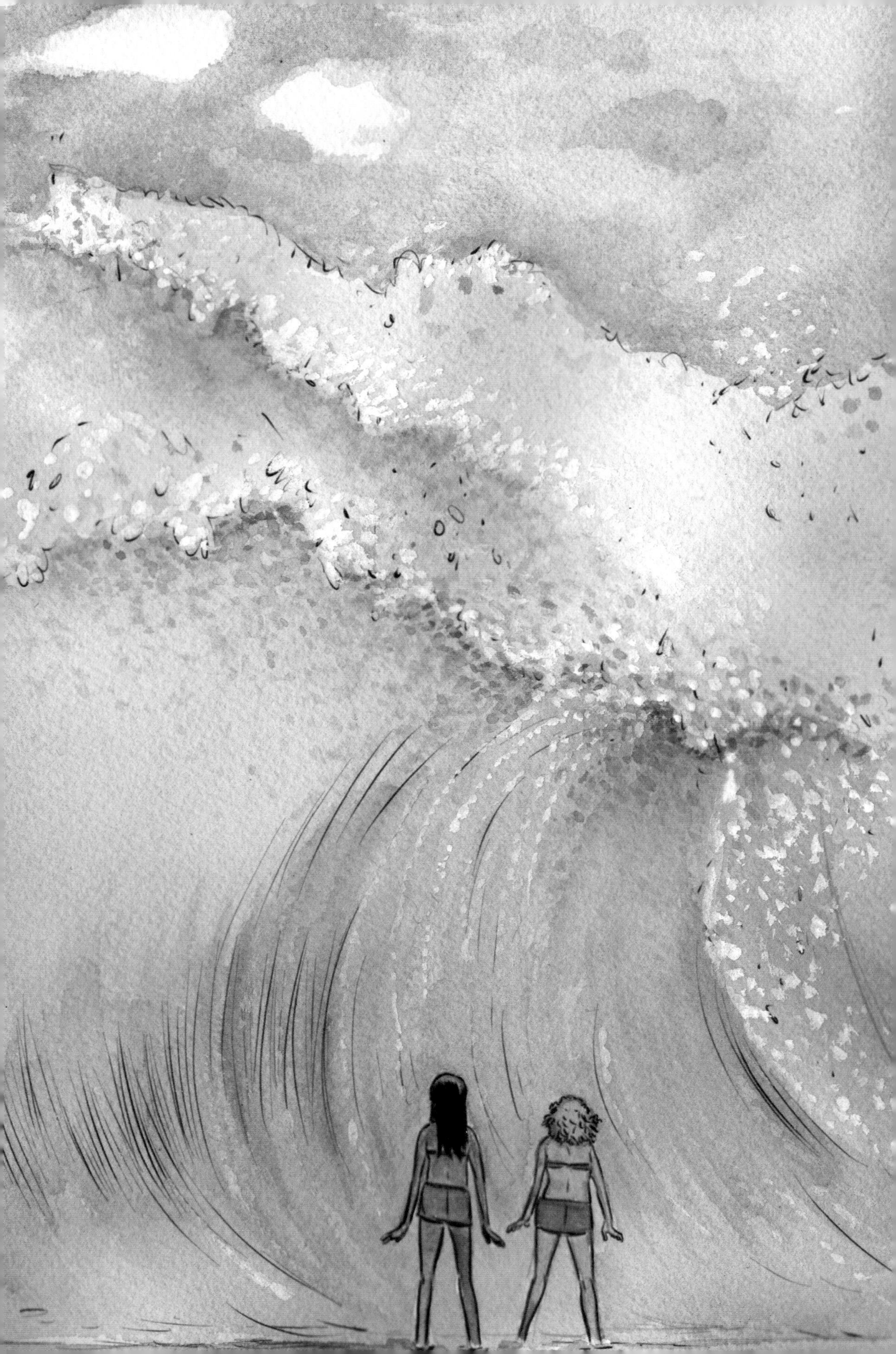

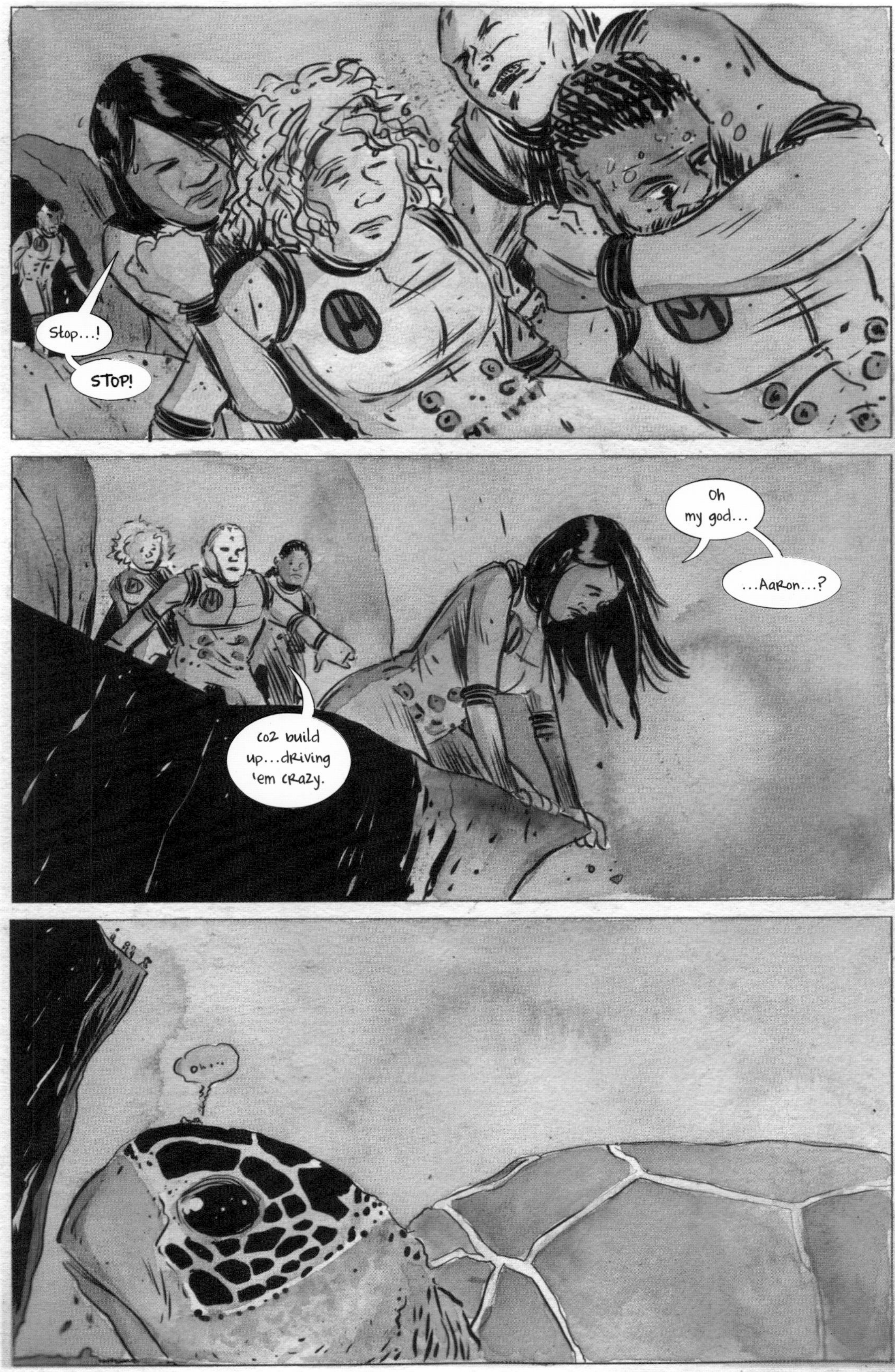
Stop...!
STOP!
Oh my god...
...Aaron...?
co2 build up...driving 'em crazy.
Oh...

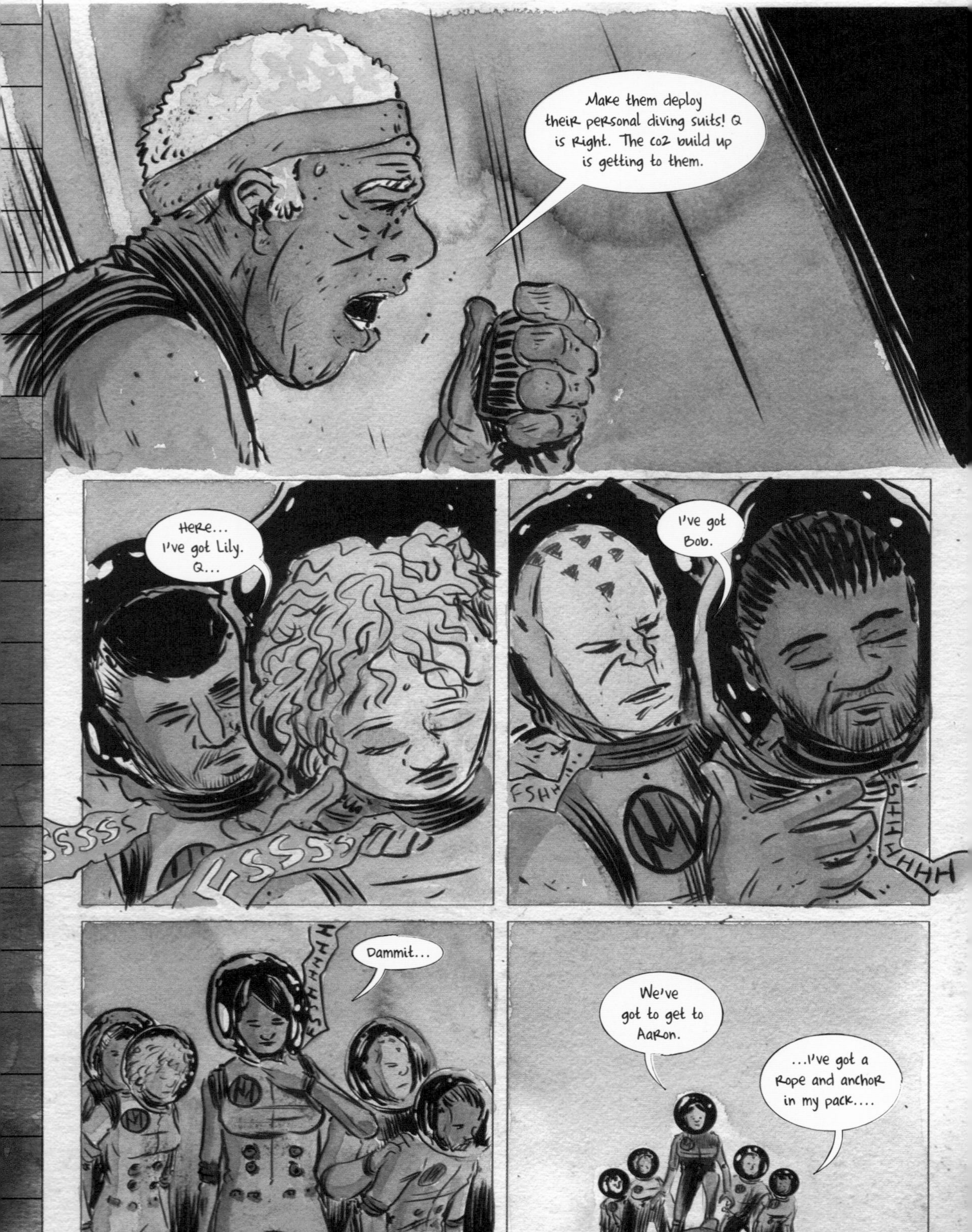
Make them deploy their personal diving suits! Q is right. The co2 build up is getting to them.
Here... I've got Lily. Q...
I've got Bob.
FSHH
Dammit...
We've got to get to Aaron.
...I've got a rope and anchor in my pack....

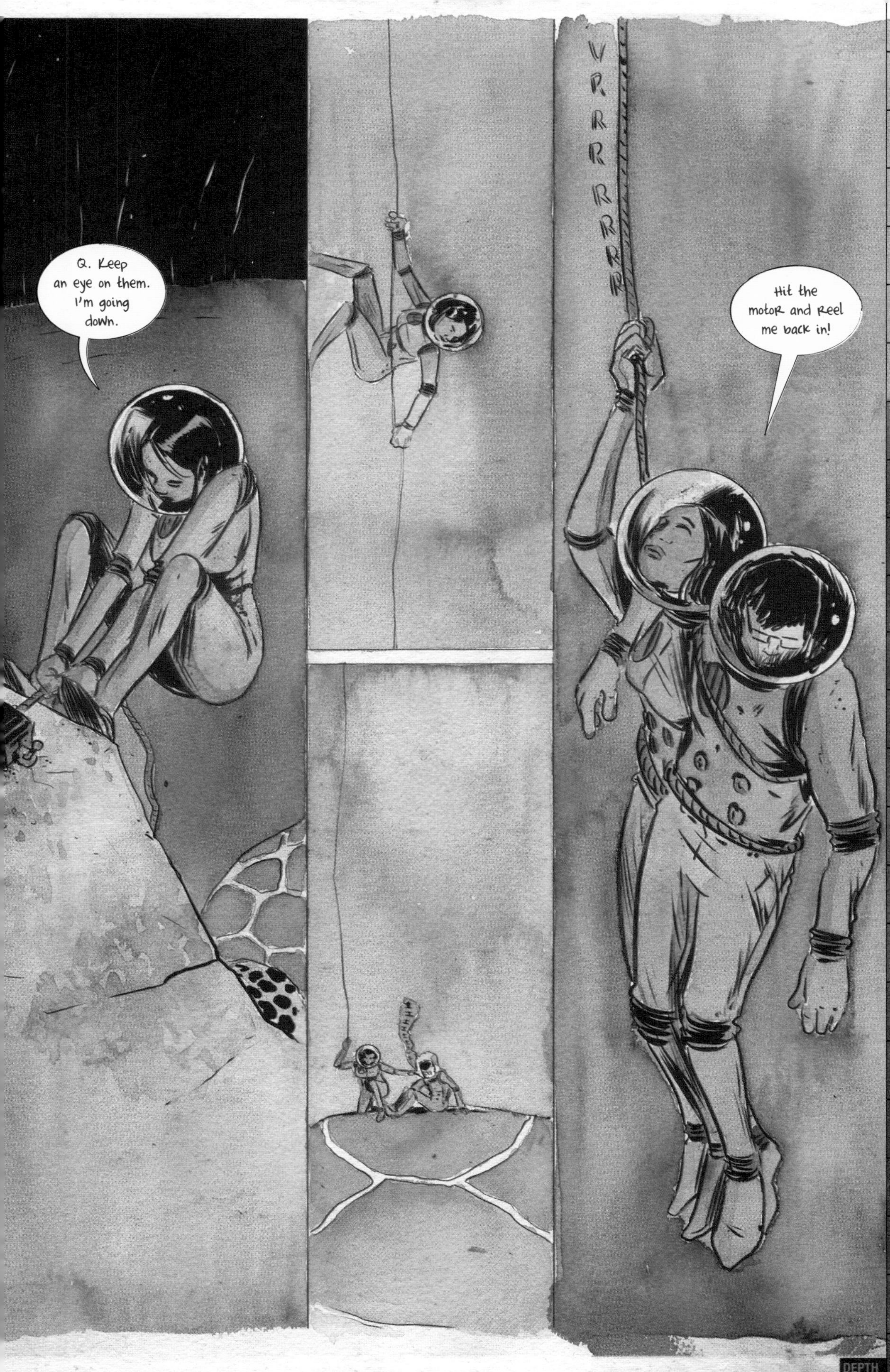
Q. Keep an eye on them. I'm going down.
VRRRRRRR
Hit the motor and reel me back in!

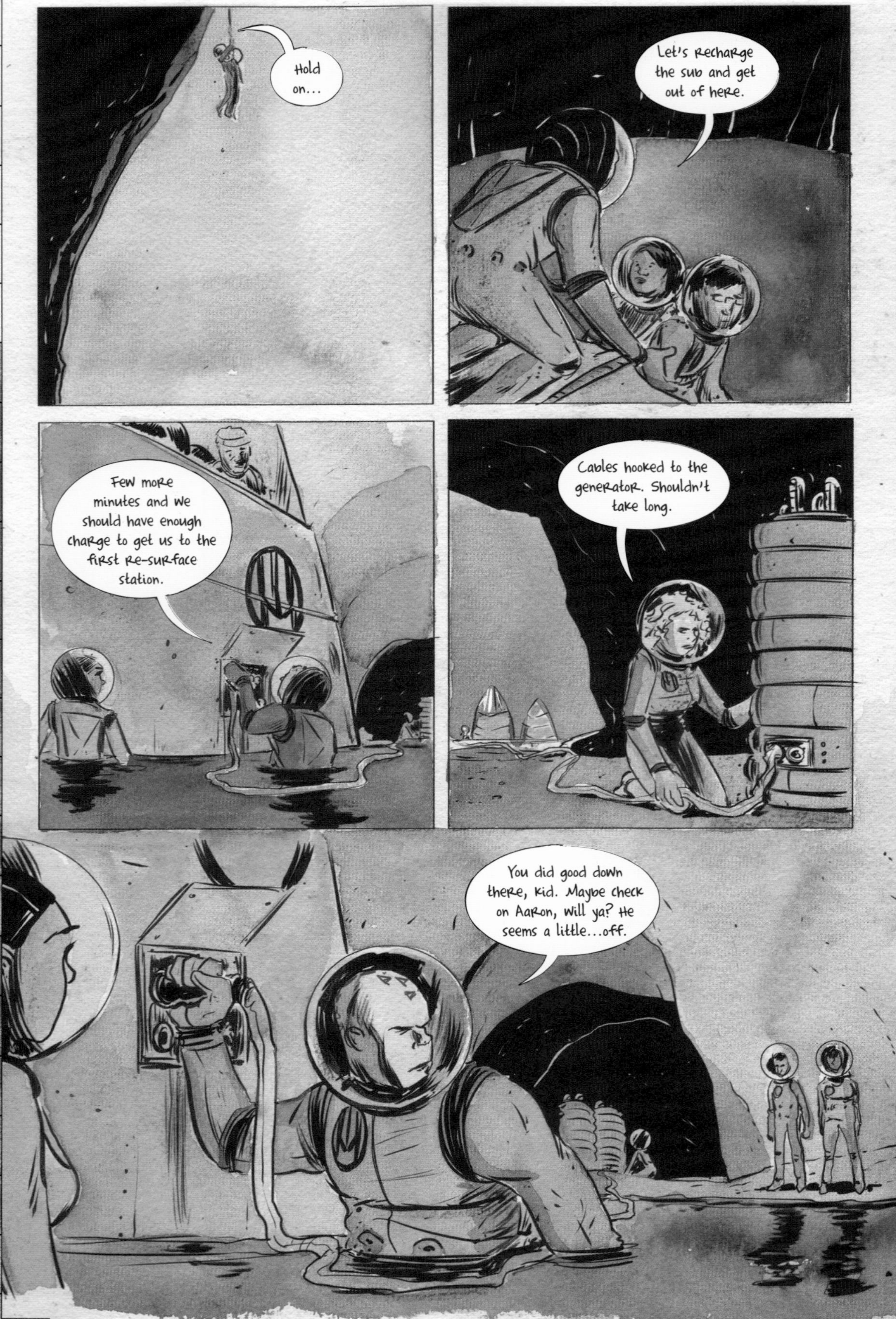
Hold on...
Let's recharge the sub and get out of here.
Few more minutes and we should have enough charge to get us to the first re-surface station.
Cables hooked to the generator. Shouldn't take long.
You did good down there, kid. Maybe check on Aaron, will ya? He seems a little...off.

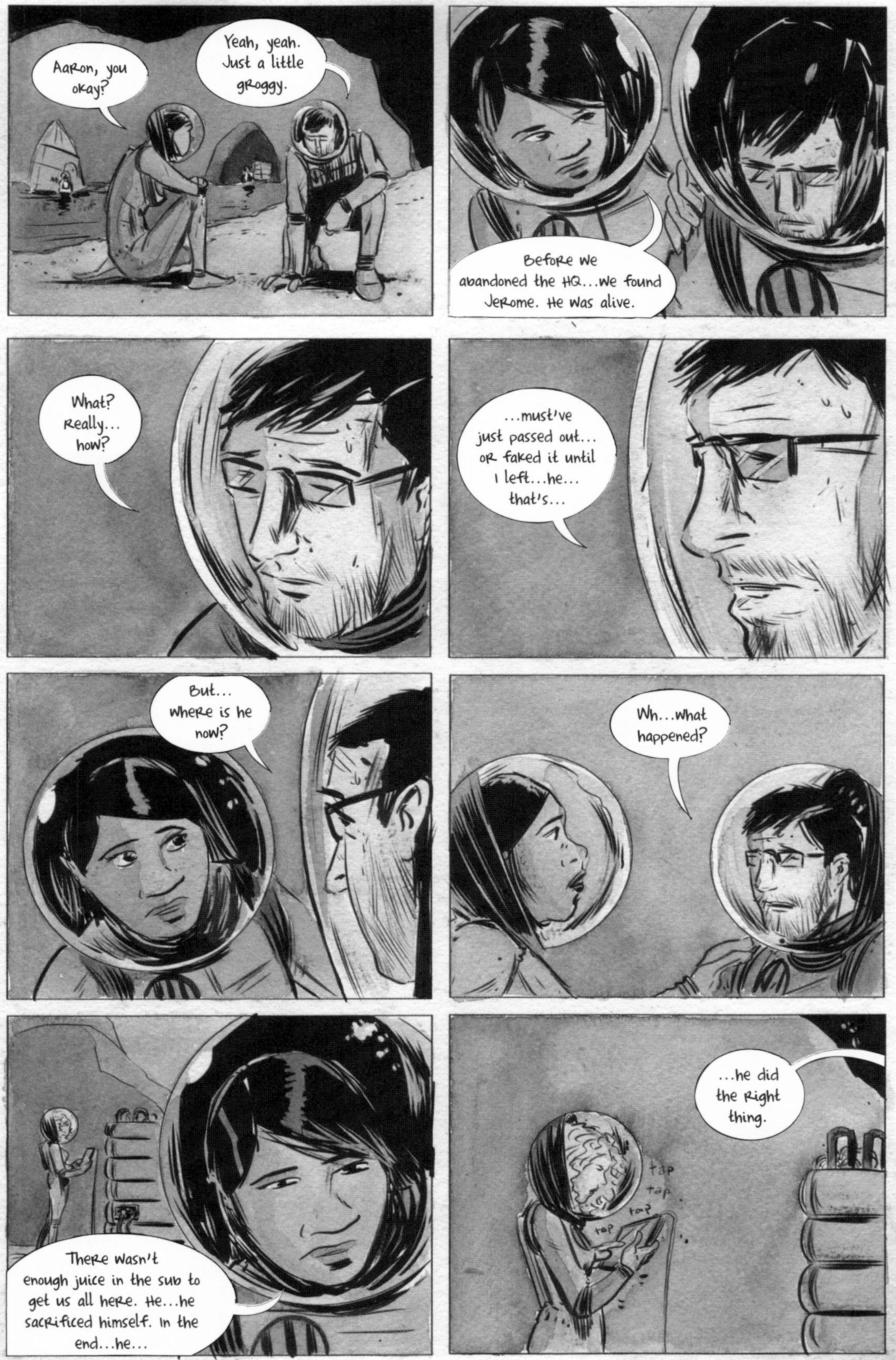
Aaron, you okay?
Yeah, yeah. Just a little groggy.
Before we abandoned the HQ...we found Jerome. He was alive.
What? Really... how?
...must've just passed out... or faked it until I left...he... that's...
But... where is he now?
Wh...what happened?
There wasn't enough juice in the sub to get us all here. He...he sacrificed himself. In the end...he...
...he did the right thing.
tap
tap
tap
tap

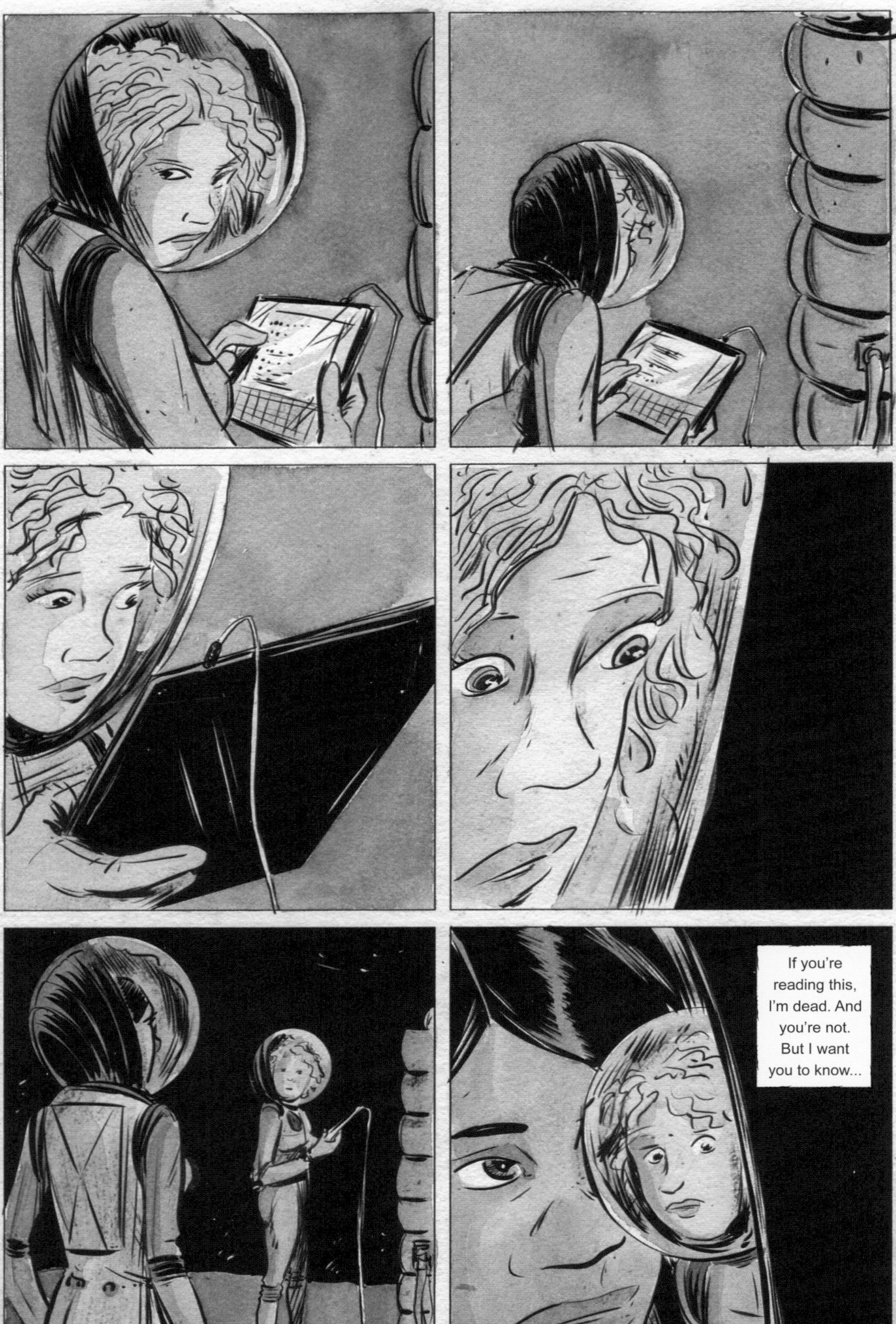
If you're reading this, I'm dead. And you're not. But I want you to know...

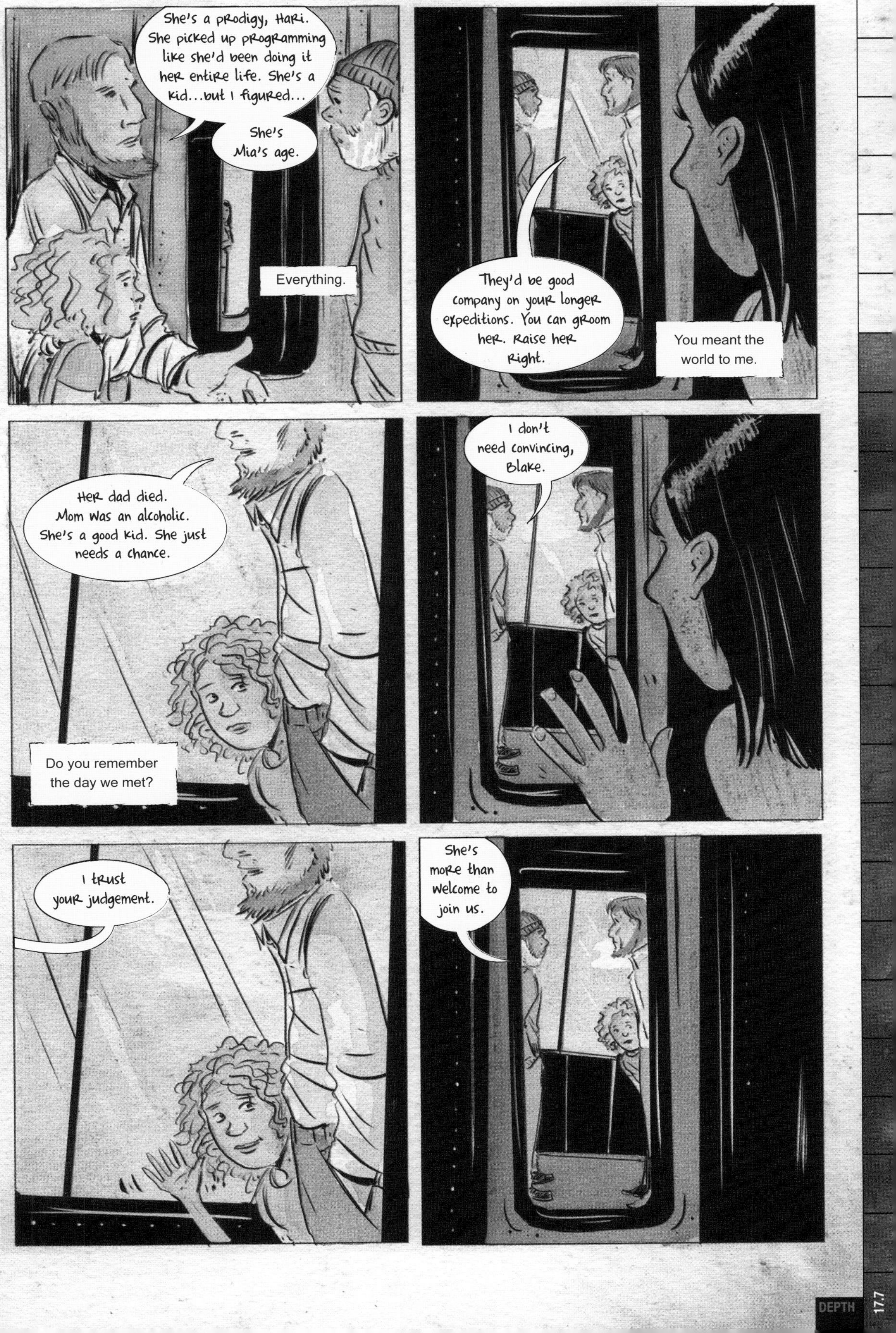
She's a prodigy, Hari. She picked up programming like she'd been doing it her entire life. She's a kid...but I figured...
She's Mia's age.
Everything.
They'd be good company on your longer expeditions. You can groom her. Raise her right.
You meant the world to me.
Her dad died. Mom was an alcoholic. She's a good kid. She just needs a chance.
Do you remember the day we met?
I don't need convincing, Blake.
I trust your judgement.
She's more than welcome to join us.

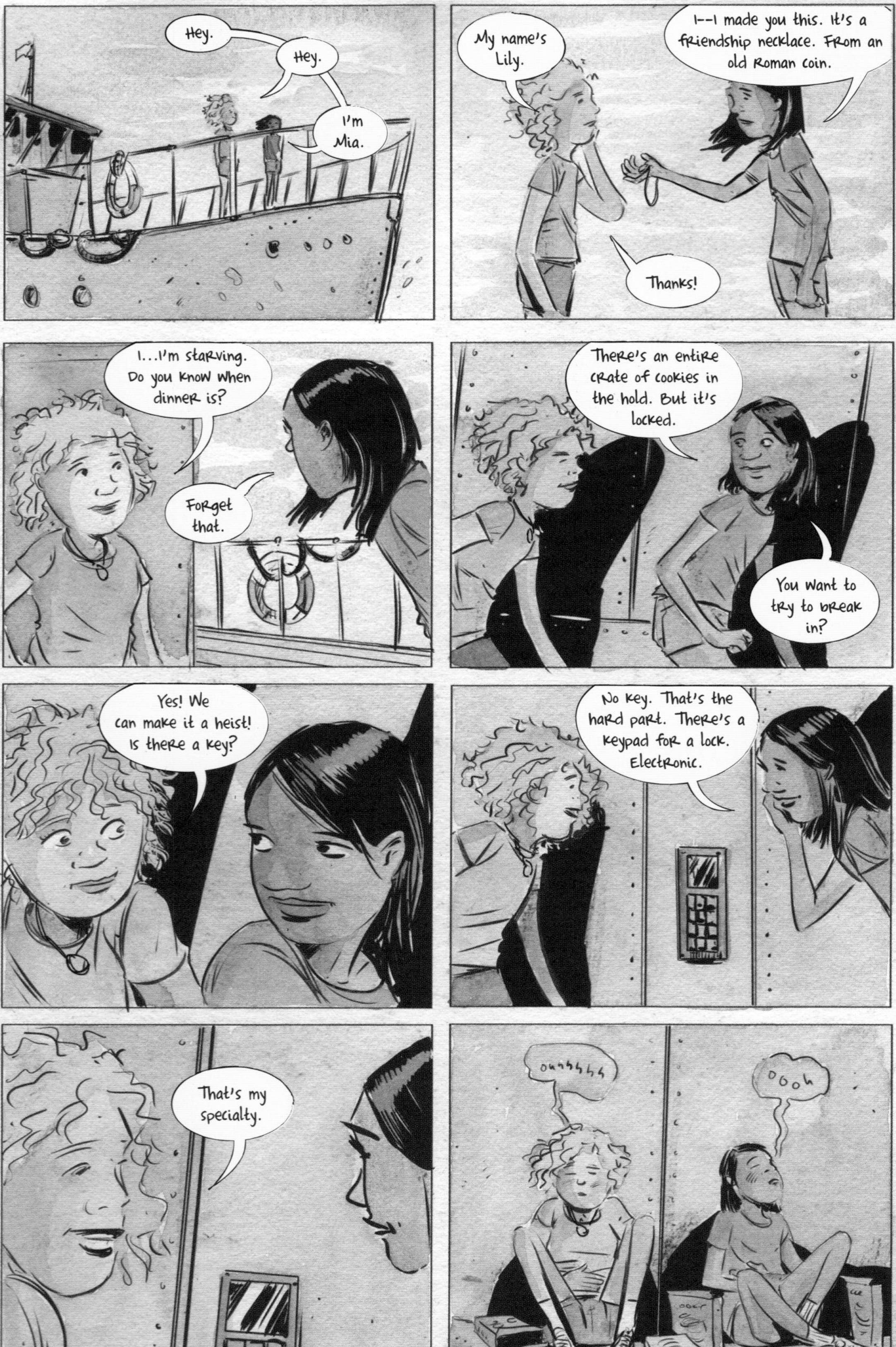
Hey.
Hey.
I'm Mia.
My name's Lily.
I--I made you this. It's a friendship necklace. From an old Roman coin.
Thanks!
I...I'm starving. Do you know when dinner is?
Forget that.
There's an entire crate of cookies in the hold. But it's locked.
You want to try to break in?
Yes! We can make it a heist! Is there a key?
No key. That's the hard part. There's a keypad for a lock. Electronic.
That's my specialty.
ouhhhhh
Oooh

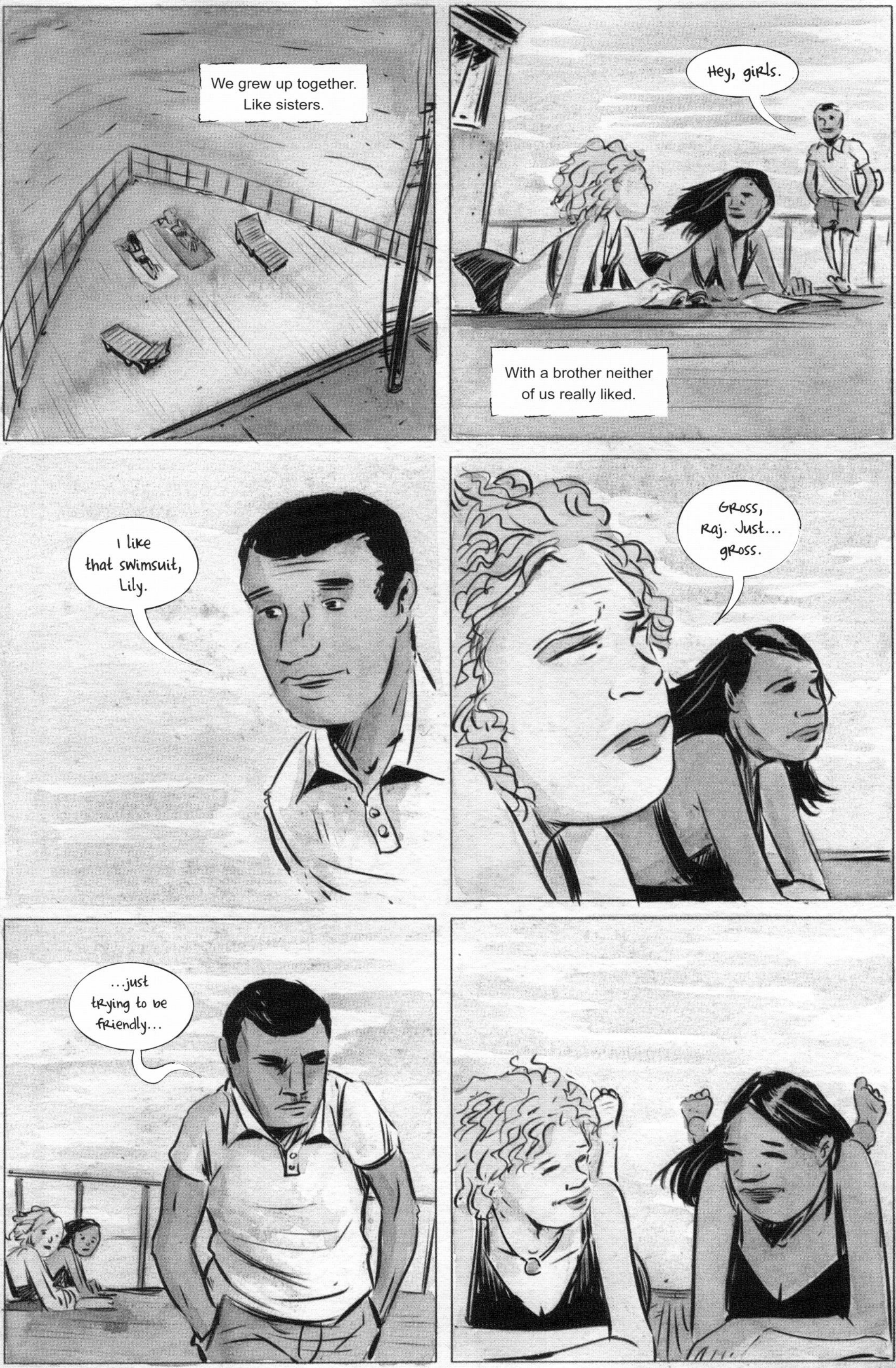
We grew up together. Like sisters.
Hey, girls.
With a brother neither of us really liked.
I like that swimsuit, Lily.
Gross, Raj. Just... gross.
...just trying to be friendly...

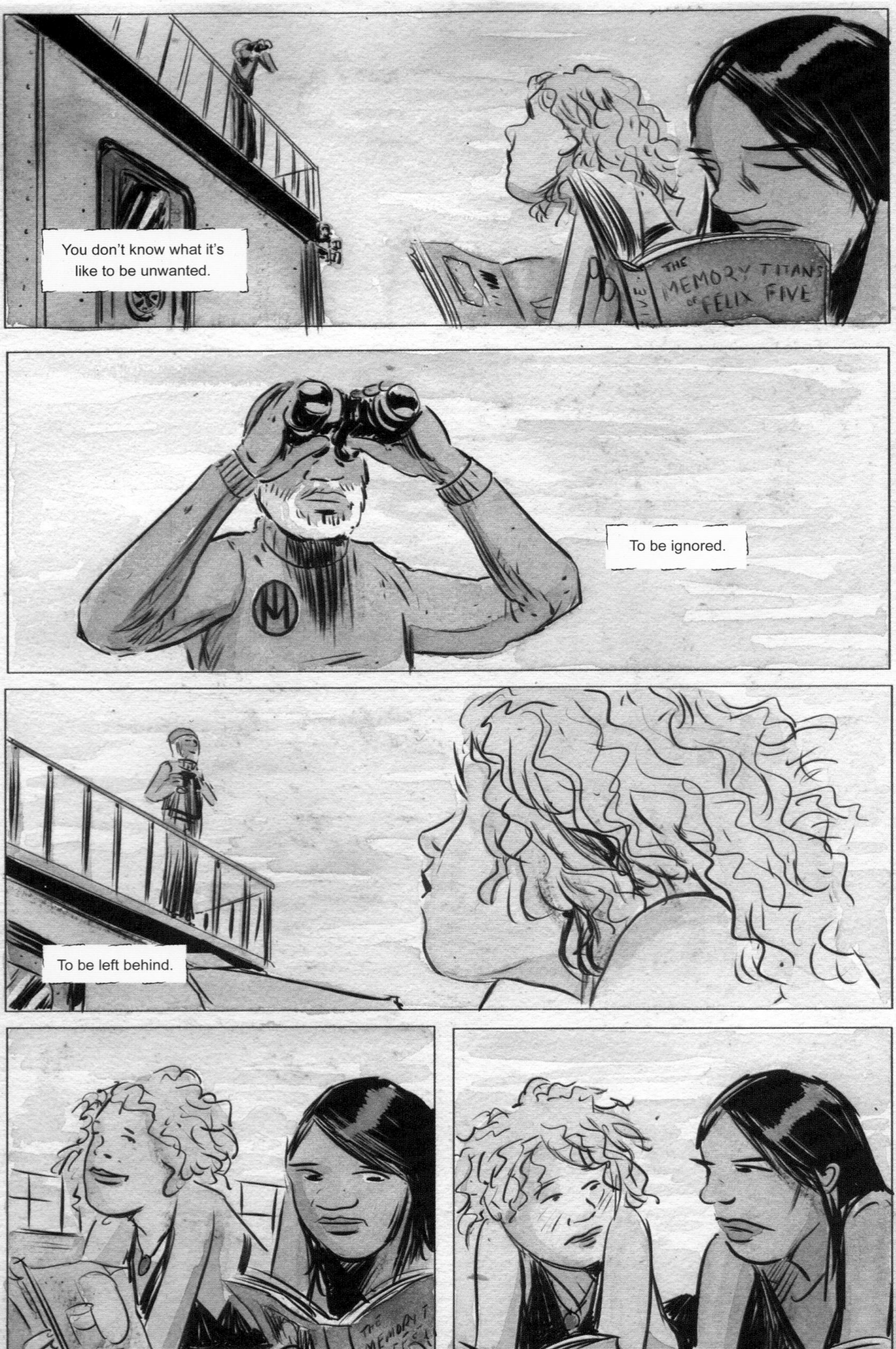
You don't know what it's like to be unwanted.
THE MEMORY TITANS OF FÉLIX FIVE
To be ignored.
To be left behind.

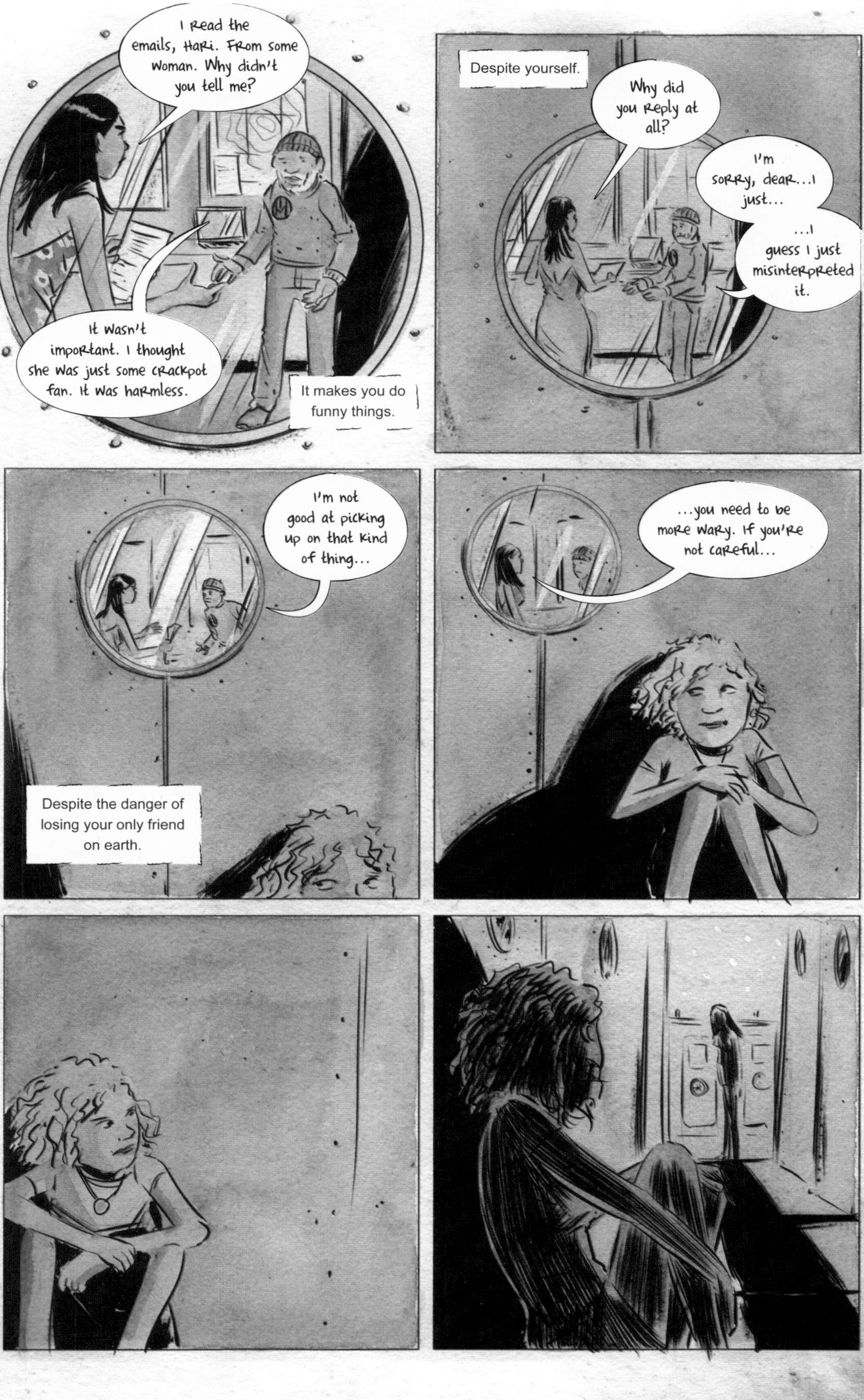

I read the emails, Hari. From some woman. Why didn't you tell me?
It wasn't important. I thought she was just some crackpot fan. It was harmless.
It makes you do funny things.
Despite yourself.
Why did you reply at all?
I'm sorry, dear... I just...
...I guess I just misinterpreted it.
I'm not good at picking up on that kind of thing...
Despite the danger of losing your only friend on earth.
...you need to be more wary. If you're not careful...

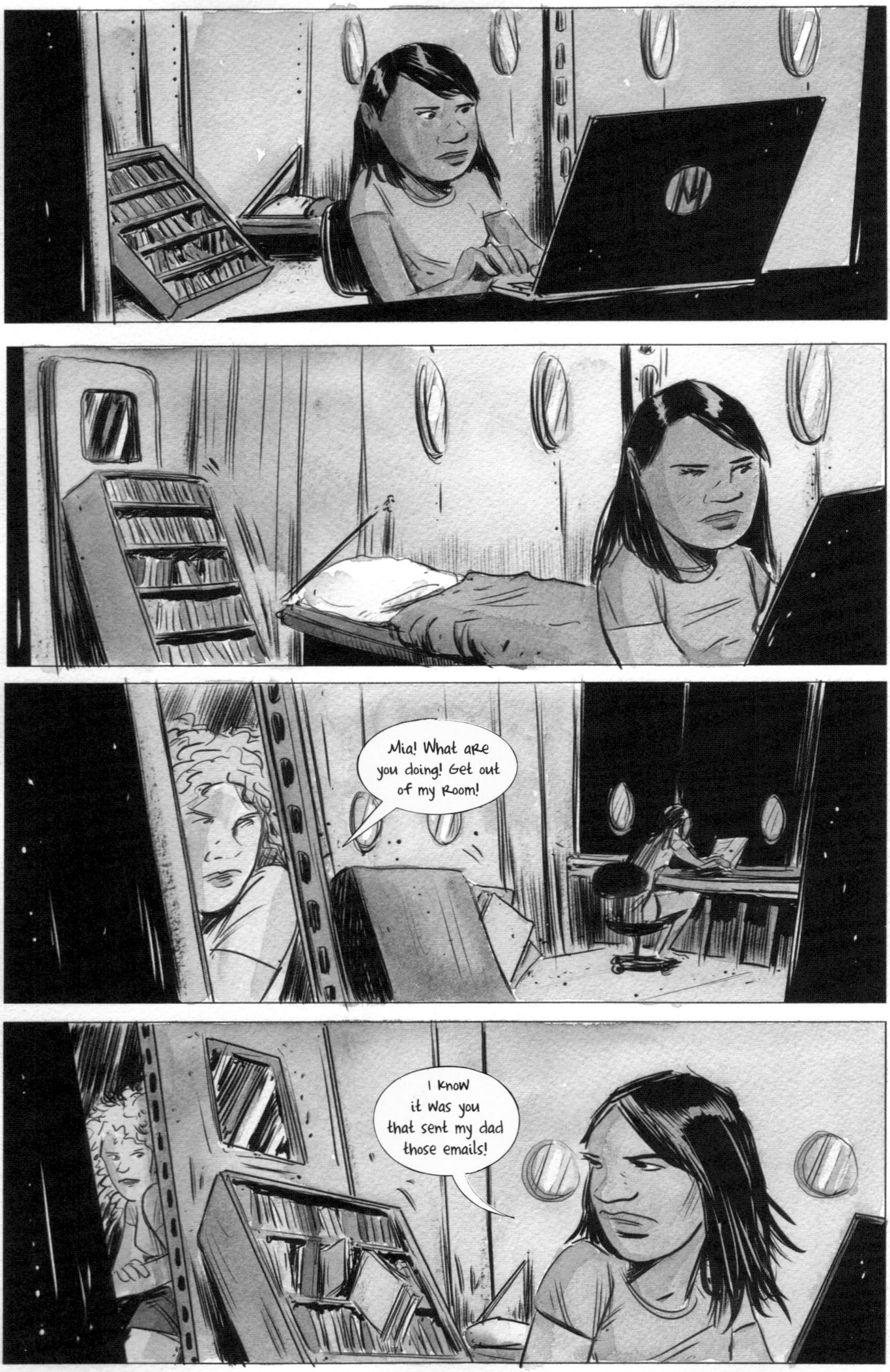
Mia! What are you doing! Get out of my Room!
I Know it was you that sent my dad those emails!

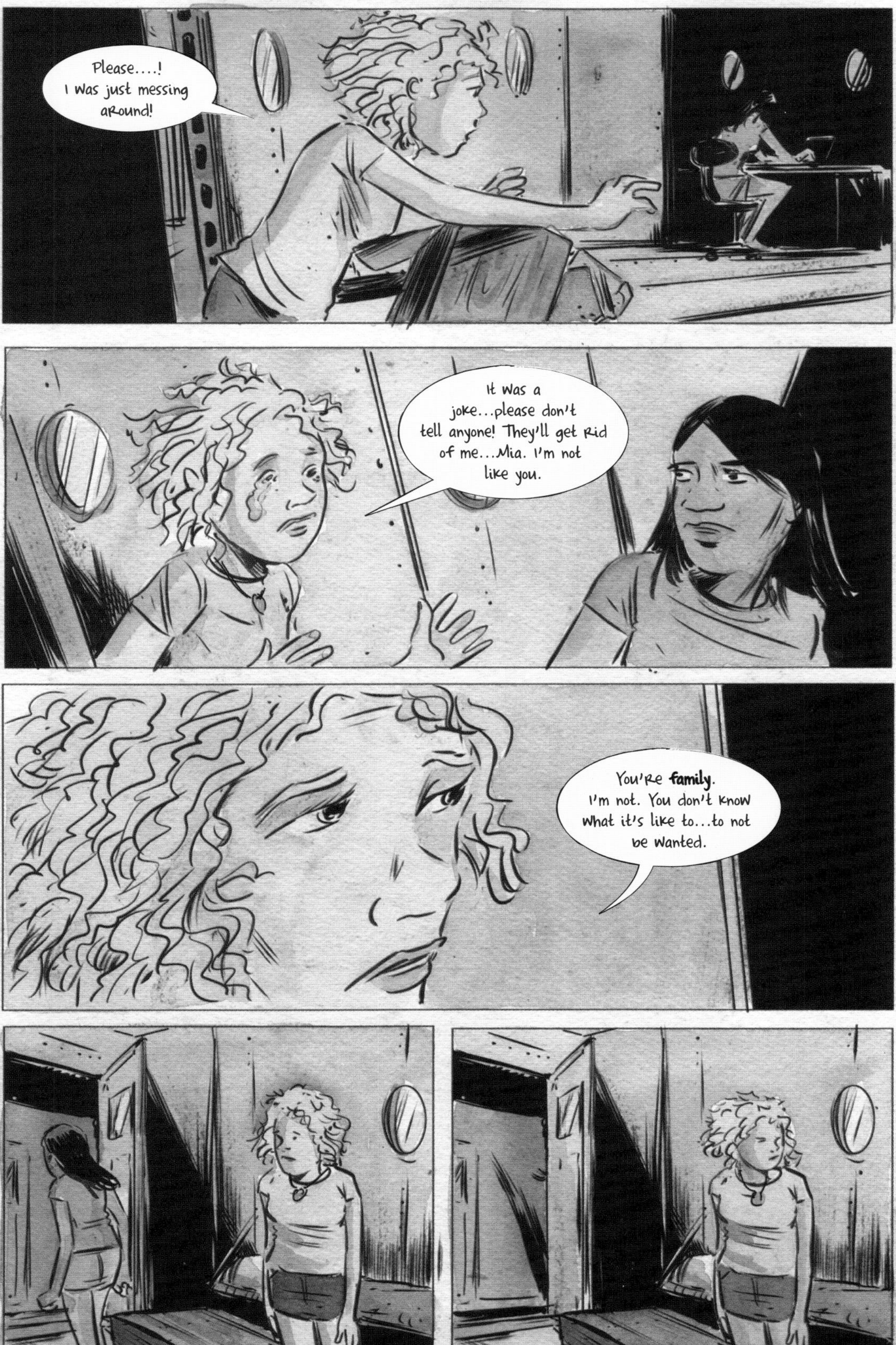
Please....! I was just messing around!
It was a joke...please don't tell anyone! They'll get rid of me...Mia. I'm not like you.
You're **family**. I'm not. You don't know what it's like to...to not be wanted.

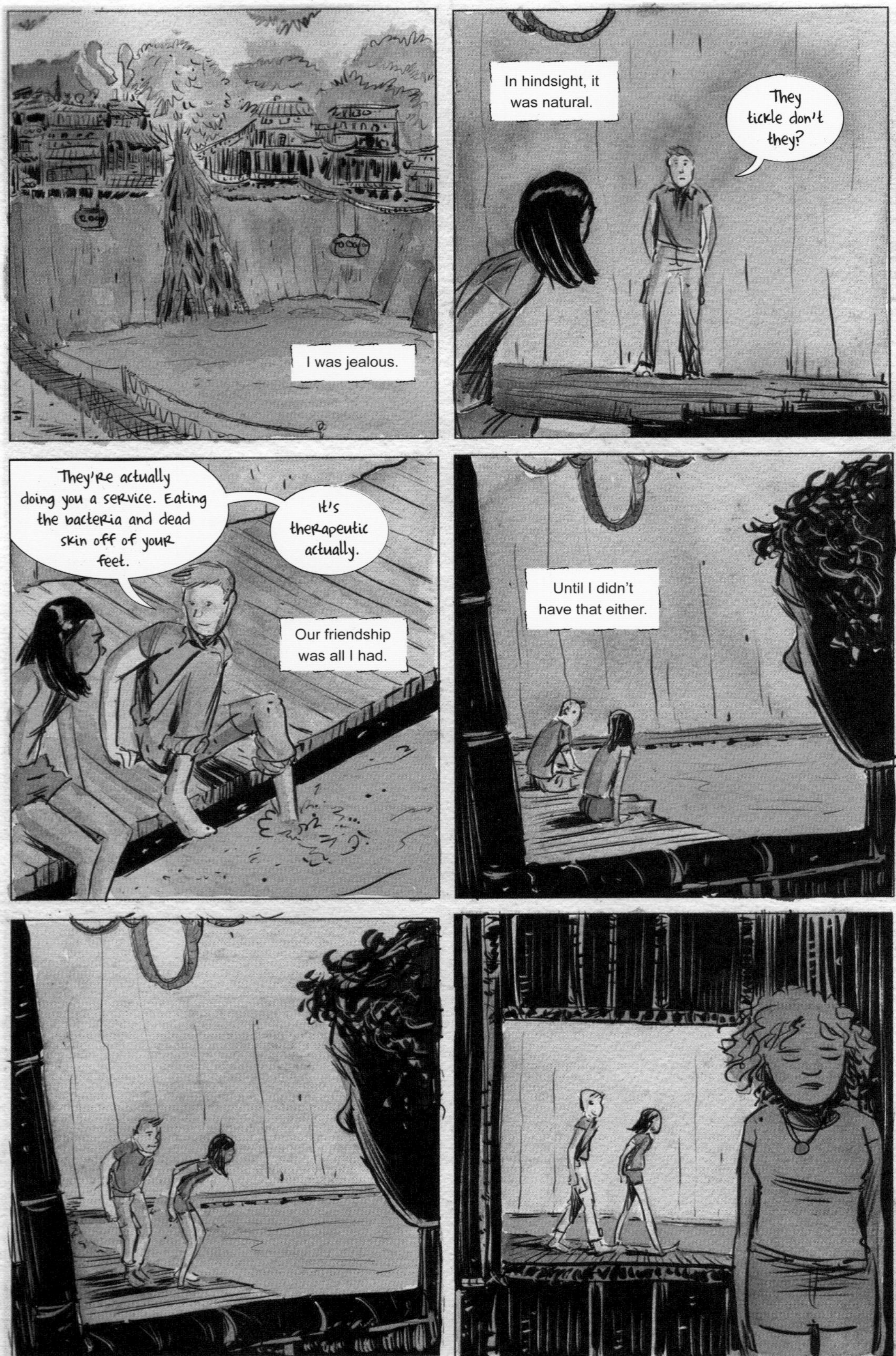

I was jealous.
In hindsight, it was natural.
They tickle don't they?
They're actually doing you a service. Eating the bacteria and dead skin off of your feet.
It's therapeutic actually.
Our friendship was all I had.
Until I didn't have that either.

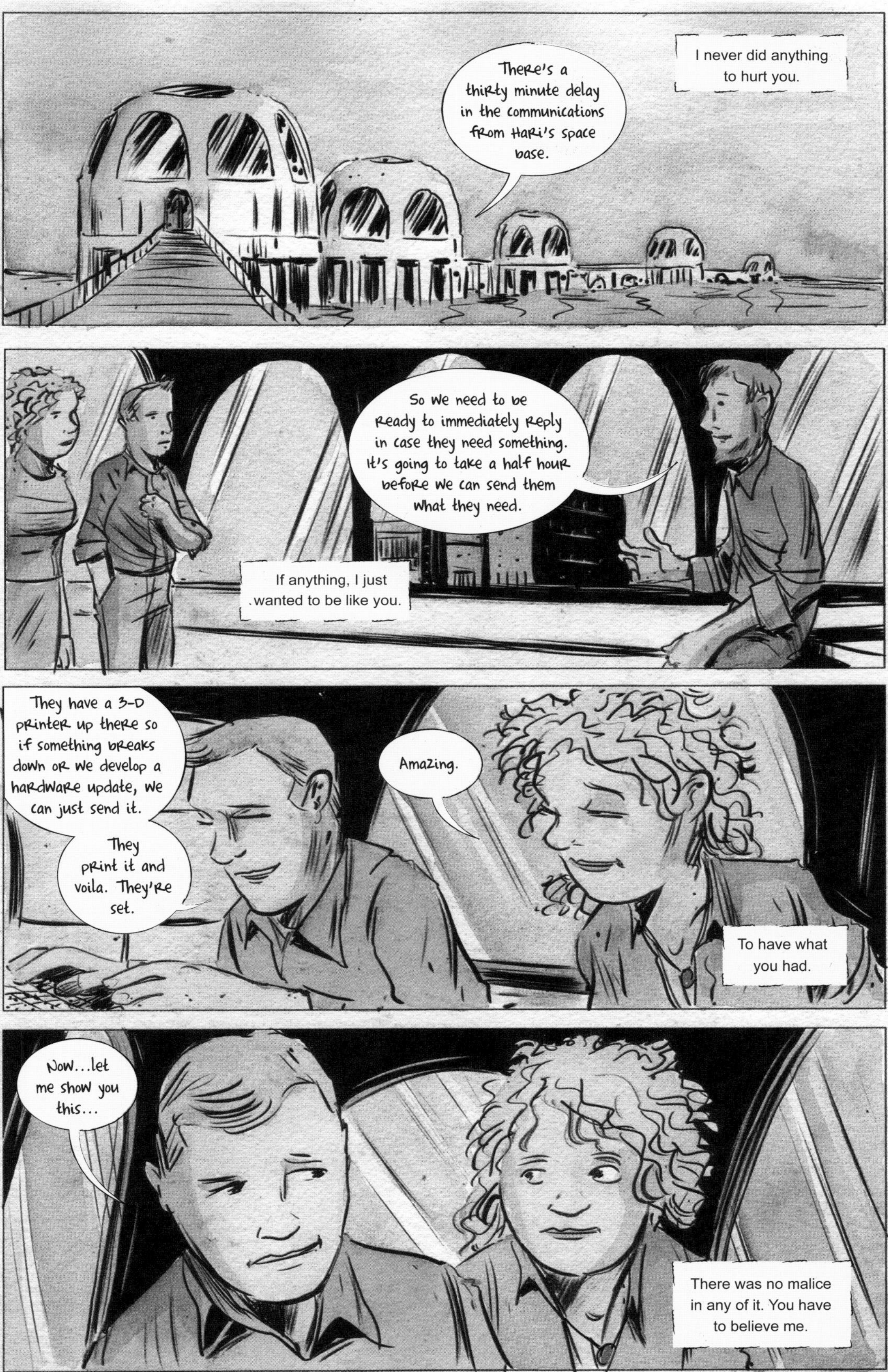

I never did anything to hurt you.
There's a thirty minute delay in the communications from Hari's space base.
So we need to be ready to immediately reply in case they need something. It's going to take a half hour before we can send them what they need.
If anything, I just wanted to be like you.
They have a 3-D printer up there so if something breaks down or we develop a hardware update, we can just send it.
They print it and voila. They're set.
Amazing.
To have what you had.
Now...let me show you this...
There was no malice in any of it. You have to believe me.

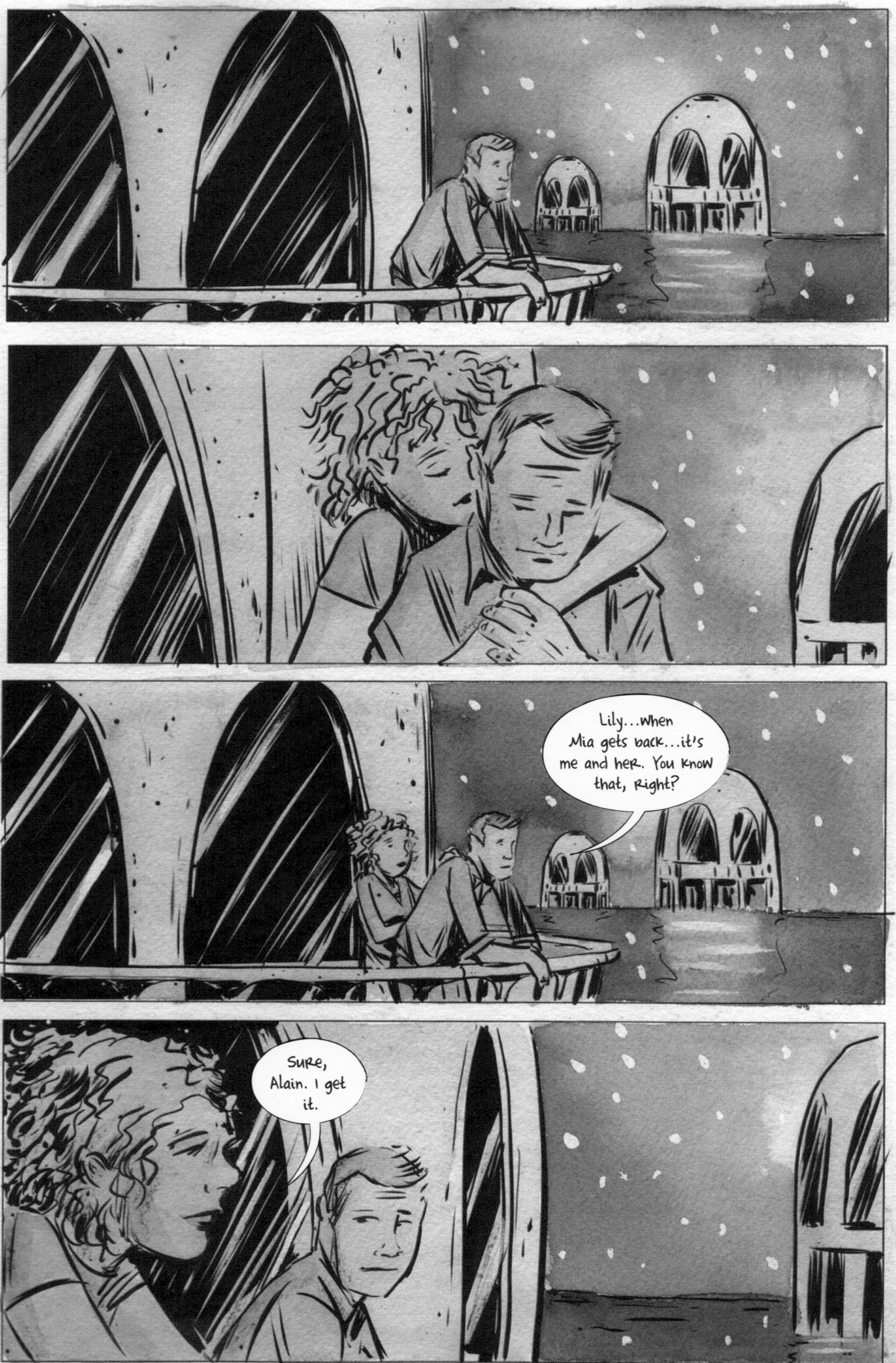
Lily...When Mia gets back...it's me and her. You know that, Right?
Sure, Alain. I get it.

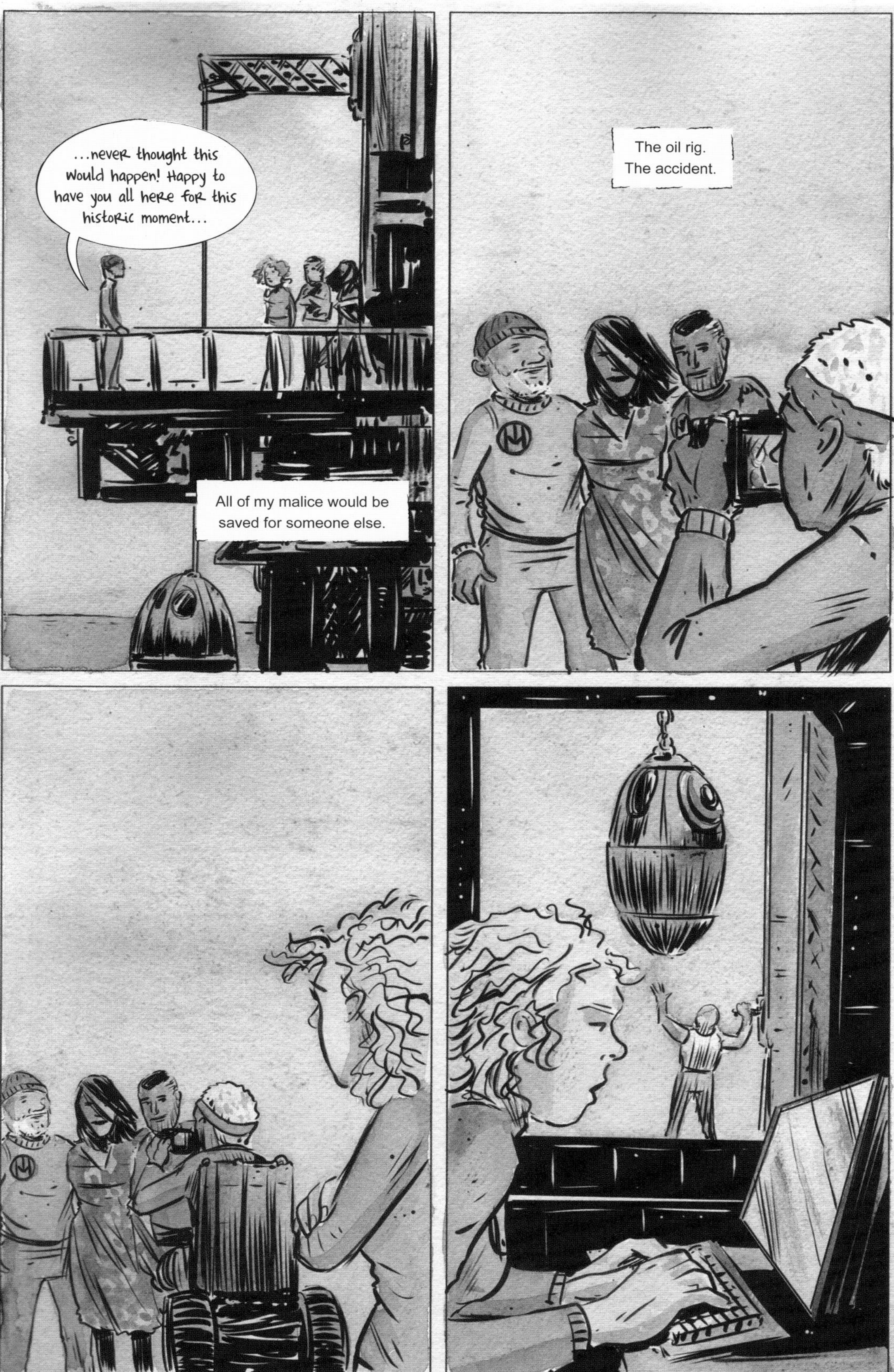
...never thought this would happen! Happy to have you all here for this historic moment...
All of my malice would be saved for someone else.
The oil rig.
The accident.

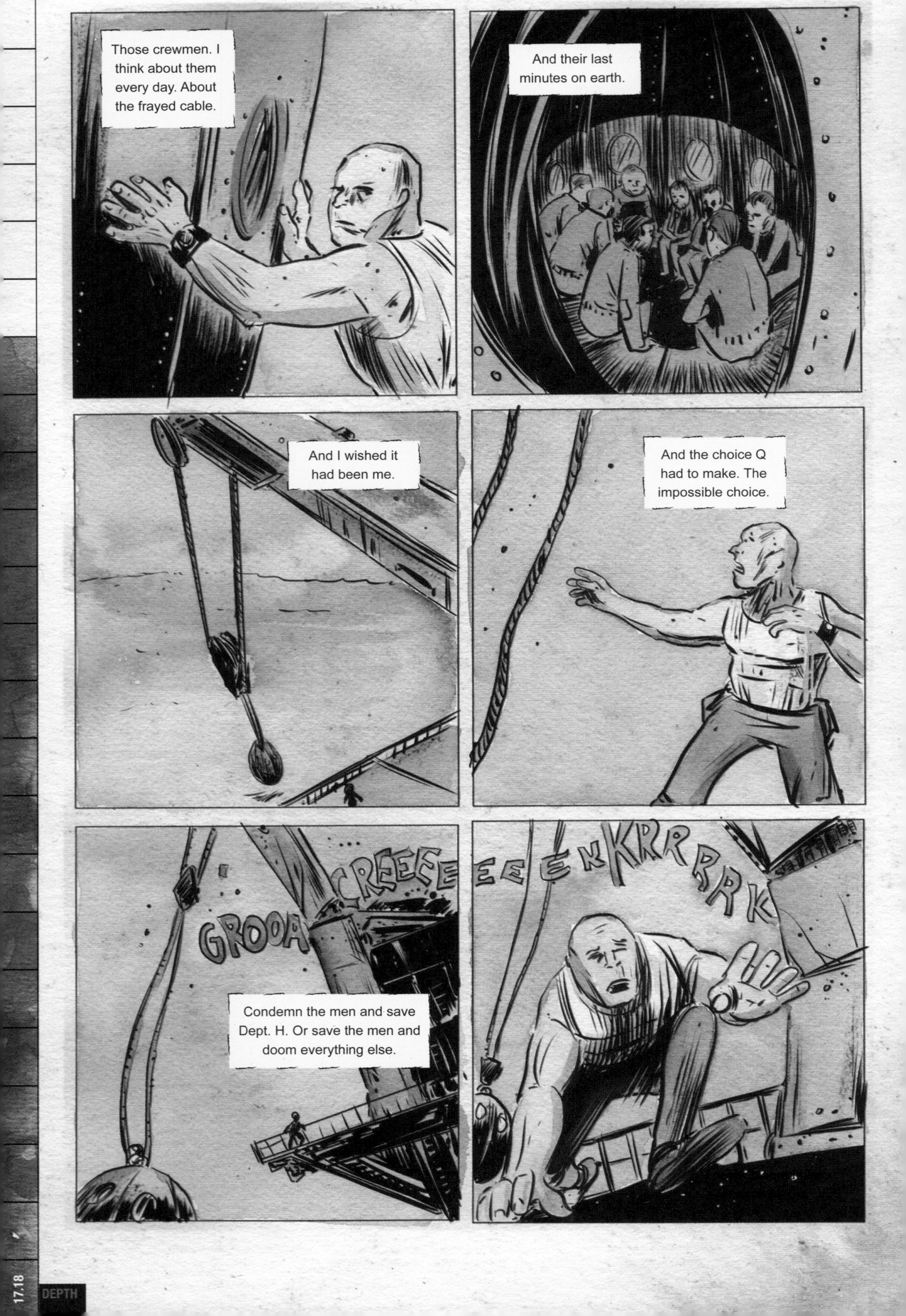

Those crewmen. I think about them every day. About the frayed cable.
And their last minutes on earth.
And I wished it had been me.
And the choice Q had to make. The impossible choice.
GROOA
CREEEEEEEEEKKRRRRRK
Condemn the men and save Dept. H. Or save the men and doom everything else.

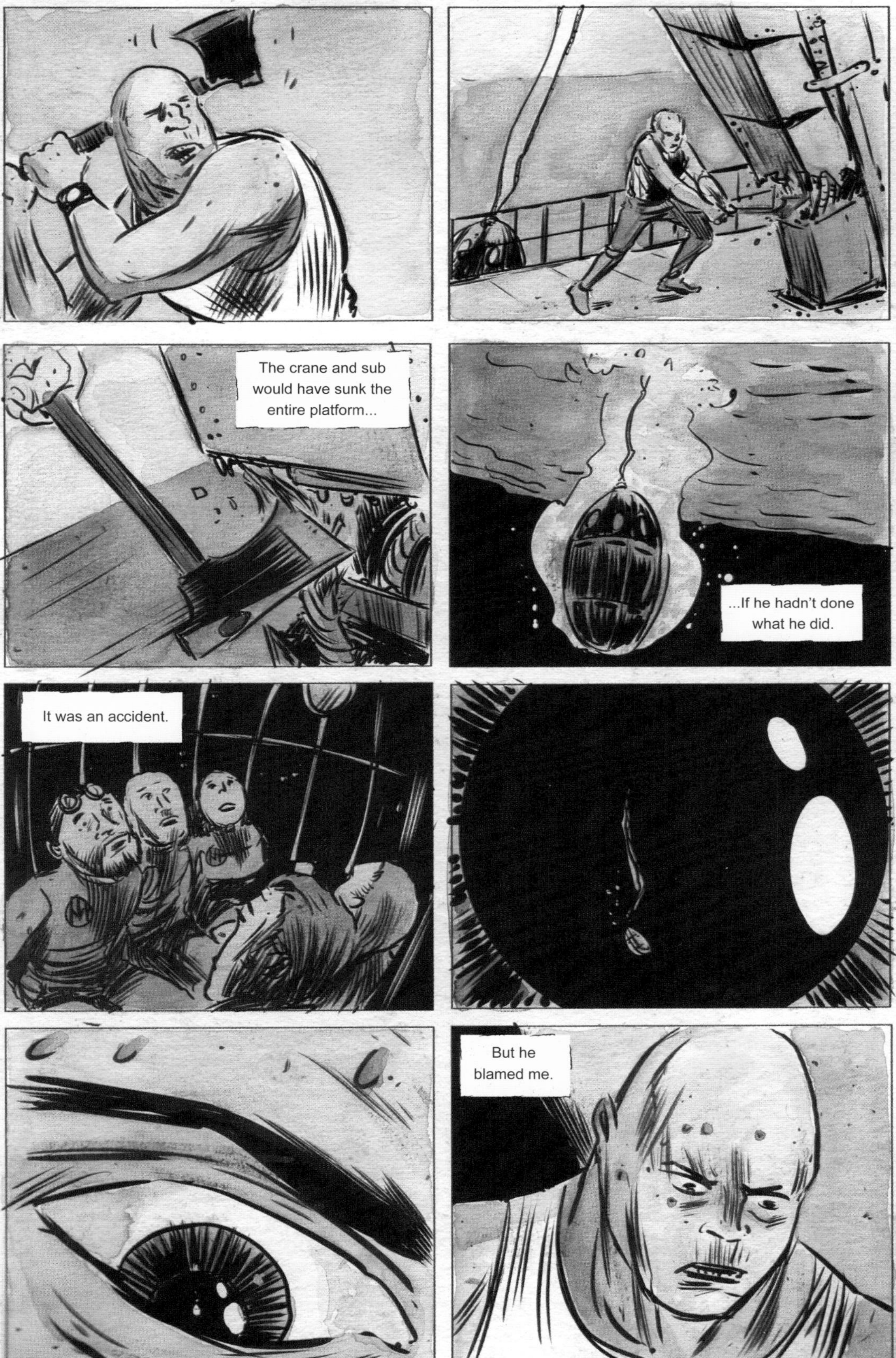
The crane and sub would have sunk the entire platform...
...If he hadn't done what he did.
It was an accident.
But he blamed me.

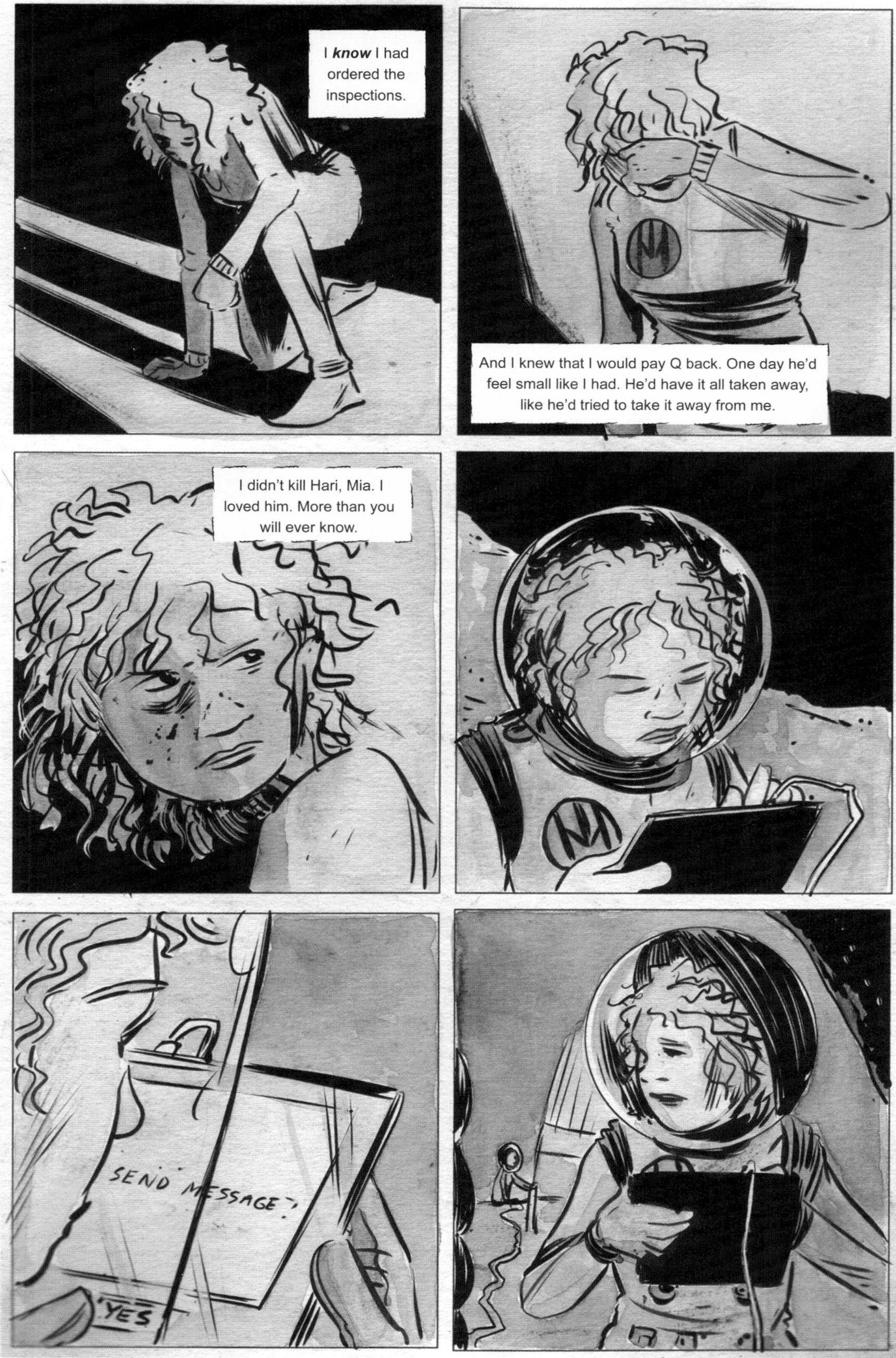
I **know** I had ordered the inspections.
And I knew that I would pay Q back. One day he'd feel small like I had. He'd have it all taken away, like he'd tried to take it away from me.
I didn't kill Hari, Mia. I loved him. More than you will ever know.
SEND MESSAGE?
YES

I was able to access my email...I've got news from the surface...something bad has happened...

Brief us on the way. We gotta get outta this cave.

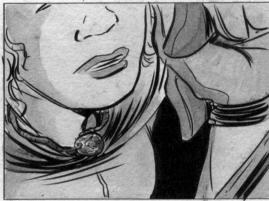

There's been another outbreak. The China epidemic made the jump to the other continents.

The H-virus is everywhere. It's... reports of mayhem all over the globe...

Then why are they worried about us surfacing? We've got what might be the cure! And they're afraid of us? It doesn't make sense.

To: mia@depth.com

From: lily@depth.com

Subject:

If you're reading this, I'm dead. And you're not. But I want you to know...Everything. You meant the worl[d]

Do you remember the day we met? We grew up together. Like sisters. With a brother neither of us reall[y]

liked. You don't know what it's like to be unwanted. To be ignored. To be left behind. It makes you do fu[...]

things. Despite yourself. Despite the danger of losing your only friend on earth. I was jealous. In hinds[ight]

it was natural. Our friendship was all I had. Until I didn't have that either. I never did anything to hurt y[ou]

If anything, I just wanted to be like you. To have what you had. There was no malice in any of it. You h[ave to]

believe me. All of my malice would be saved for someone else. The oil rig. The accident. Those crew[...]

I think about them every day. About the frayed cable. And their last minutes on earth. And I wished it[...]

been me. And the choice Q had to make. The impossible choice. Condemn the men and save Dept[...]

the men and doom everything else. The crane and sub would have sunk the entire platform...If he[...]

done what he did. It was an accident. But he blamed me. Accused me of not having the inspections[...]

At the time I couldn't remember if I'd had the inspections done or not. There was so much to do.[...]

And he was intent on shifting his guilt at any cost. I admitted guilt...just to get rid of him.

Out of fear...I was in shock. I **know** I had ordered the inspections. And I knew that I woul[d]

pay Q back. One day he'd feel small like I had. He'd have it all taken away, like he'd trie[d]

to take it away from me. I didn't kill Hari, Mia. I loved him. More than you will ever know.

But I hated Q with everything in me.

-L

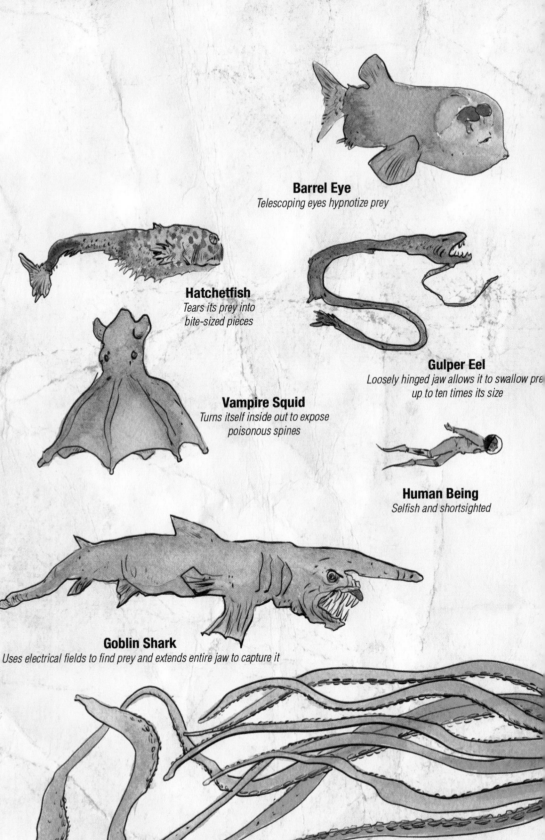

Barrel Eye
Telescoping eyes hypnotize prey

Hatchetfish
*Tears its prey into
bite-sized pieces*

Gulper Eel
*Loosely hinged jaw allows it to swallow prey
up to ten times its size*

Vampire Squid
*Turns itself inside out to expose
poisonous spines*

Human Being
Selfish and shortsighted

Goblin Shark
Uses electrical fields to find prey and extends entire jaw to capture it

THE MOST DANGEROUS CREATURES IN THE OCEAN

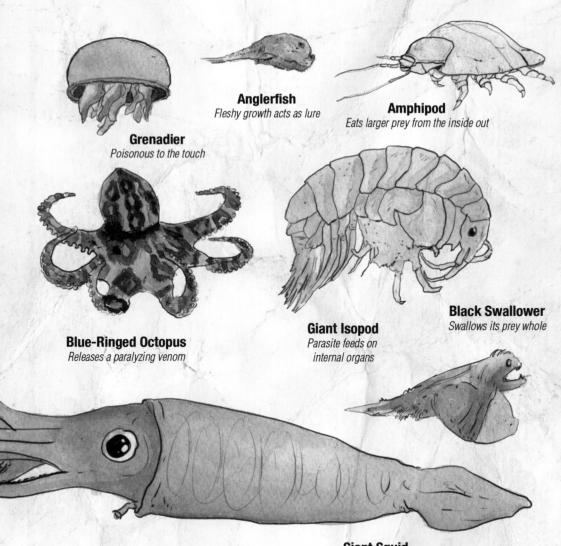

Anglerfish
Fleshy growth acts as lure

Amphipod
Eats larger prey from the inside out

Grenadier
Poisonous to the touch

Black Swallower
Swallows its prey whole

Blue-Ringed Octopus
Releases a paralyzing venom

Giant Isopod
Parasite feeds on internal organs

Giant Squid
Pulls its prey down to lethal depths

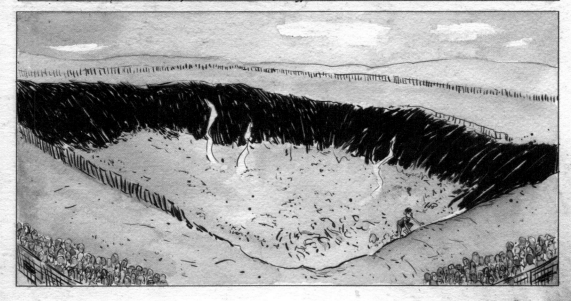

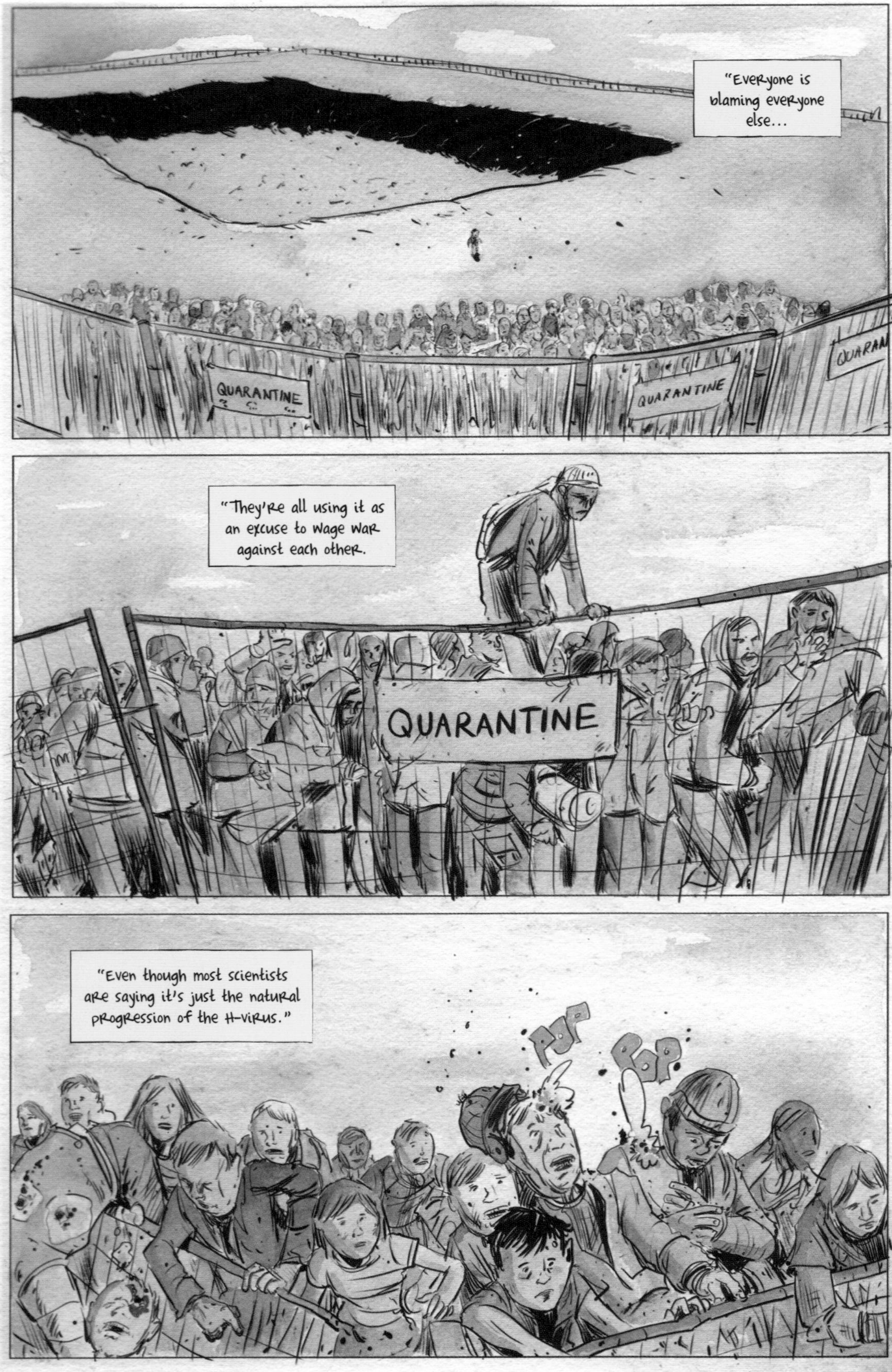
"Everyone is blaming everyone else…
QUARANTINE
QUARANTINE
"They're all using it as an excuse to wage war against each other.
QUARANTINE
"Even though most scientists are saying it's just the natural progression of the H-virus."
POP
POP

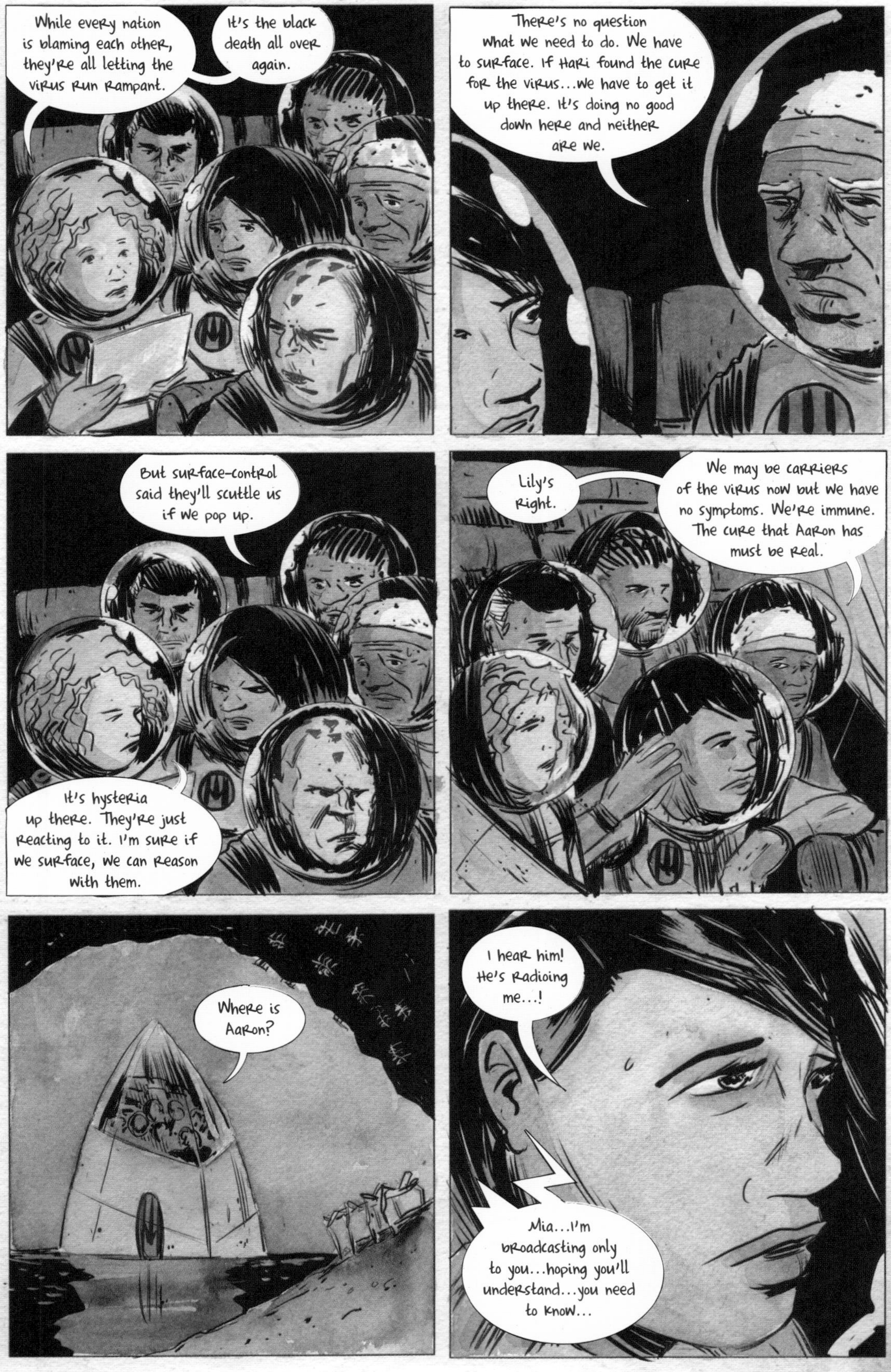
While every nation is blaming each other, they're all letting the virus run rampant.
It's the black death all over again.
There's no question what we need to do. We have to surface. If Hari found the cure for the virus...we have to get it up there. It's doing no good down here and neither are we.
But surface-control said they'll scuttle us if we pop up.
It's hysteria up there. They're just reacting to it. I'm sure if we surface, we can reason with them.
Lily's right.
We may be carriers of the virus now but we have no symptoms. We're immune. The cure that Aaron has must be real.
Where is Aaron?
I hear him! He's radioing me...!
Mia...I'm broadcasting only to you...hoping you'll understand...you need to know...

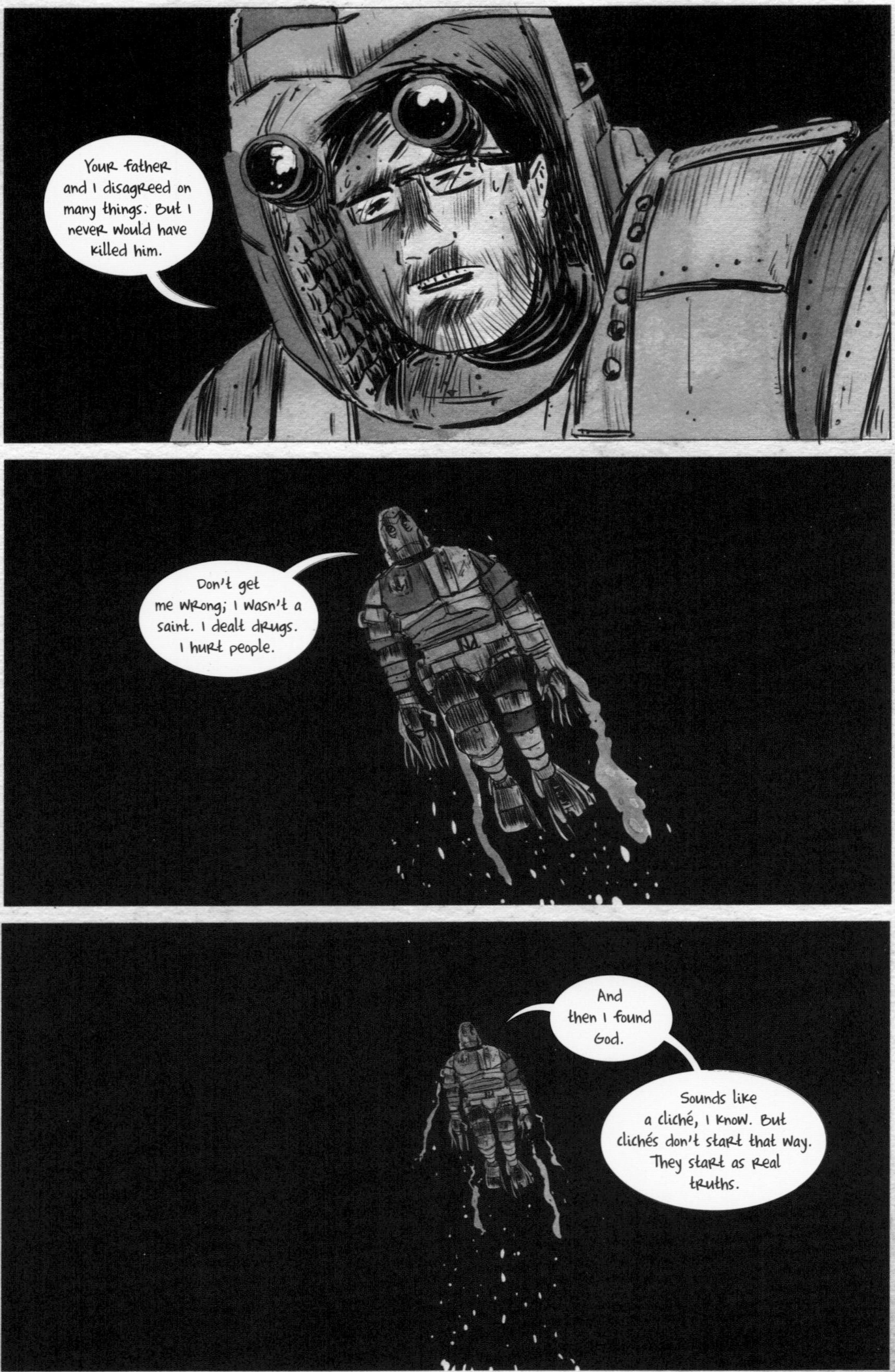
Your father and I disagreed on many things. But I never would have killed him.
Don't get me wrong; I wasn't a saint. I dealt drugs. I hurt people.
And then I found God.
Sounds like a cliché, I know. But clichés don't start that way. They start as real truths.

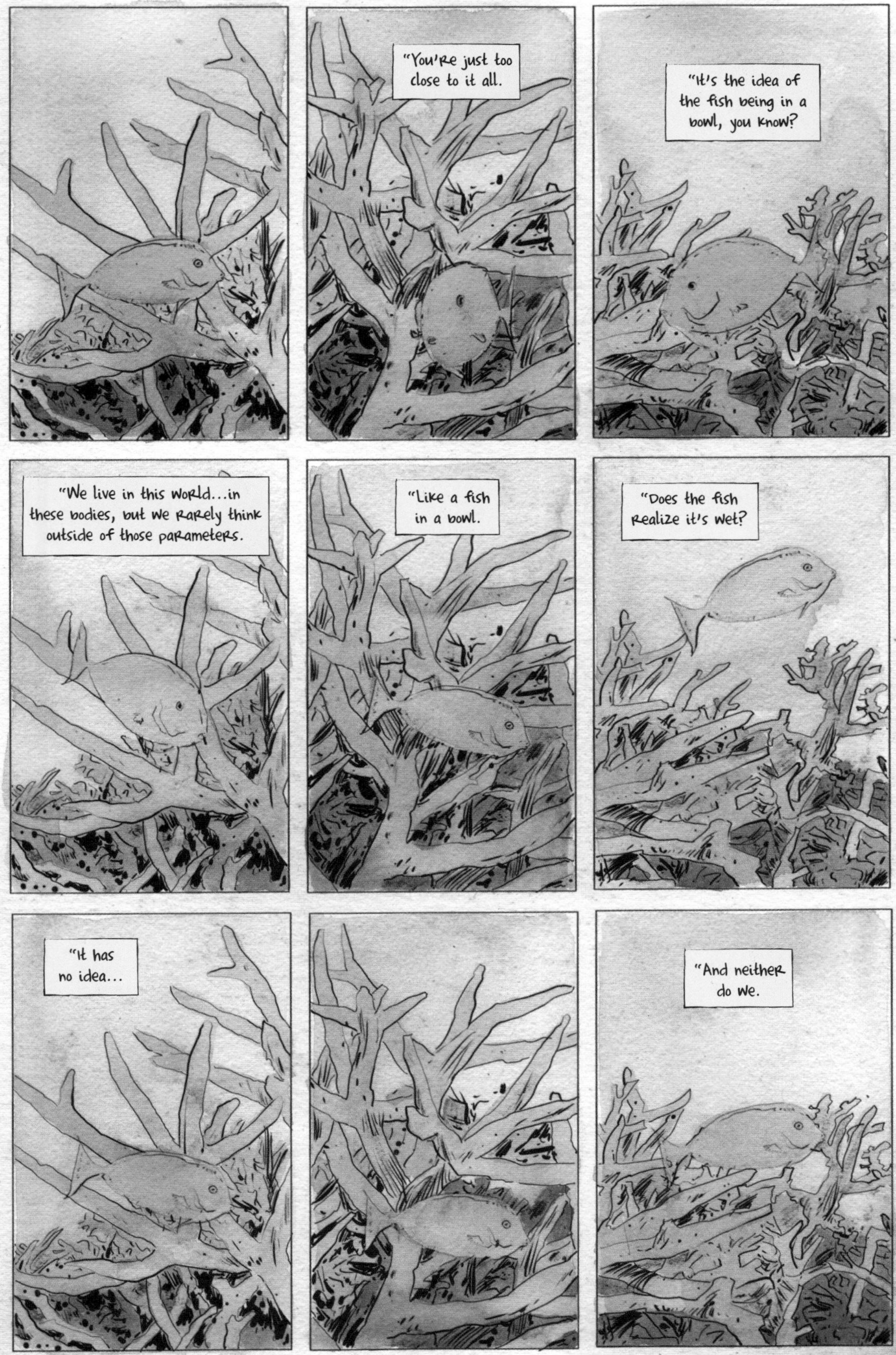
"You're just too close to it all.
"It's the idea of the fish being in a bowl, you know?
"We live in this world...in these bodies, but we rarely think outside of those parameters.
"Like a fish in a bowl.
"Does the fish realize it's wet?
"It has no idea...
"And neither do we.

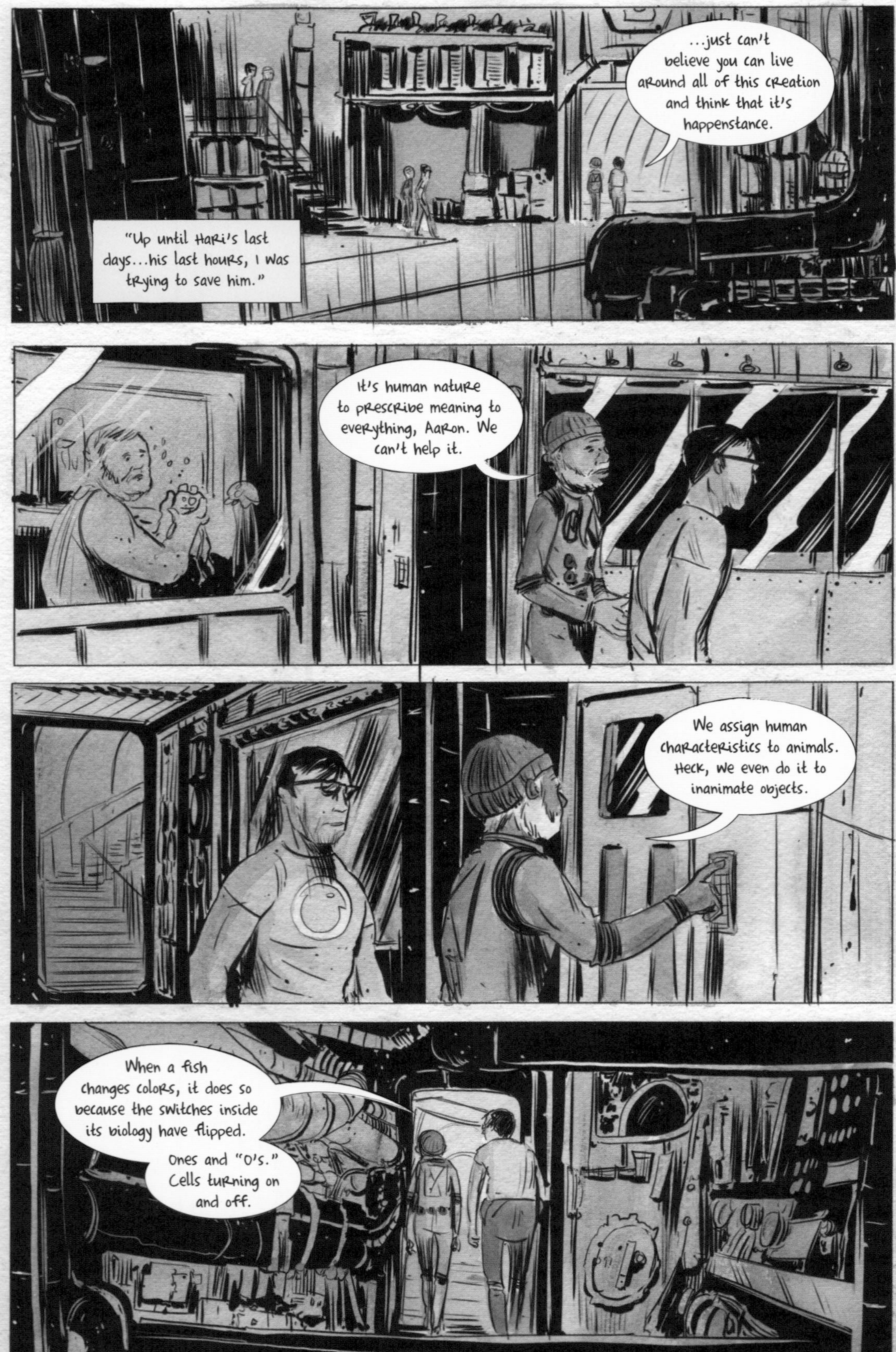
...just can't believe you can live around all of this creation and think that it's happenstance.
"Up until Hari's last days...his last hours, I was trying to save him."
It's human nature to prescribe meaning to everything, Aaron. We can't help it.
We assign human characteristics to animals. Heck, we even do it to inanimate objects.
When a fish changes colors, it does so because the switches inside its biology have flipped.
Ones and "0's." Cells turning on and off.

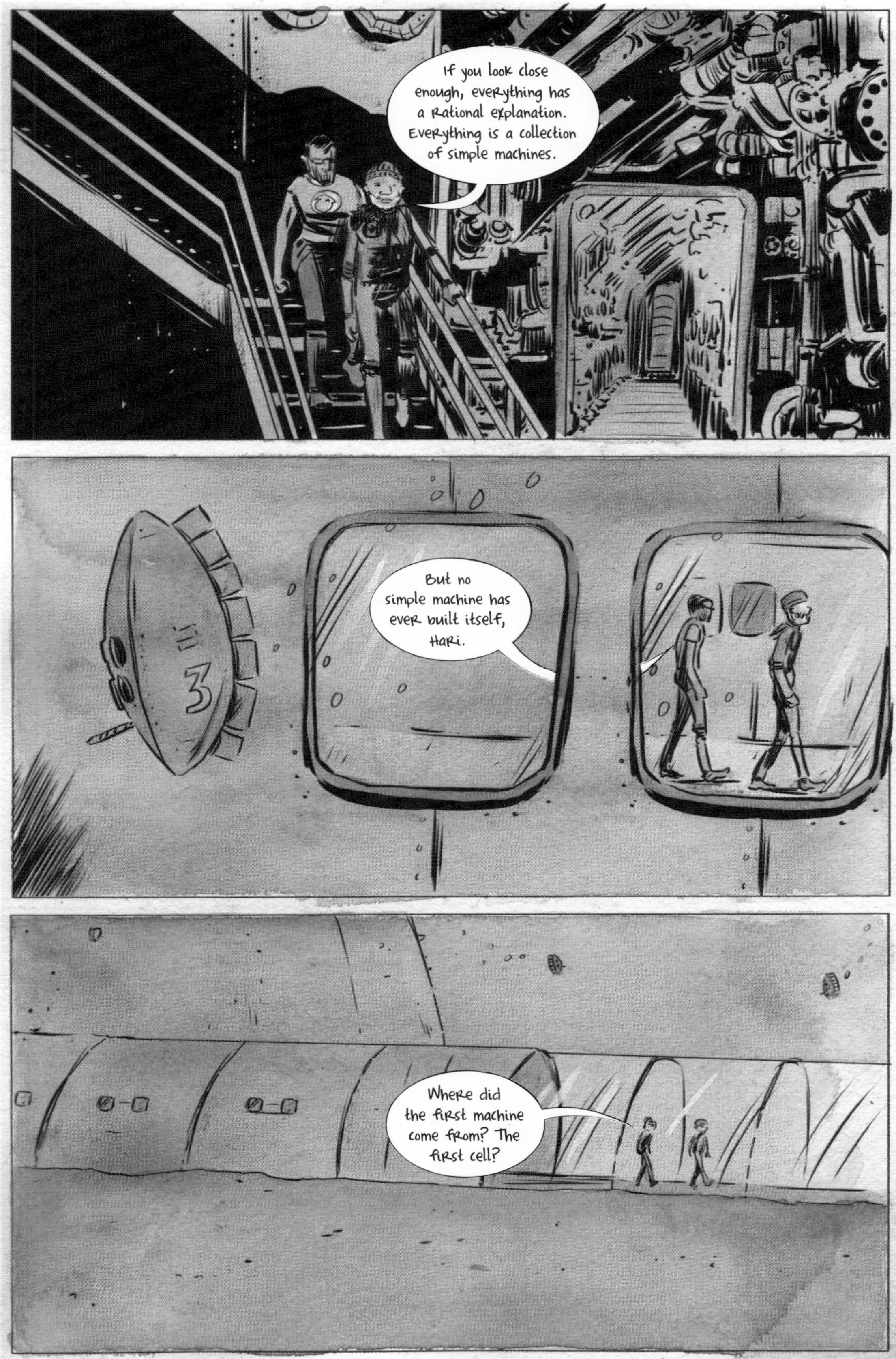
If you look close enough, everything has a Rational explanation. Everything is a collection of simple machines.
But no simple machine has ever built itself, Hari.
3
Where did the first machine come from? The first cell?

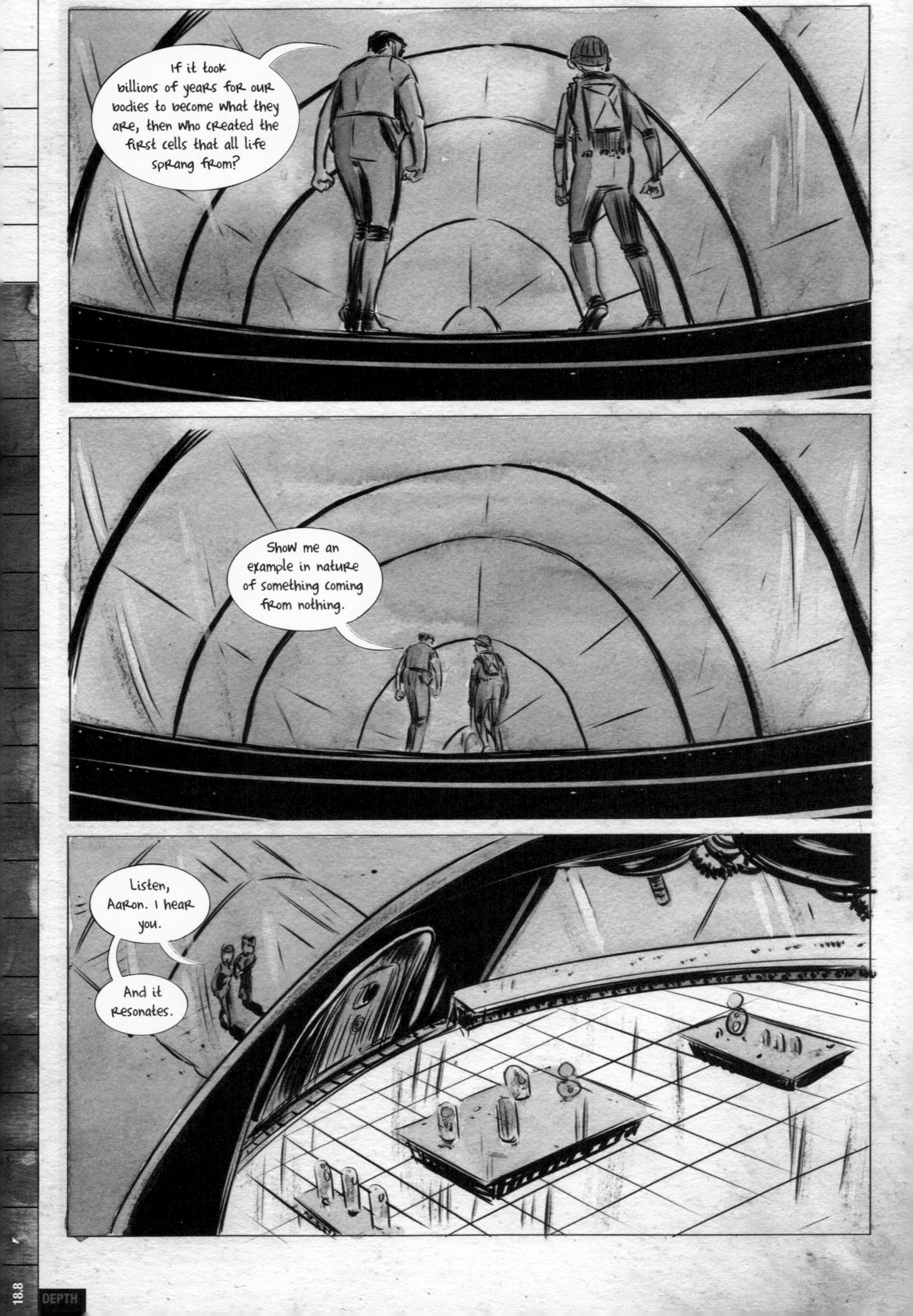
If it took billions of years for our bodies to become what they are, then who created the first cells that all life sprang from?
Show me an example in nature of something coming from nothing.
Listen, Aaron. I hear you.
And it resonates.

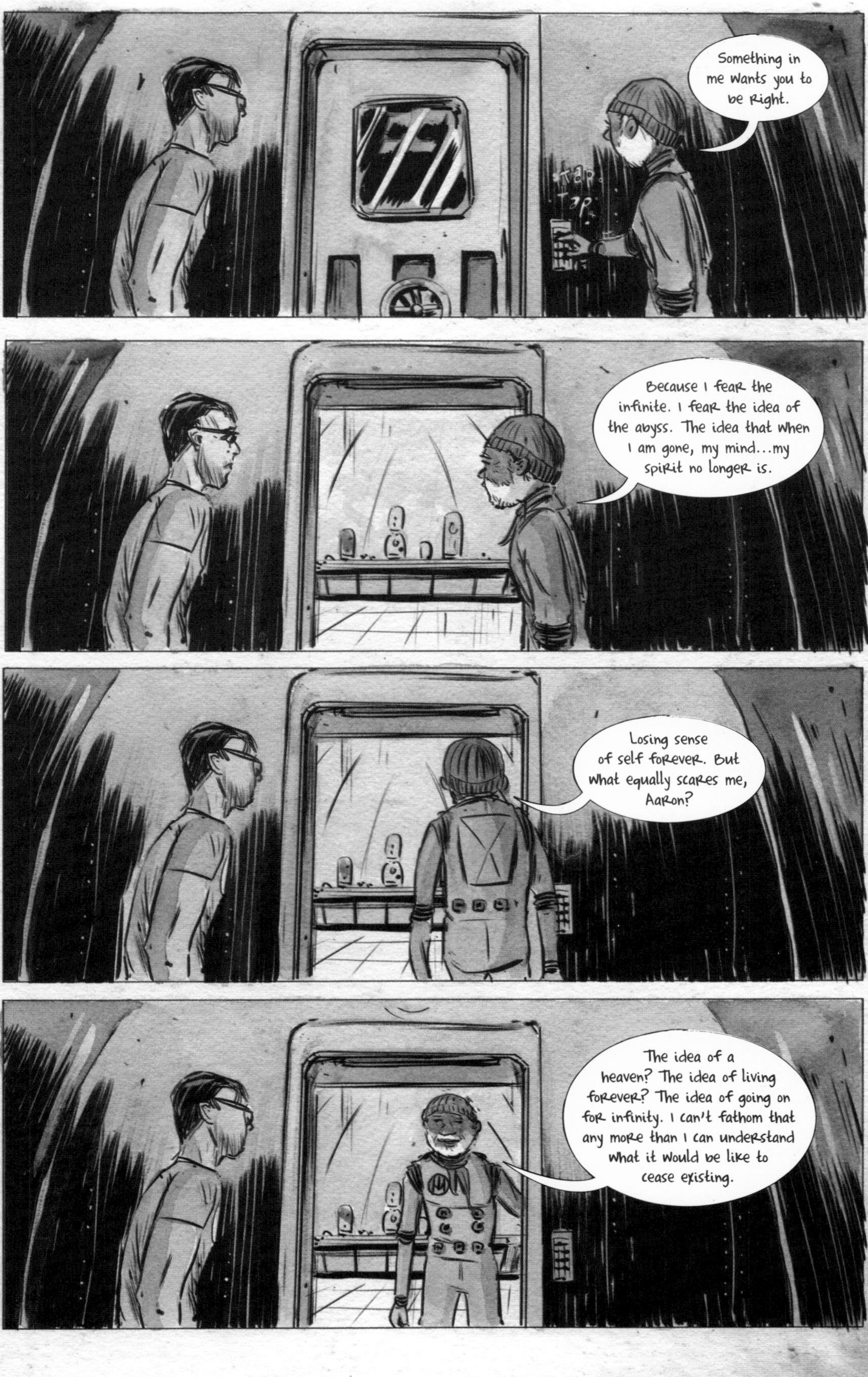
Something in me wants you to be right.
tap. tap.
Because I fear the infinite. I fear the idea of the abyss. The idea that when I am gone, my mind...my spirit no longer is.
Losing sense of self forever. But what equally scares me, Aaron?
The idea of a heaven? The idea of living forever? The idea of going on for infinity. I can't fathom that any more than I can understand what it would be like to cease existing.

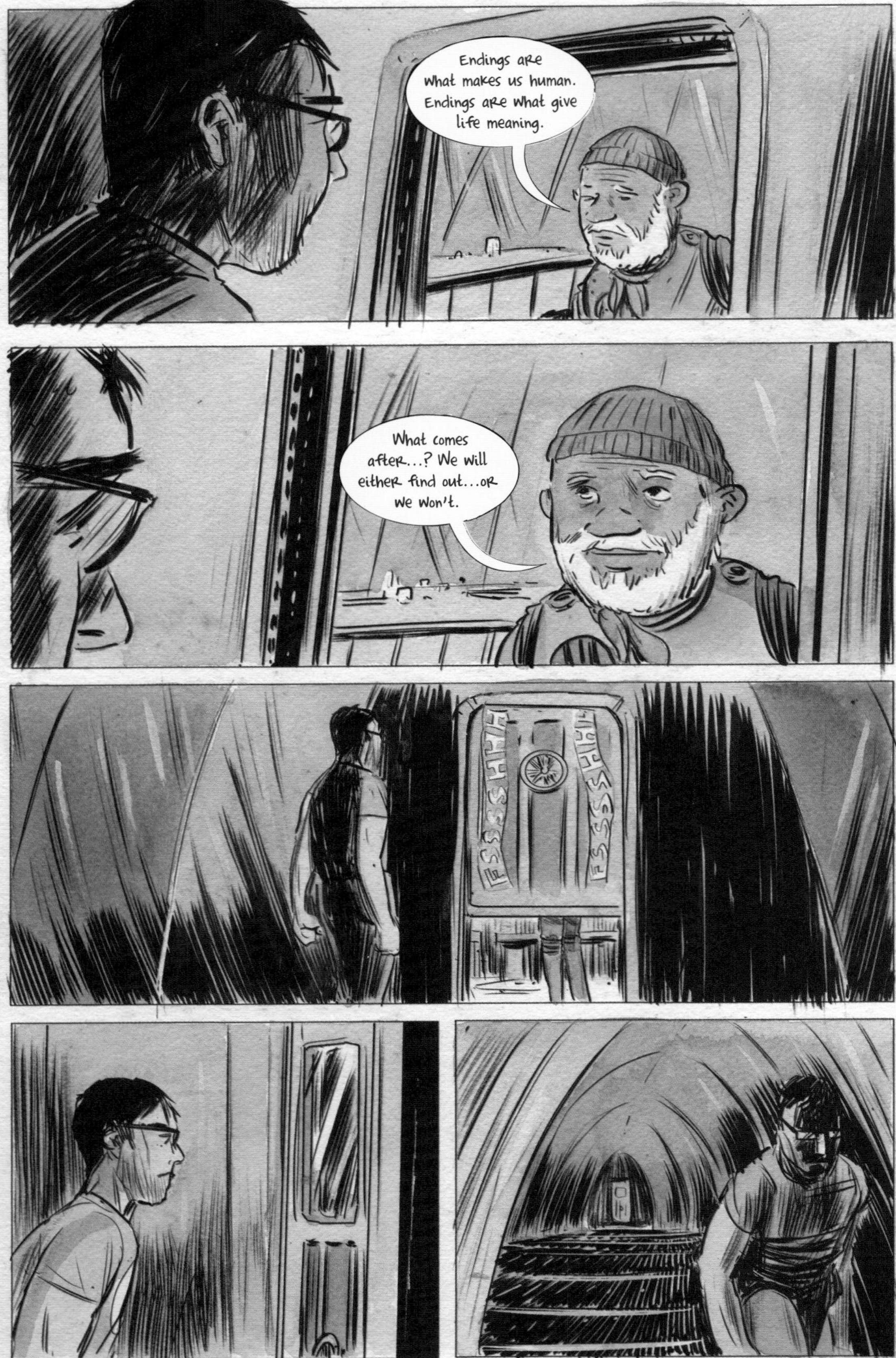
Endings are what makes us human. Endings are what give life meaning.
What comes after...? We will either find out...or we won't.
FSSSSHHH
FSSSSHHH

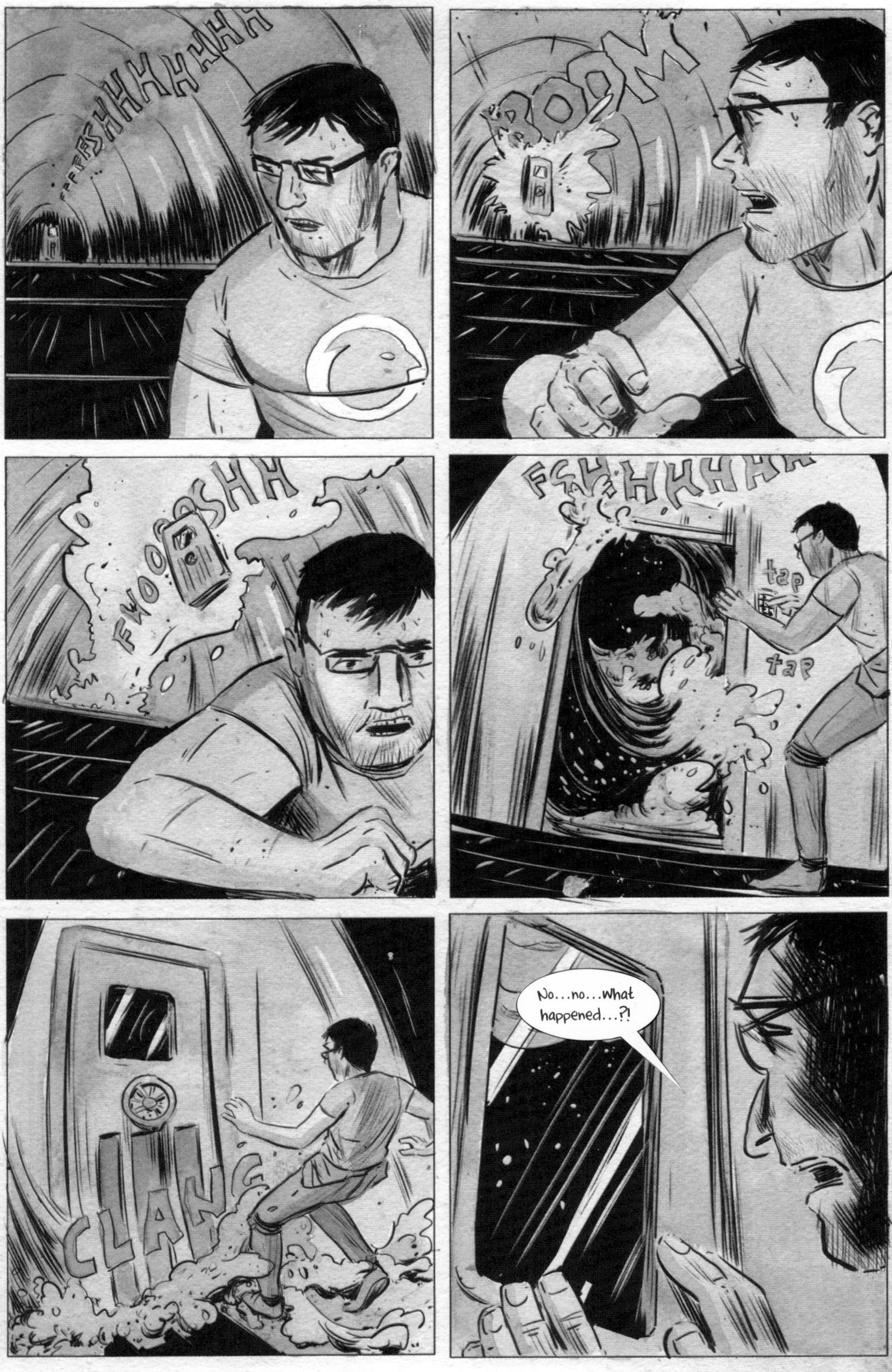
BOOM
tap
tap
CLANG
No...no...what happened...?!

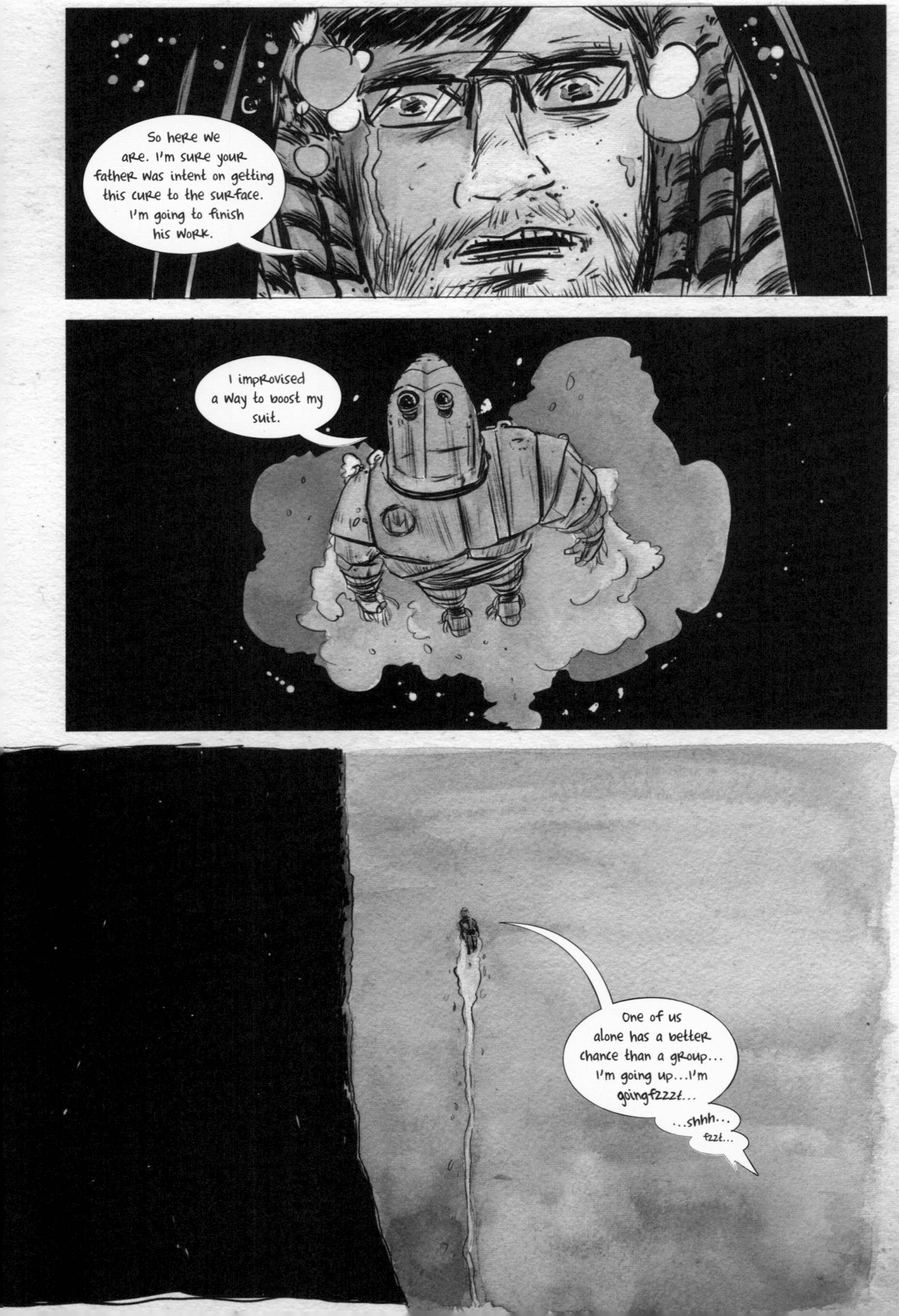
So here we are. I'm sure your father was intent on getting this cure to the surface. I'm going to finish his work.
I improvised a way to boost my suit.
One of us alone has a better chance than a group... I'm going up...I'm goingfzzzt...
...shhh...
fzzt...

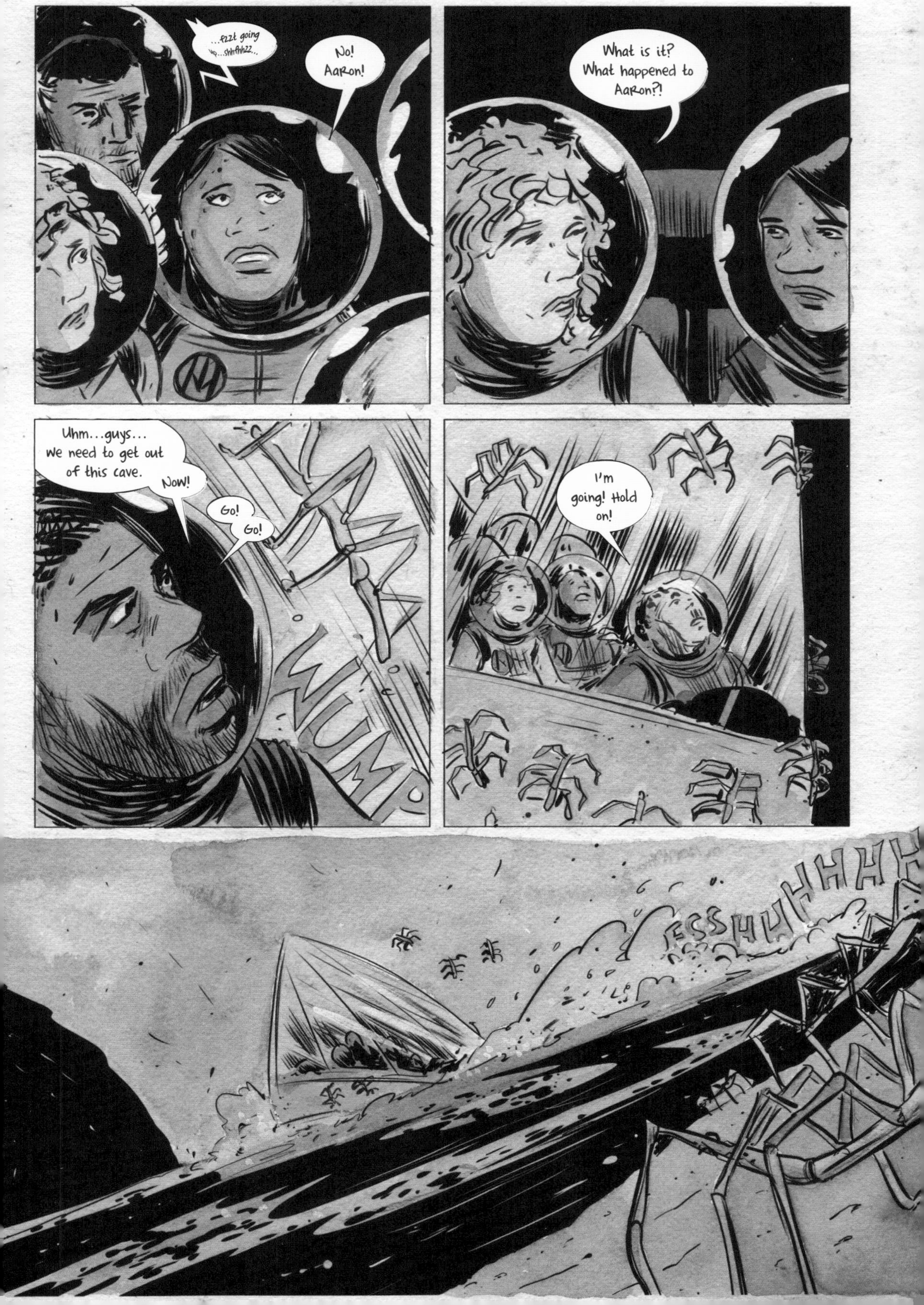
...fzzt going up...shhfhhzz...
No! Aaron!
What is it? What happened to Aaron?!
Uhm...guys... we need to get out of this cave.
Now!
Go!
Go!
WUMP
I'm going! Hold on!
ESSHHHHHH

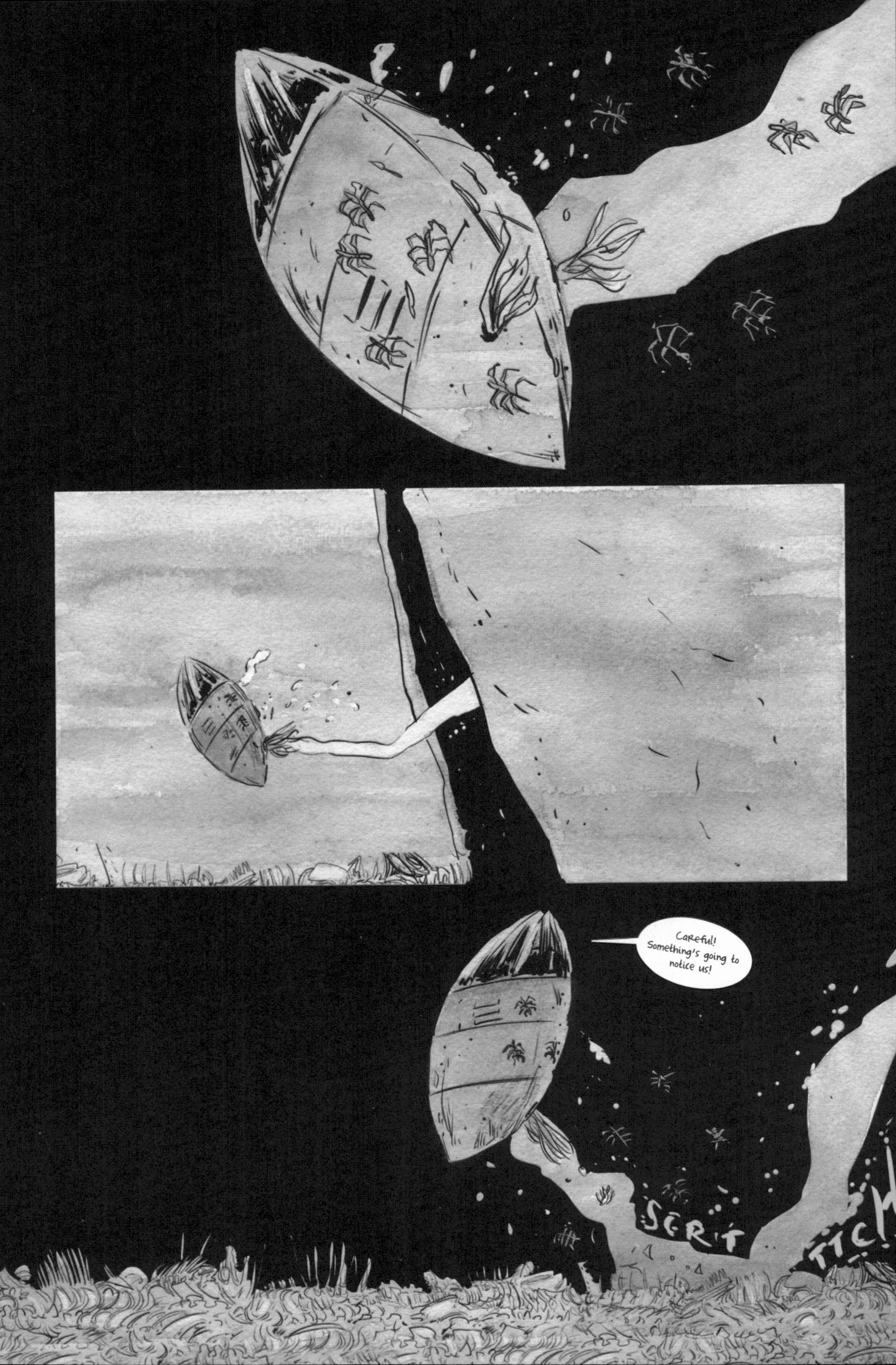
Careful! Something's going to notice us!
SCRT
TTCH

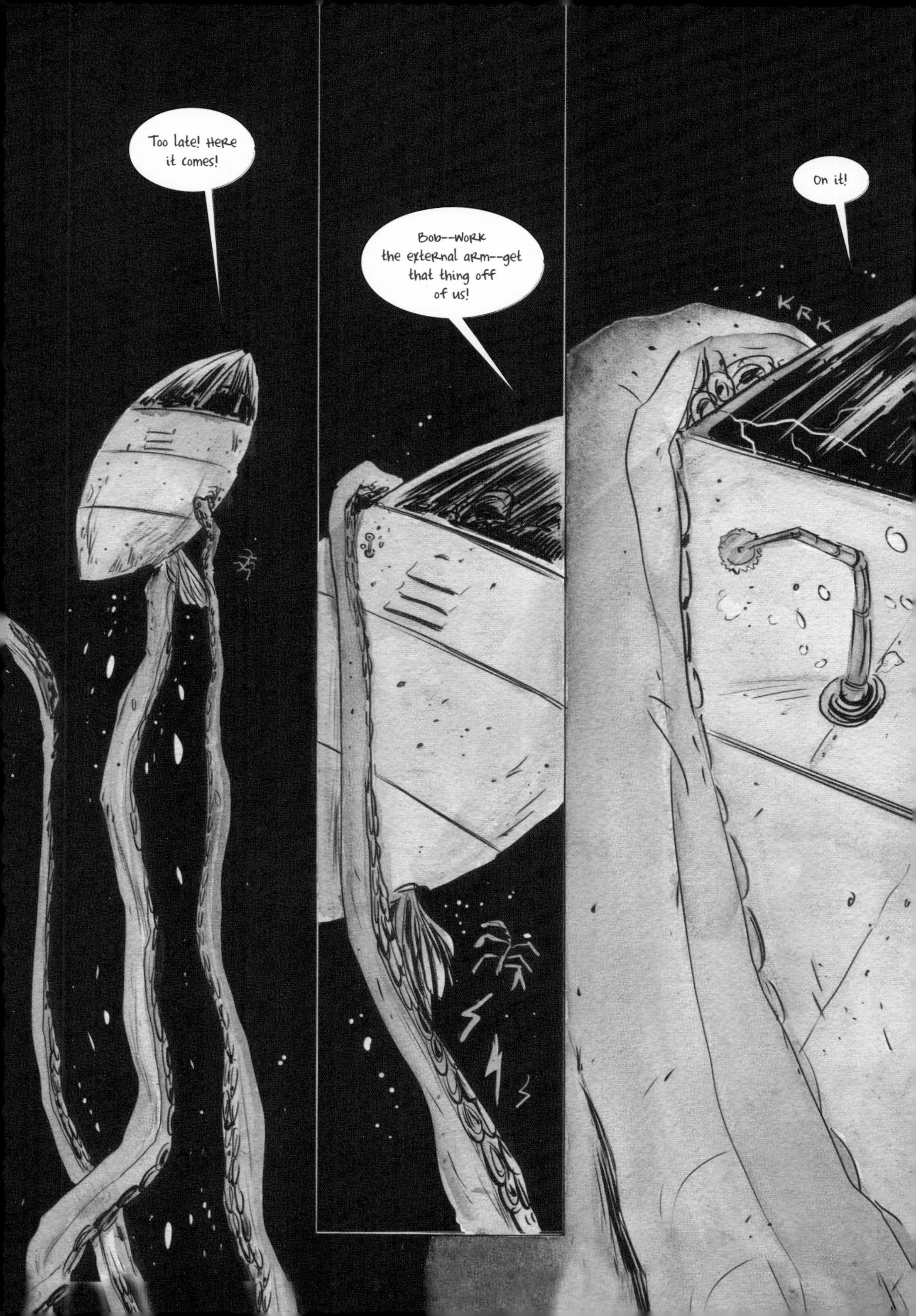
Too late! Here it comes!
Bob--work the external arm--get that thing off of us!
On it!
KRK

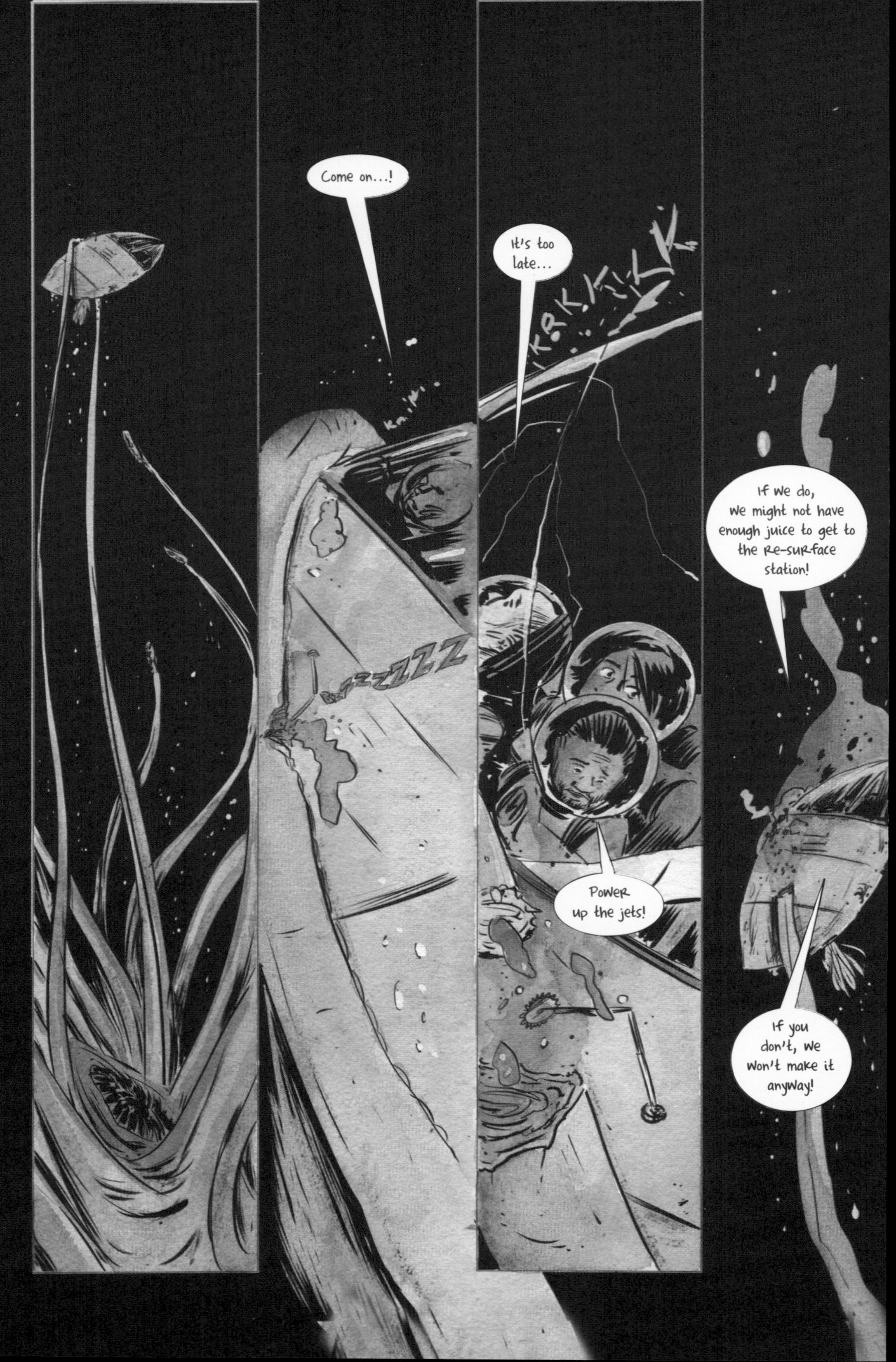
Come on...!
Knipi
It's too late...
KRKKKKK
BZZZZZZ
Power up the jets!
If we do, we might not have enough juice to get to the re-surface station!
If you don't, we won't make it anyway!

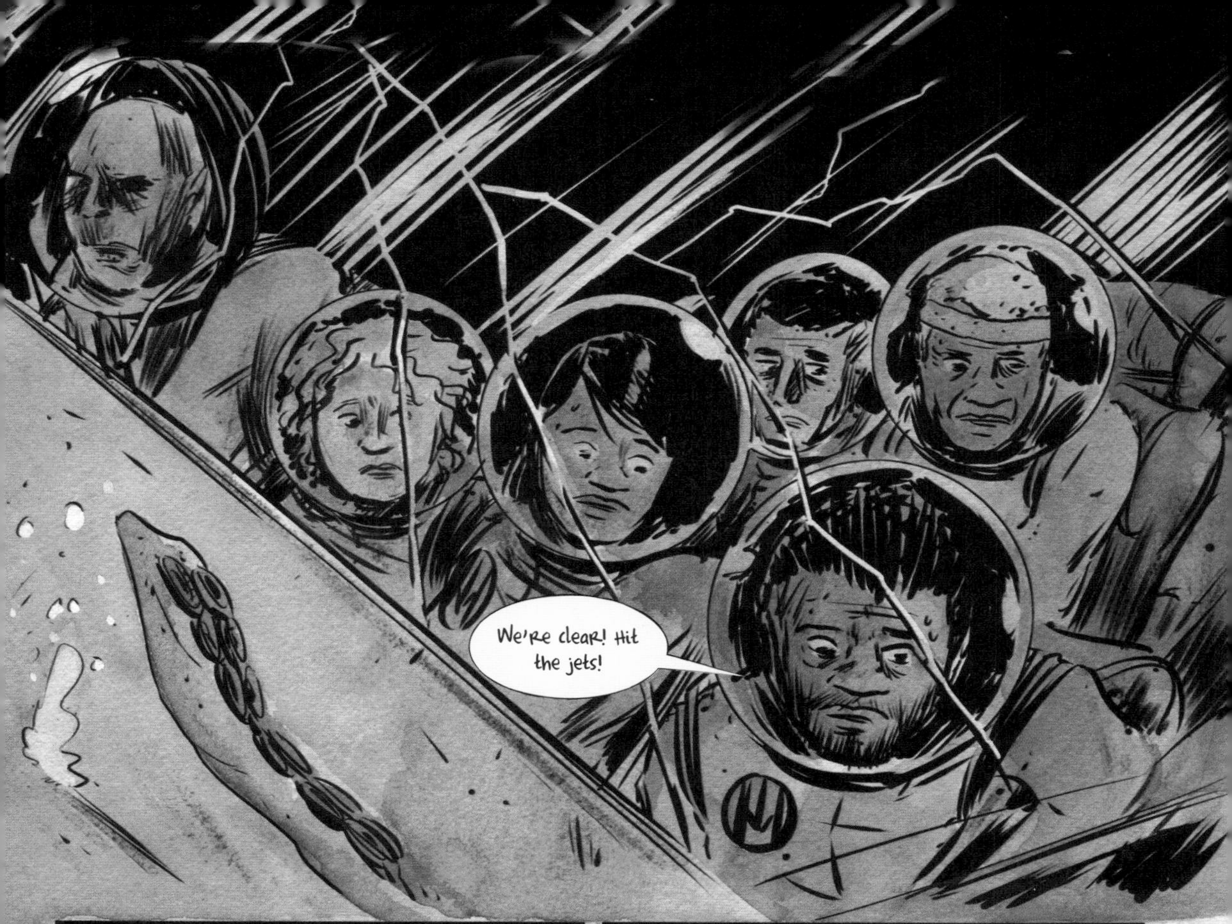
We're clear! Hit the jets!

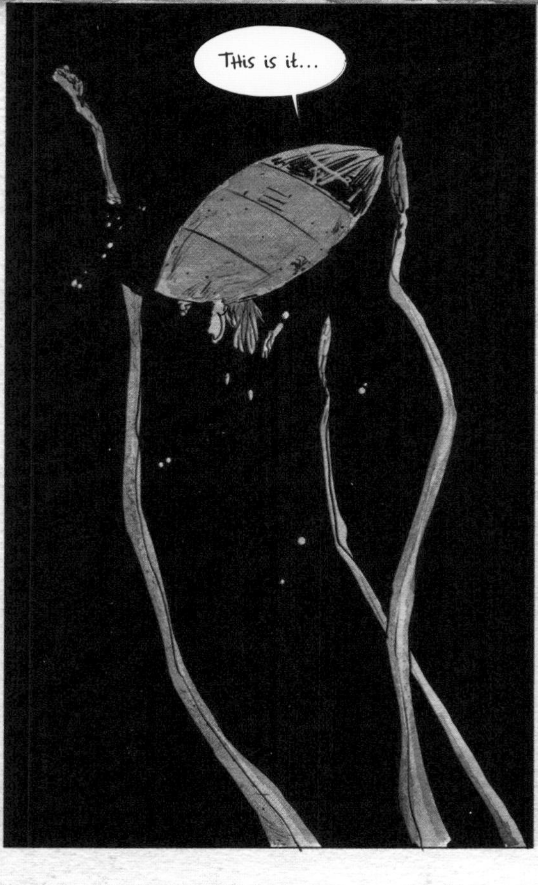
This is it...

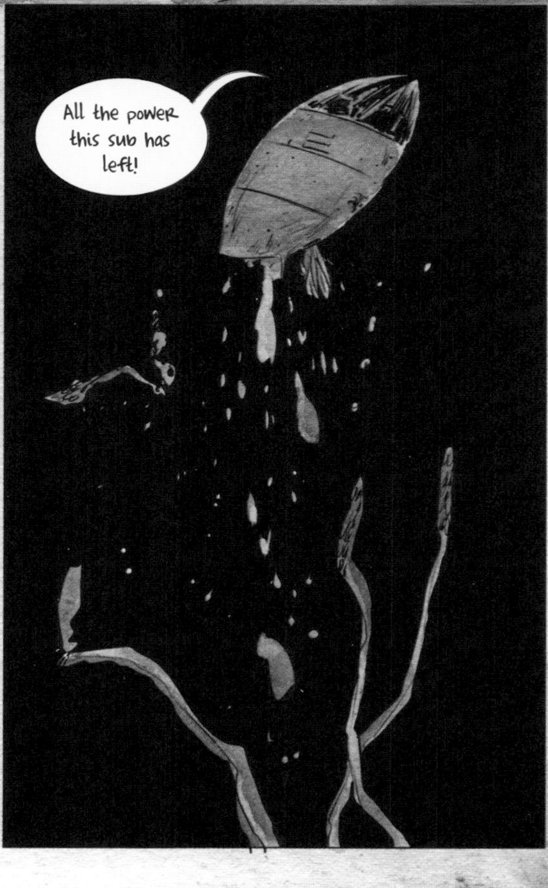
All the power this sub has left!

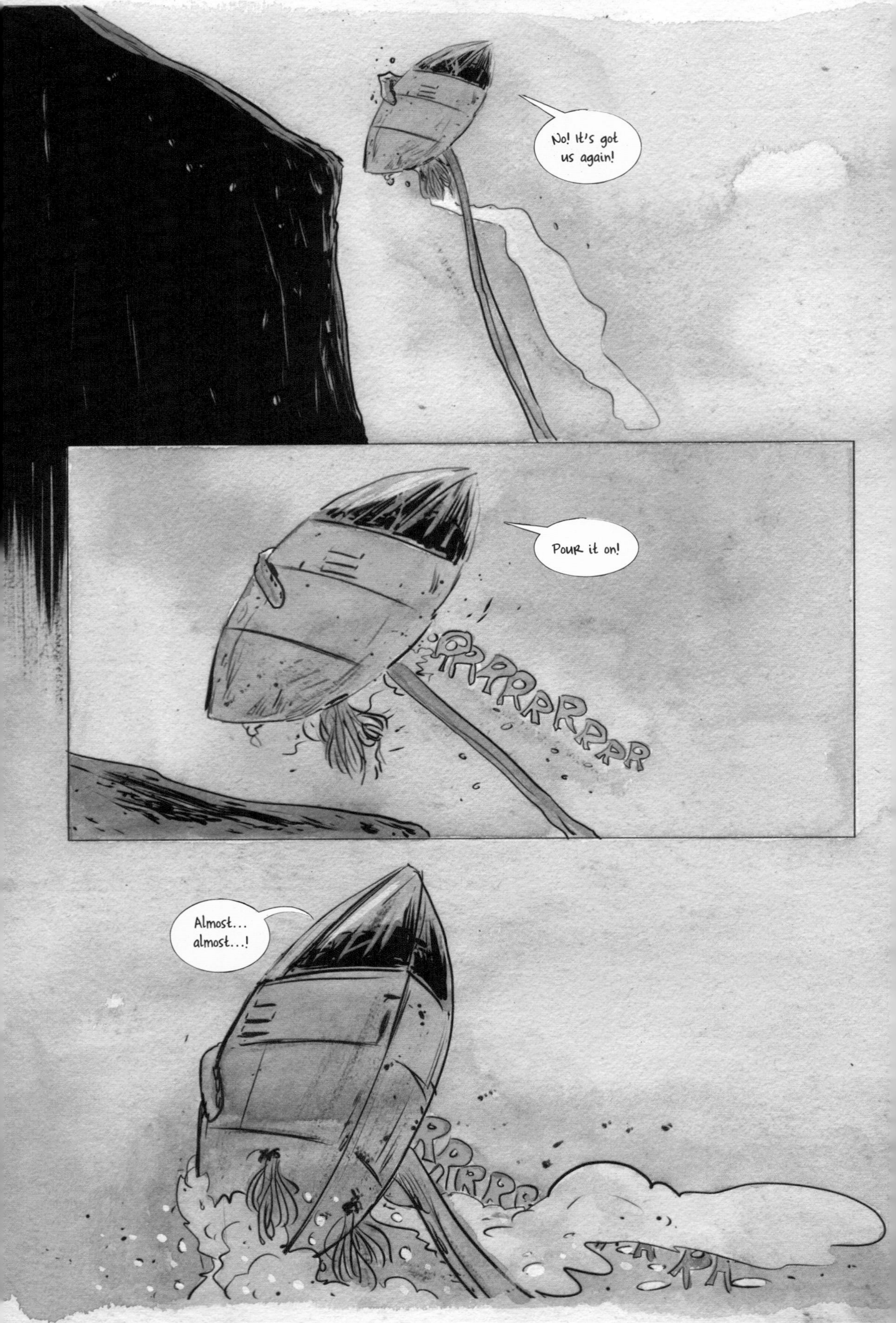
No! It's got us again!
Pour it on!
RRRRRRRRRRRR
Almost... almost...!

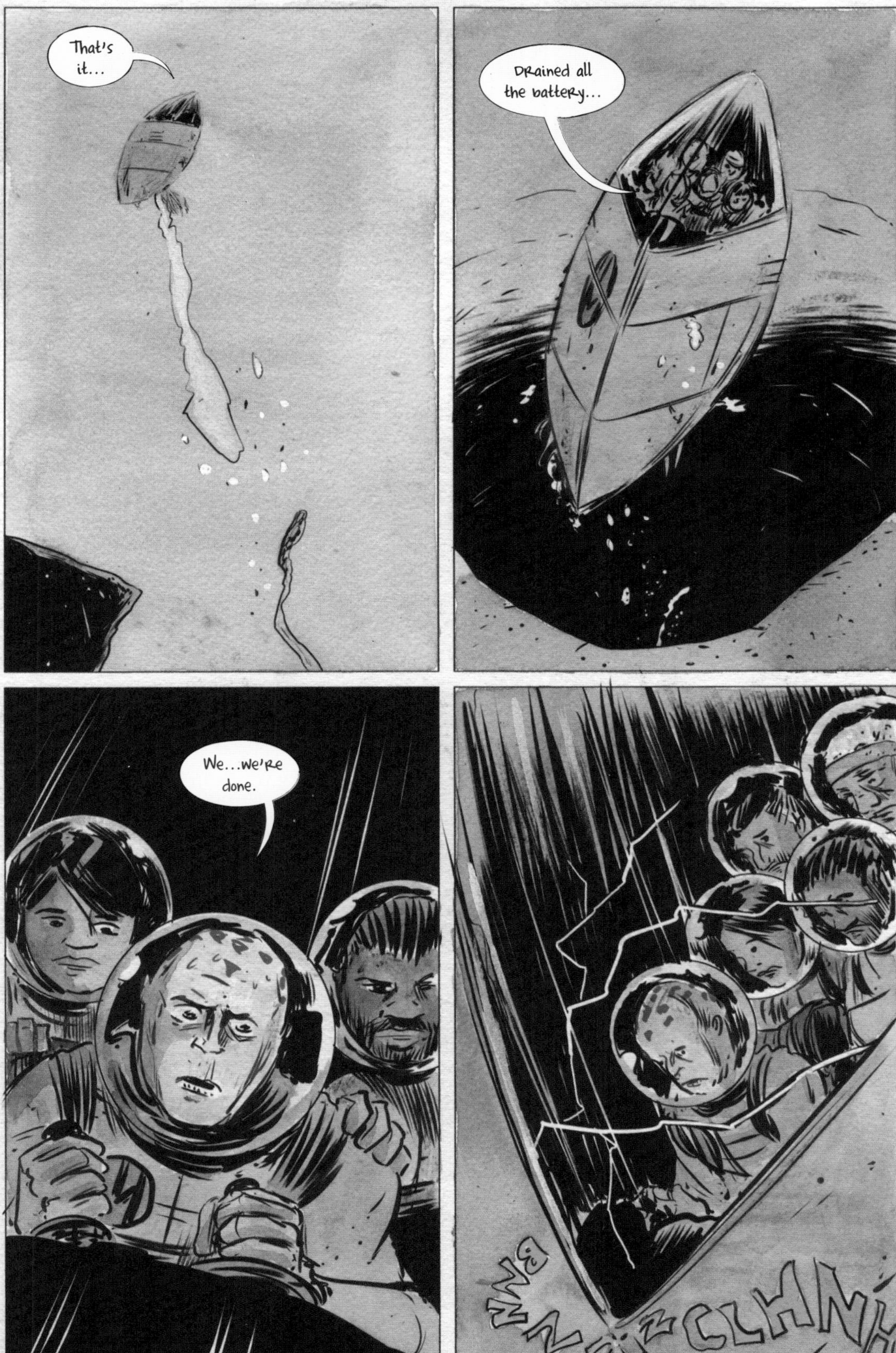
That's it...
Drained all the battery...
We...we're done.
BWNZZZCLHNH

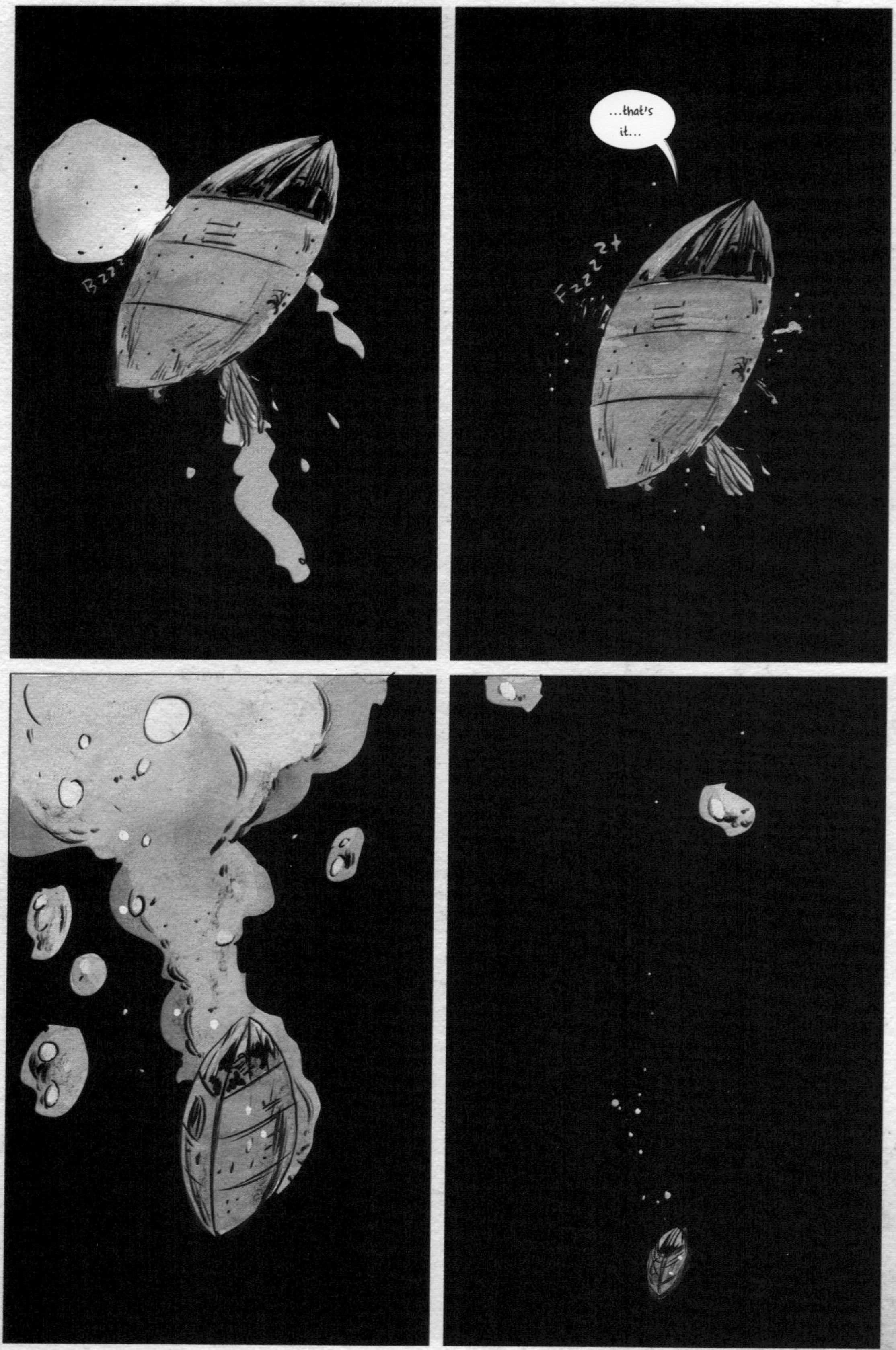
Bzzz
...that's it...
Fzzzzt

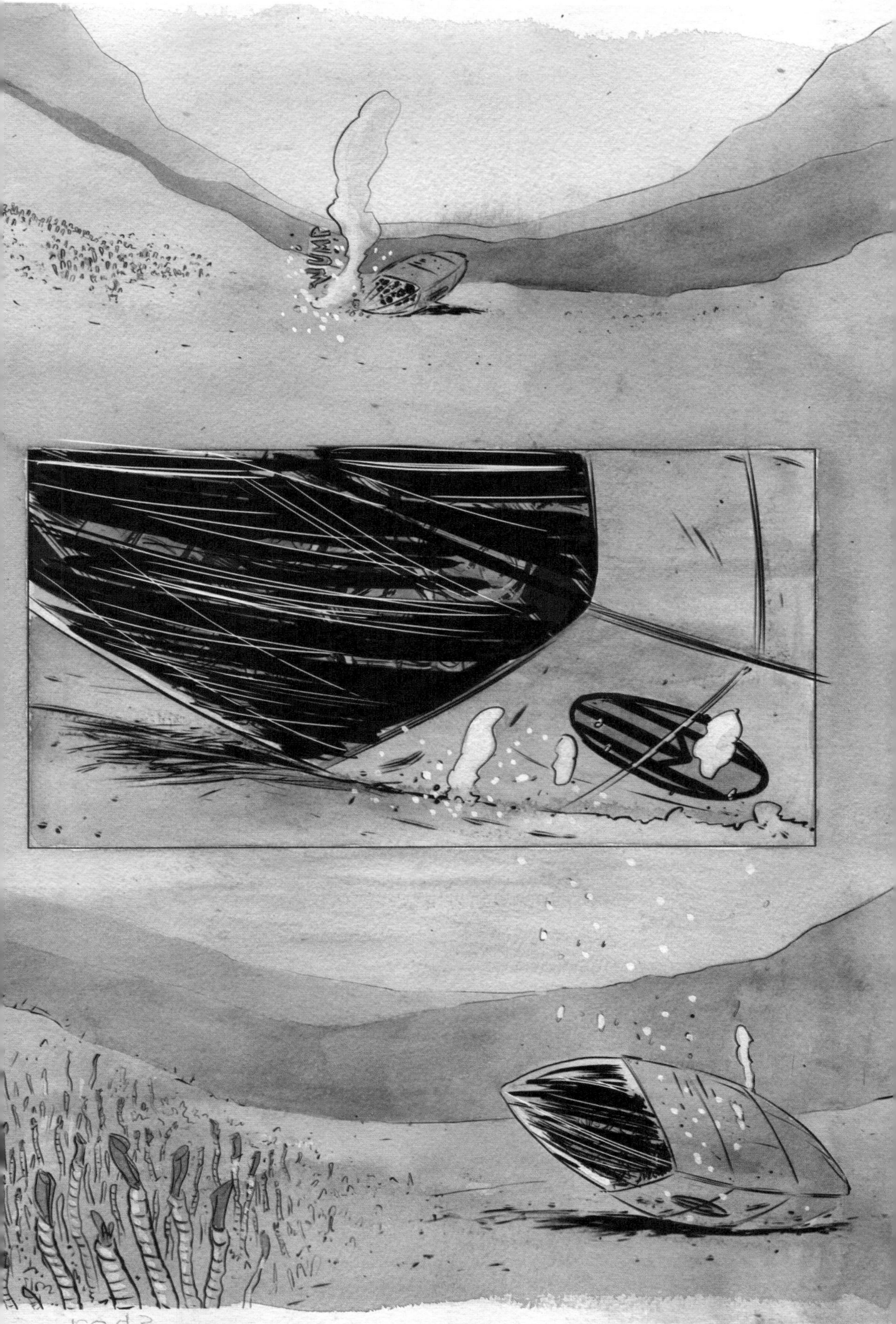
WUMP

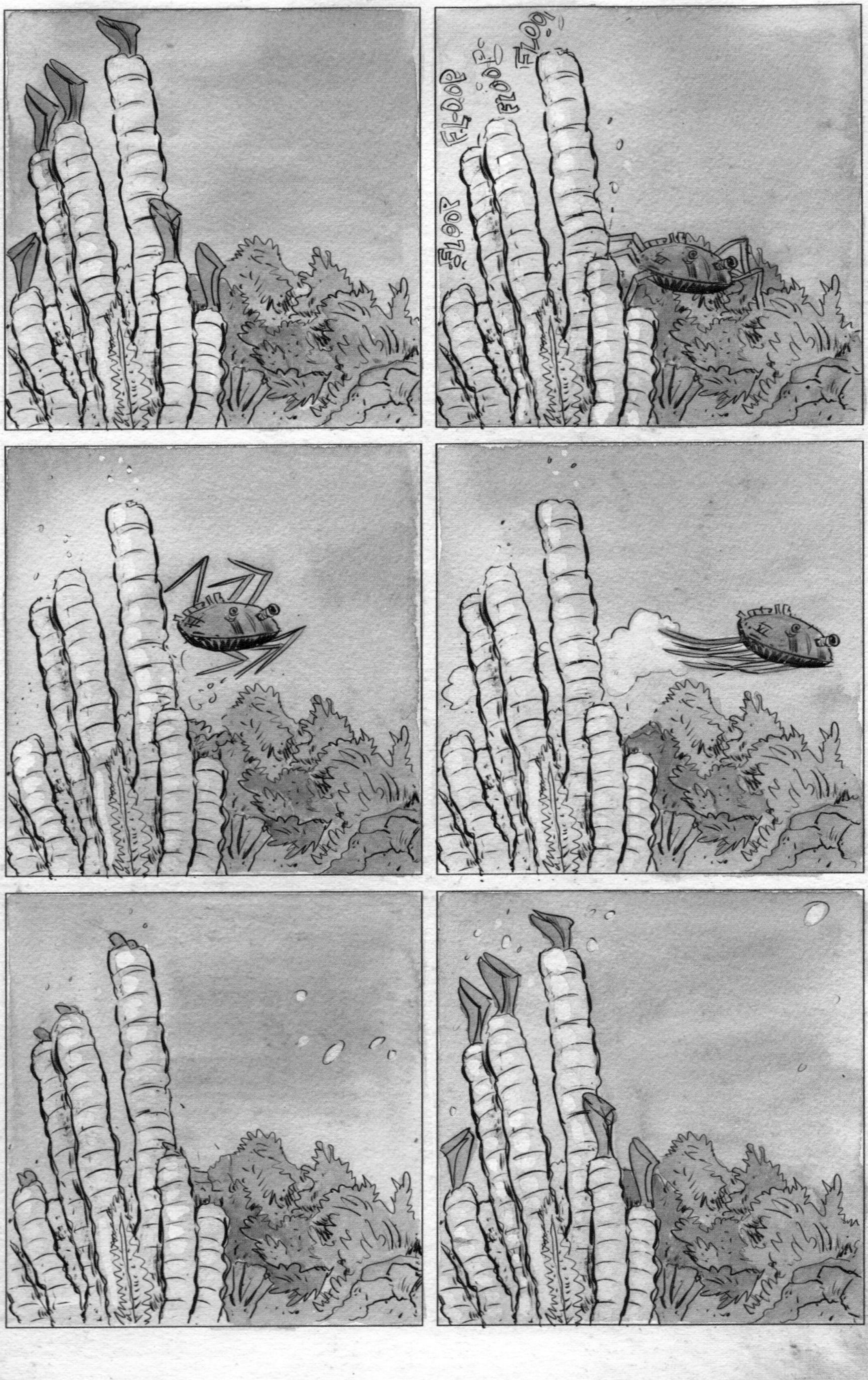
FLOOR
FL-OOP
FLOOP
FLOOP!

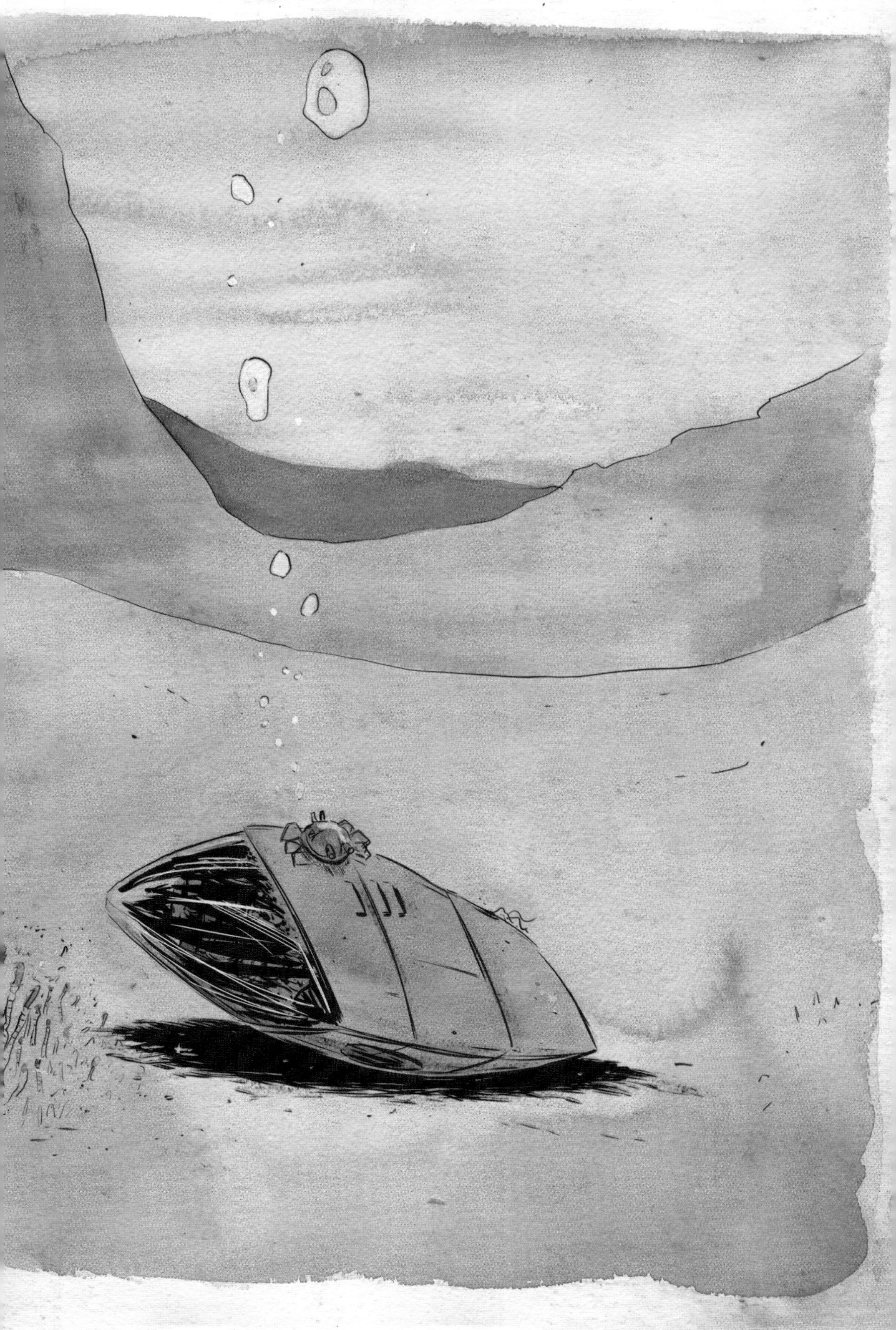

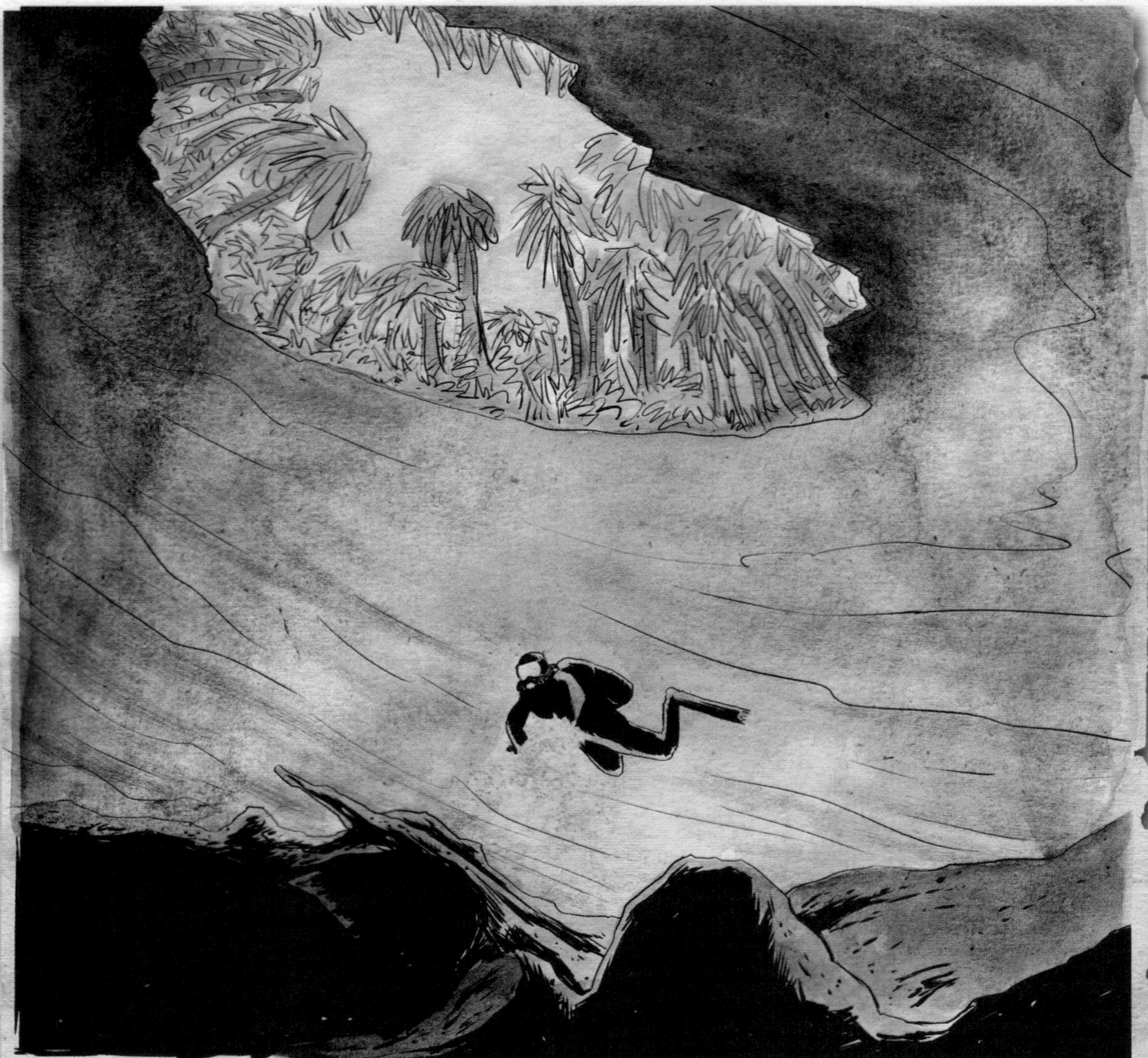

DIVING FOR HOPE

Looking for global cures in the world's most dangerous places.

The "green holes" of South America may potentially yield cures for many of the problems that are plaguing our modern society. So hopes one of the world's preeminent scientists and explorers, Hari Hardy, who has spent his life extending his reach into the stars and plumbing the depths of the oceans.

While the green holes may yield a trove of scientific information, the holes make for some of the most dangerous diving exploration on earth.

As one descends, the green turns to gray and then slowly to black as handheld lights struggle to penetrate the deep. In addition, toxic clouds of gas must be navigated, clouds generated by thousands of years of decaying organic matter and bacterial colonies the likes of which no one has ever encountered. It is these bacterial colonies that Hardy hopes to exploit. Through collection, study, and experimentation, he believes that most of today's epidemics and diseases can be cured by mining this untapped

(continued on next page)

mom doesn't talk as much as she used to.

seems like she's looking for something?
Is she sick?
Is she mad at Hari?
I think Raj did something that made her mad.
She only talks to Roger.

Blake, Philip & Hari
Green Hole Prelim. Expedition

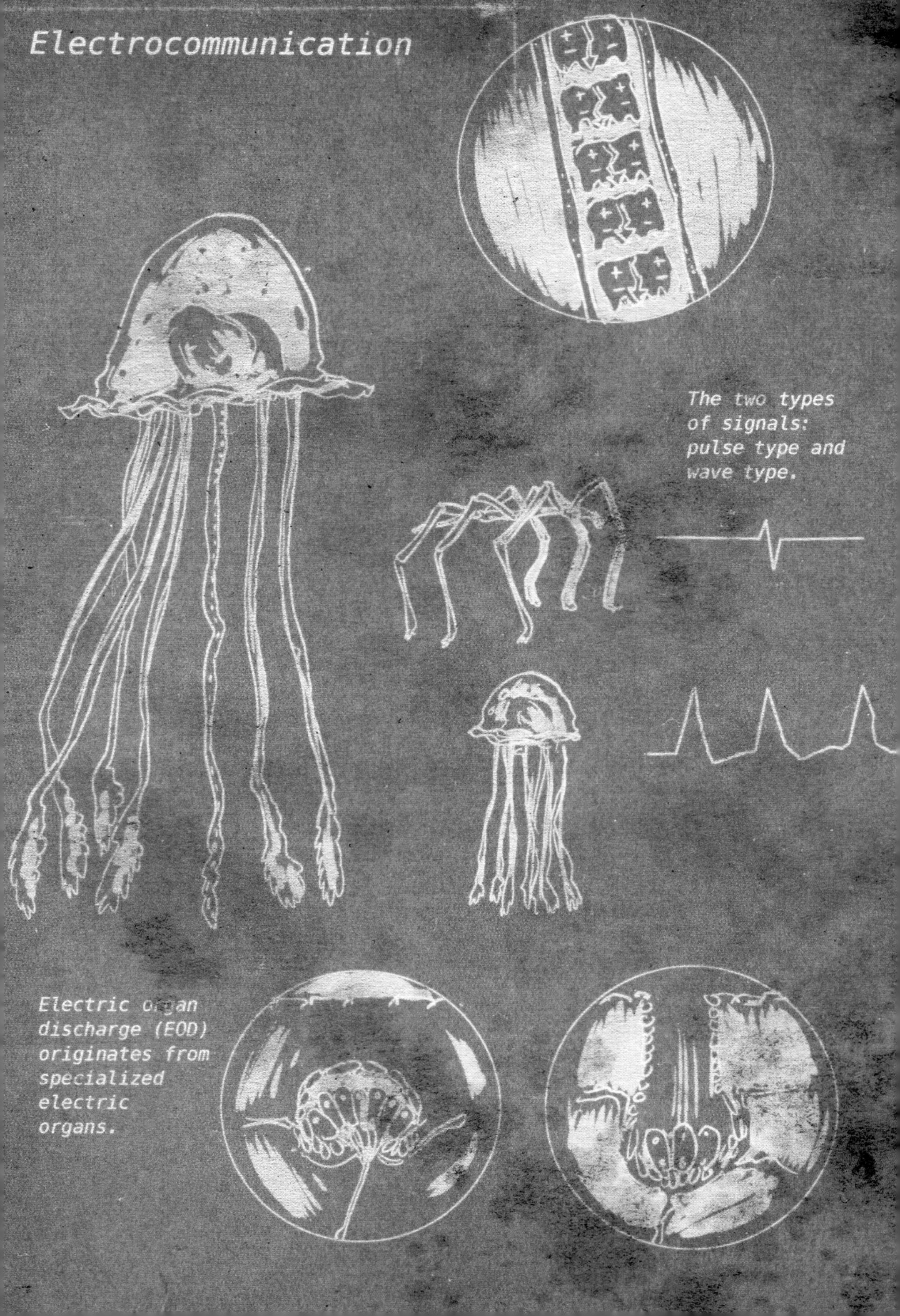

Electrocommunication

The two types
of signals:
pulse type and
wave type.

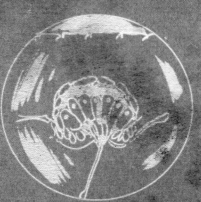

Electric organ
discharge (EOD)
originates from
specialized
electric
organs.

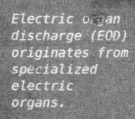

THE CONTAGION RACES

United States (alleged)
Protothecosis: accidentally released during development—airborne disease mutated to jump from dog and cat carriers to humans.

Russia (alleged)
Paramyxoviridae: threat of virus spread via specialized carrier pigeons.

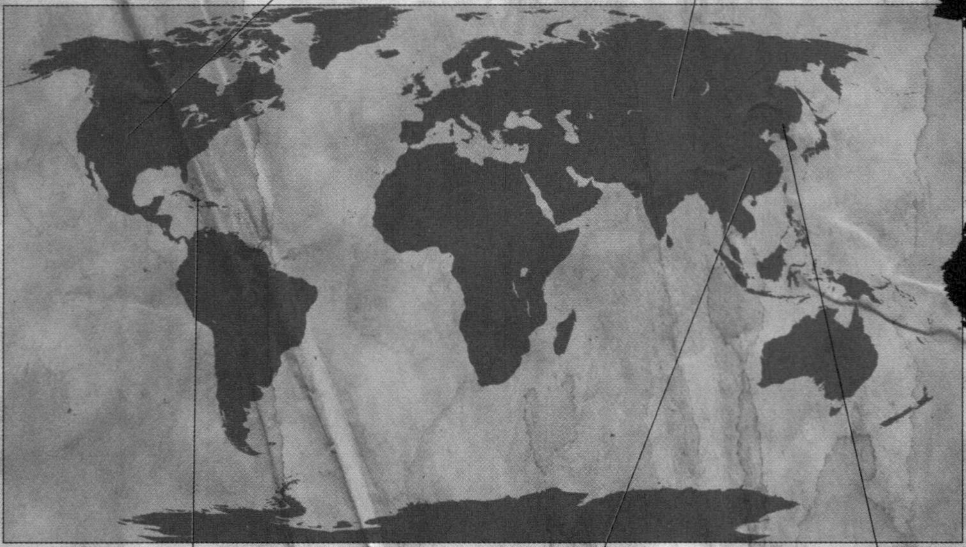

Cuba
Saprophytes: plant-based fungus thought to be delivered via corpses.

China (alleged)
Flaviviridae: capable of being dropped on enemy territories via artificially infected ticks.

North Korea (alleged)
Picornaviridae: able to be weaponized via fish and various other aquatic life.

Some believe the current epidemics were brought on either purposely or inadvertently by humanity and its modern biological weapons race.

Junior Exploration Team

Meet the inaugural JET (Junior Exploration Team). This is a special program funded by Hari Hardy that is working to train elite groups of teens in all of the specialty sciences and skills required to explore extreme aquatic locations, from submerged volcanoes to endangered reefs, around the world.

When questioned about his reasoning for funding this team, Hari was candid:

"There is more on this Earth than humanity can ever hope to fully study and explore. The only way we can even begin to tackle all of the wonders that nature holds for us is to work as a team. Peers, but a team that consists of future generations. My work doesn't stop and start with what I am doing with Dept. H. We are laying the groundwork for future generations, just as this youing team will one day pass the baton to their successors. Exploration is ultimately a selfless act. We work not for this generation, but for the next thousand years of humanity."

1. **Kristyn M.** Underwater Photography
2. **Zoe D.** Team Cuisine Expert
3. **Sophie D.** Dolphin Training
4. **Ada F.** Aquatic Medical Technician
5. **Ella K.** Specimen Collection Specialist

6. **Jane C.** Journalism Liason
7. **Alex B.** Security & Demolitions Expert
8. **Pippa N.** Marine Biologist
9. **Bob** Gecko Mascot

Dept. H Salvage/Recovery Catalog

Item # 1818
Description:

Paper fragment — believed to be crew-member Aaron's handwriting — unconfirmed.

Jonah

The cure is with us
2 And said, I cried by reason of mine affliction
unto the LORD, and he heard me: out of the belly of
hell cried I, *and* thou heardest my voice.
3 For thou hadst cast me into the deep, in the
midst of the seas; and the floods compassed me
about: all thy billows and thy waves passed over
me. Making my way up
4 Then I said, I am cast out of thy sight; yet I will
look again toward thy holy temple. If I
5 The waters compassed me about, *even* to the
soul: the depth closed me round about, the weeds
were wrapped about my head. don't make
6 I went down to the bottoms of the mountains;
the earth with her bars *was* about me for ever: yet
hast thou brought up my life from corruption, O
LORD my God. it — know this that
7 When my soul fainted within me I remembered
the LORD: and my prayer came in unto thee, into
holy temple. is